France Turns the Tide

France Turns the Tide

The Battle of the Marne 5-12 September 1914

George Herbert Perris

LEONAUR

France Turns the Tide
The Battle of the Marne 5-12 September 1914
by George Herbert Perris

FIRST EDITION

First published under the title
The Battle of the Marne

Leonaur is an imprint
of Oakpast Ltd

Copyright in this form © 2014 Oakpast Ltd

ISBN: 978-1-78282-337-7 (hardcover)
ISBN: 978-1-78282-338-4 (softcover)

http://www.leonaur.com

Contents

IN MEMORIAM
N. F. P.
+
E. L. P.

Preface

The great war has entered into history. The restraints, direct and indirect, which it imposed being gone with it, we return to sounder tests of what should be public knowledge—uncomfortable truths may be told, secret places explored. At the same time, the first squall of controversy in France over the opening of the land campaign in the West has subsided; this lull is the student's opportunity. No complete history of the events culminating in the victory of the Marne is entirely possible, or soon to be expected. On the German side, evidence is scanty and of low value; on that of the Allies, there is yet a preliminary work of sifting and measuring to undertake ere definitive judgments can be set down. Any narrative conceived in a scientific, not an apologetic or romantic, spirit may claim to further this end.

The difficulty lies less in following the actual movements of that great encounter—the most important of which, and their part in the result, can now be traced pretty accurately—than in estimating the factors that produced and moulded it. Yet, if we are right in holding the Battle of the Marne to be essentially the completion of a chapter, the resultant of certain designs and certain misadventures, a vast strategical reversal and correction, such an estimate is necessary to the subject. How did the two chief antagonists envisage the process of modern warfare? Why was the action which was to close the first phase of the war, and largely to shape its after-course, fought not near the northern or eastern frontiers, but between Paris and Verdun? Why and how were the original plans of campaign modified to reach this result? What conditions of victory existed on the Marne that had been lacking on the Sambre? In a word, the key to the meaning of the battle must be sought in the character of the forces in play, their comparative numbers, organisation, and training, armament and equipment, leadership and inspiration.

No sooner is such an inquiry opened than a number of derivative problems appear. Where exactly lay the German superiority of force at the outset, and why was it not maintained? Was the first French concentration justifiable? If not, was it promptly and soundly changed? Could the northern frontier have been defended? Was Lanrezac responsible for Charleroi, and, if so, why not Castelnau for Morhange? Was the German plan of envelopment exaggerated? Could the British have done more at Mons, and were they slow and timorous when the hour arrived to turn about? Was Paris ever in danger? And, coming to the battle itself, how was it decided? What parts did Gallieni, Von Kluck, Sir John French, and Foch play? Was Joffre really master of the field? It may be too soon to answer fully such questions as these; it is too late to evade them.

Outside the mass of official and semi-official bulletins, dispatches, and explanations, much of it now best left to oblivion, a considerable literature has accumulated in France, including personal narratives by combatants of all arms, and critical essays from points of view the most diverse. With the rather cruel sincerity of the French intelligence, the whole military preparation of the Republic has been challenged; and, in the consequent discussion, many important facts have come to light. Thus, we have the texts of the most decisive orders, and many details of the dispositions of troops. We have Marshal Von Bülow's valuable diary of field movements, and the critical reflections of distinguished officers like Lt.-Col. de Thomasson, Generals Malleterre, Berthaut, Verraux, Percin, Canonge, Bonnal, Palat, Cherfils, and Col. Feyler. Fragmentary statements by General Joffre himself, by Generals Foch, Lanrezac, and Maunoury, the Ministers of War, MM, Messimy and Millerand, by Generals von Freytag-Loringhoven, Von Kluck, and other German officers and men, give useful indications. We are also indebted to the more systematic works of MM. Hanotaux, Reinach, Engerand, and Babin; and, with regard to the British Force, the volumes of Marshal French and Major-General Maurice are important. These and other sources are cited in the notes, in which some questions of detail, especially relating to the preparation of the battle, are discussed.

Having been privileged to watch the war in France from beginning to end, and to live with the French armies (as correspondent attached to General Headquarters) for more than two years, the writer has also had exceptional opportunities of studying the terrain, and of discussing the drama as a whole and in detail with officers and men from the highest to the most humble. To name all those from whom he has received aid would be impossible; to name any might seem to associate them with conclusions for which he is solely responsible; but he may record his deep gratitude to the French Government, the Headquarters Staff, and the various Army Staffs, for the rare experience of which this volume is unworthy fruit.

February 1920.

German units are throughout numbered in Roman capitals ("the XX Corps"), Allied in ordinary figures ("the 20th Corps").

Douai

Arras

Doullens Cambrai

Albert

AMIENS Peronne

SOMME St Quentin

Ham

Roye

Montdidier Noyon

Lassigny OISE La Fère

ST. GOBAIN

Clermont Compiègne Soissons

Verberie Vic

Creil Crépy V. Cotterets

Chantilly Senlis Ferté Milon OURCQ

Dommartin Nanteuil Lizy Chau Thierry

PARIS Meaux Varreddes

Lagny Crécy

Coulommiers GD. MORIN

Brie C te Robert La Ferté G.

Melun Naugis Provins

Fontainebleau R. SEINE Nogent

Montereau

Sens

Condé Mons Charleroi

Valenciennes Thuin

le Quesnoy Maubeuge

Bouchain SAMBRE

Solesmes Avesnes Philippeville

FST. OF Givet

le Cateau Landrecies MORMAL

Chimay Fumay

Guise Hirson VIROUAIN

Rocroy Charlevil

Ribémont Vervins

May R. SERRE Mezières Se

Signy l'Abbaye MEUSE

Laon Sissonne Novion-Porcien Ste

Craonne C. Porcien Rethel Gd. Pré

AISNE ARGO

Braisne Berry-au-Bac Vouziers ONNE

Fismes Berru

Fère en- REIMS Souain Ste Mene

Tardenois Verzy Suippes

Dormans R. MARNE Valmy Triaucou

Condé-en-Brie Epernay Châlons

Montmirail MARNE Revigny

Fromentières Vertus

Champaubert IV

Sézanne Fère Champ se Vitry

Mailly Sommesous Blesmes

Arcis Vassy

AUBE Joinvil

Troyes

Bar-sur-Au

Bar-sur-Seine Chaum

0 10 20 50 100

MEUSE · uur · III · Malmédy

nant · Marche · OURTHE

B · *E* · *L* · *G* · IV · Bastogne · LUXEMBOURG

liseuil · SEMOY · Neufchâteau · Trèves

dan · Arlon · M · V

CHIERS · Virton · Luxembourg

Montmédy · Longwy

nay · Longuyon · Thionville

MOSELLE

Dun · ORNAIN · Spincourt · Briey · NIED · Saarbruck · VI

ntfaucon · Etain · Conflans · ORNE · Saarguemines

Varennes · AIRE · VERDUN · **METZ**

hould · **3** · Vigneulles · F.TROY · Souilly · Thiaucourt

pt · Vaubécourt · St.Mihiel · Pont-à-Mousson · R.SAAR · Phalsbourg

Brabant-le-Roi · Nomeny · Saverne

rmaize · Commercy · Amance · VI · Château-Salins · Saarebourg · VII

Bar-le-Duc · Toul · NANCY · Remeréville · Avricourt · Strasbourg

t.Dizier · **2** · Lunéville · Blamont · MT DONON · Molsheim

Gondréc't · MEURTHE · Gerbéville · VII · Badonviller · Schirmeck · Mutzig

le · Bayon · Baarat · Raon l'E. · Saales · Schlettstadt

Neufchâteau · Charmes · St.Dié · St.Marie

be · Mirecourt · Ramber · I · MEURTHE · Mandray

ont · Epinal · Bruyeres · Munster · Colmar

Remiremont · N.Brisach

150 · 200 · Miles · 250

General Map
showing

POSITION of
the ARMIES

on the Eve of the
Battle: and the
central German
lines of approach

German Armies.
I-Von Kluck. II-Von Bülow.
III-Von Hausen. IV-Duke of
Würtemberg. V-Imperial
Crown Prince. VI-C.Prince
of Bavaria (& troops from Metz)
VII- Von Heeringen

French & British Armies:
6-Maunoury.. B.E.F. British
5-F.d'Esperey.. 9-Foch.....
4-De Langle de Cary. 3-Sarrail
2-De Castelnau. 1-Dubail...

CHAPTER 1

The Deluge

August 25, 1914: three weeks after Von Emmich opened the war
before Liège; five days after the French Army of Lorraine was trapped
at Sarrebourg and Morhange; two days after Namur fell, and Charleroi
and Mons were abandoned. On this black day, the 25th, while Louvain
was burning, the 80,000 men of the old British regular Army made an
average of 20 miles under a brazen sun, pursued by the enormous mass
of Von Kluck's marching wing. The 1st Corps under Haig came into
Landrecies at 10 p.m., and, after a stiff fight and two or three hours'
sleep, trudged on to Guise; while the 2nd, Smith Dorrien's, at Le Cateau and towards Cambrai, spent most of a showery night in preparing
for the battle of the morrow, which was to save the western flank of
the Allies, On the British right, the French 5th Army, Lanrezac's, surprised in the Charleroi-Namur-Dinant triangle by the onset of Von
Bülow and the cleverly secreted approach of Von Hansen, had struck a
wild blow, and then reeled back; the two German commanders were
now driving it over the Belgian frontier from Avesnes to Rocroi.

The 4th Army, under de Langle de Cary, no less heavily punished
between Paliseul and Neufchateau in the Belgian Ardennes, was just
reaching the French Meuse between Sedan and Stenay, there to dispute the passages against the Duke of Würtemberg. Eastward again,
Ruffey, beaten back on a wide crescent from Virton to Briey in the
Woevre by the Imperial Crown Prince, was standing better against
a relaxed pressure, from toward Montmédy, through Spincourt, to
Etain, Thus, Sarrail, in taking over the command of the 3rd Army,
was able to make ready, though with inadequate means, for the three-
sided defence of Verdun. On the eastern border, Castelnau and Dubail,
withdrawing hardly from ill-starred adventures in Lorraine and Alsace,
were rallying the 2nd and 1st Armies around the Nancy hills and on

both sides of the Gap of Charmes. Mulhouse, twice captured, was finally abandoned by General Pau, with all save a corner of Alsace and the southern passes of the Vosges. The official *communiqué* of August 26 said:—

> It is a cruel necessity which the Army of Alsace and its chief have submitted to with pain, and only at the last extremity.

They had discovered that "the decisive attack "had to be met" in the north." At that moment, in fact, a hardly less "decisive" attack was being met in the heart of Lorraine.

It was everywhere the same bitter story of defeat—defeat by surprise, by locally superior numbers, by superior armament, sometimes by superior generalship; and everywhere the retreat was accompanied and hampered by the flight of masses of peasantry and townsfolk whose flaming homes lit upon the horizon behind a warning to hasten their feeble steps.

Before we seek the Staffs in their shifting quarters, to explain this extraordinary situation, let us see what it meant for the commonalty of the armies, without whose strength and confidence the best plans must be as chaff in the wind. Over a million strong, they had left their homes, and gathered at their depots during these three weeks, to be whirled off to the frontiers and the first scarcely imaginable trial of modern conscript systems. It was a new thing in the world's history, this sudden tremendous clash of the whole manhood of highly developed nations, armed with the most murderous machinery science could devise, and supported by vast reserves of wealth.

It had fallen swiftly upon them, the doom that many learned men had declared to be impossible in the twentieth century; yet its essential nature was crude enough to be immediately understood, and the intelligence of France, though shocked, was not stunned. This million of peasants and workmen, merchants, manufacturers, priests, artists, idlers, and the nation behind them, were unanimous as never before. They knew the issue was not of their making; they knew equally that it could not be refused, but must be fought out, and that it would be a hard fight. The Napoleonic wars were to be eclipsed; and there was now no Little Corporal to flash his genius like a searchlight across Europe. The enemy had no less advantage in prestige than in effectives, preparation, initiative.

Few of the million guessed, as yet, that most of them were marked down for sacrifice. The general opinion was that it would be all over by Christmas, at latest. A four months' war seemed tragic enough in those first days. With the unwonted agreement, an unwonted gravity spread across the sunny lands from the Channel to the Alps where the crops were ripening. If international idealism lay shattered, national democracy rose well to the trial—never better. No recrimination (even the murderer of Jaurès was set aside), no conspiracy, no guillotine, marked the great revival of the republican spirit. England would at least guard the coasts, and keep the seaways open. France went into the struggle without wavering or doubt.

And so, "*Aux armes, Citoyens!*"—for these, mark you, are, in very fact, citizen armies, independent, freethinking, high-spirited fellows, no emperor's "cannonfood." From the smallest hamlet to the *boulevards* of the great city, every pulse of life is feverishly concentrated upon their gathering and departure. At the barracks the reservists, clad, armed, equipped, are ready to entrain. Crowds of women, whose red eyes belie their brave words, children at their skirts, surround the gates, and run forward with bunches of flowers and tricolour rosettes. The officers carry bouquets at their saddle-bows, the men cap their rifles with roses and ribbons. At the railway station, long lines of goods-vans, with a few passenger carriages; more flowers and little flags; allied colours in front of the engine; a wag chalks up the direction: "*Berlin, aller et retour.*" The horses and guns are aboard: the men jostle in the open doorways, and exchange cries with the crowd. A *stanza* of the "*Marseillaise*" is broken by last *adieux*, shouts of "*Vive la France!*" and the curtain falls upon the first memorable act.

Interminable journeys follow, by road and rail, toward the frontiers, then from town to village, and from farm to farm of countrysides more and more deserted and desolate. In the passes of the Vosges, the hills and fiats of Lorraine, the woods of the French Ardennes, the men accustom themselves uneasily to the oppressive heat of day and the chill and damp of night; to sore feet and chafed shoulders; to spells of hunger due to late or lost convoys; to the deprivation of accustomed comfort, and the thousand minor ills which in all times have been the ground-stuff of the showy tapestries of war. Superfluous graces of civilised life vanish before the irreconcilable need of economy in every effort. Officers begin to be honoured not for rank or show, but for the solid talents of leadership; pals are chosen, not from effusion of heart, but for assurance of help in emergency.

The mantles of the chasseurs are still blue, the breeches of the infantry red, the uniforms of the artillery and engineers nearly black; but already bright colours tend to disappear, and every other tone to as-similate with the dust of the high roads. By day and night there is but one traffic throughout these northern and eastern departments—files of cavalry, batteries of field-guns, columns of heavy-laden men, convoys of Parisian autobuses and hooded carts, pass incessantly through the silent forests out into the open plains. The civilian population steadily diminishes, even in the larger towns; the *gendarmerie* keep those who remain under suspicion of espionage.

The frontier villagers welcome the marching troops hospitably, until local food supplies are exhausted, and until news comes in from the front of reverses and of foul cruelty to the peasants on the part of the enemy. Only a fortnight has gone by when the national confidence in a speedy victory receives this heavy blow. Bad news gathers and reverberates. It is a little difficult, after years of bloodshed, to recover the fresh sense of these first calamities. Men were then not yet broken to the pains, the abominable spectacles, of war. That their self-offering to the fatherland should win them an honoured grave might well be. But defeat at the outset, the shame of retreat almost before a blow could be struck, this was an incredible, monstrous, intolerable thing.

The incredible, however, generalised itself over all the highways of Lorraine and Belgium. Take any typical scene on the march-routes of August 22 or the following days. (See note end of chapter). The roads are black with columns of troops retreating west-and southward, more or less broken, linesmen, *chasseurs*, artillerymen, supply and special services, with their guns, munition wagons, Red Cross detachments, convoys of heavy-laden carts with wounded men sitting on top or clinging behind; and, in the breaks, crowds of panic-stricken peasants, in farm wagons or on foot, old men, women, and children, with bedding, boxes, bird-cages, and other strange belongings. Dismay broods like a palpable cloud over these pitiful processions. There is an incessant jostling. Drivers flog their horses cruelly. Wounded men drop by the wayside and lie there untended, their haggard faces stained with mire and powder, blood oozing through their coats, trickling out into the litter of torn knapsacks and broken arms. The sun blazes inexorably, the air is poisoned with of dust, or drenching showers of rain produce another sort of misery; and ever the long stream of failure and fear flows on, eddying here and there into acute confusion as some half-mad woman sets up a cry: "The Prussians"

Night follows day: soldiers and country-folk, hungry and exhausted, fall into the corners of any sheltered place they can find—an

17

empty barn, the nave of a village church—for an unsatisfying sleep, or, too sick to sleep, watch the fantastic shadows and fugitive lights dancing upon the walls, mocking their anguished thoughts of the morrow. The batteries and convoys have gone on through the darkness, men rolling from side to side with fatigue on their horses or gun-carriages, as though drunk. With daybreak the greater trek recommences. The enemy has not been idle: in the distance behind rolls the thunder of heavy guns; pillars of smoke and flame rise from burning villages. And as, day after day, a new stage of retirement—increasingly controlled, it is true—is ordered, the question pierces deeper: What is to become of France?

Those who have lived at the centre as well as on the skirts of armed hosts become habituated to one enveloping condition: the rank and file, and even most of the officers, know little or nothing of what is passing outside their own particular spheres. It is in the nature and necessity of military operations, especially at the beginning and in a phase of rapid movement, that it should be so. Perhaps it is also a necessity of the psychology of endurance. Of these republican armies, only a small minority of the men were old soldiers; most of them had all they could do to adapt themselves, day by day and hour by hour, to the new world of violence, squalor, and general unreason in which they were now prisoned.

They had to learn to bear fatigue and pain such as they had never known; to overcome the spasm of fear that grips the stoutest heart in unaccustomed emergencies; to thrust the bayonet not into a sand-bag, but into soft, quivering flesh, and draw it forth again; to obey men who were incompetent and stupid, as well as born leaders. The German heavy shells, aeroplanes, motor transport, the formidable entrenchments and fields of wire—gradually they recognised these and other elements of the invader's superiority. Weaklings cried: "We are betrayed. It is 1870 over again." What could the bravest reply? Letters were few and far between. Newspapers were never so barren. What was Paris doing? What were Russia and England doing? The retreating columns marched with downcast eyes, wrapped in a moody silence.

By what revolt of the spirit did these apparently broken men become, a fortnight later, the heroes of the Marne? The answer must be that they were not broken, but were passing through the sort of experience which, in a virile race, wakens the dull-minded to their utmost effort, blows away the last traces of laxity and false idealism, and, by setting above every other fear the fear of a ruined Fatherland,

18

rallies the whole mass on the elementary ground of defence to the death. Voices, lying voices, had whispered that France was diseased, body and soul, that the Republic would surely die of its corruptions. We have since discovered the immeasurable strength of democratic communities. Then it was questioned by the few, unsuspected by the many. England and America, even more than France, had outgrown any sort of liking for war. To be driven back to that gross test was a profound surprise. For the quick, proud French mind to find itself suddenly in face of defeat and the threat of conquest was a second and severer shock. The long retreat gave it time to perceive that this calamity arose largely from its own errors, and to re-group its forces in a truer conception of the character of modern warfare.

Even Joffre may not have clearly realised this need; great instincts count in the crisis of leadership equally with powerful reasoning. Amid the tramp-tramp of the weary, dust -blinded columns, by the night bivouacs, under the rain of shrapnel and the crash of high explosive, men of the most diverse condition and character, shedding old vanities and new alarms, came down step by cruel step to the fundamental honesty, unity, and resolution of our nature. The mirage of an easy victory vanished; in its place a finer idea rose and rose till the armies saw nothing else: France must live! I may die, or be doomed to a travesty of life; at any price, France must be saved.

So the steel was tempered for the supreme trial.

★★★★★★

Note:—Many volumes of soldiers' notes and recollections have been published, and some of them have high literary merit. One of these is *Ma Pièce, Souvenirs d'un Canonnier*, by Sergeant Paul Lintier, of the 44th Artillery, who shared in the defeat of Ruffey's Army near Virton, in the south-eastern corner of Belgium, 35 miles north of Verdun. It was almost his first sight of bloodshed, and with an artist's truthfulness he records all the confusion of his mind. He writes on August 23:—

> The battle is lost, I know not how or why. I have seen nothing. It is a sheer nightmare. We shall be massacred. Anguish chokes me. . . . This boiling mass of animality and thought that is my life is about to cease. My bleeding body will be stretched upon the field. I see it. Across the sunny perspective of the future a great curtain falls. I am only twenty-one years old. What are we waiting for? Why do not our guns fire? I perspire, I am afraid . . . afraid.

This mood gradually passes away. A few days later he is trying to explain the change:—

One accustoms oneself to danger as to the cruellest privations, or the uncertainty of the morrow. I used to wonder, before the war, how the aged could live in quietude before the immanence of death. Now I understand. For ourselves, the risk of death has become an element of daily existence. One counts with it; it no longer astonishes, and frightens us less. And, besides, every day trains us to courage. The conscious and continuous effort to master oneself succeeds at length. This is the whole of military bravery. One is not born brave; one becomes so.

And this stoicism is softened and spiritualised by a new sense of what the loss of France would mean.

Another notable narrative of this period of the war is *Ce qu'a vu un Officier de Chasseurs-à-Pied,* by Henri Libermann. The writer was engaged on the Belgian frontier farther west, near where the Semoy falls out of the Ardennes into the Meuse, the region where the Saxons and the IV Army joined hands on the one side, and, on the other, the 5th French Army, Lanrezac's, touched all too lightly the 4th, that of de Langle de Cary. Some French officers have quartered themselves in an old convent, picturesquely set upon a wooded hill. They do not know it, but, in fact, the cause is already lost from Dinant to Neufchateau. All they know is that a part of the 9th Corps is in action a few miles to the north. The guns can be heard; the villagers are flying in panic; the flames of burning buildings redden the northern sky.

In the convent parlour, the table is laid with a fine white cloth, decorated with flowers, bottles covered with venerable dust, cakes whose golden crust gladdens the eyes. A brilliant Staff, the Commandant, a few *chasseur* officers. The sisters hurry about, carrying dishes. 'A little more fowl, my dear *commandant*,' says the brigadier; 'really, it is delicious. And this wine—Pontet-Canet of '74, if you please!' All of us are grateful to the good sisters, who are such delicate cooks. At dessert, as though embarrassed by an unhappy impression shared by all the guests, the general speaks: 'Rest tranquil, gentlemen. Our attack tomorrow morning will be overwhelming. Debouching between hills 832 and 725, it will take in flank the German Corps which is stopping our brave 9th, and will determine the victory.

Hardly has the toast of the morrow's triumph been drunk than a heavy step is heard outside, the click of spurs, and then a knock on the door. A captain enters, in helmet and breastplate, a bloody bandage across his forehead, dust thick upon his uniform, perspiration rolling down his face. He has ridden from Dinant with news of the defeat, and secret instructions. The *Uhlans* are near. Nevertheless, the officers go to bed. During the night they are aroused by an increasing clamour of flying peasants outside the convent. There are soldiers among them, wildly crying: "The Prussians are coming, *sauve qui peut!*" An infantry regiment had camped, the previous evening, in the village of Willerzie.

They arrived late, tired out. No thought but of rest, no scouts or outposts. On the verge of the neighbouring forest, grey-coated horsemen appeared. The sentinels fired a few shots, and they retired into the wood. The regiment then went to sleep in its false security. About 11 p.m., however, three searchlights flashed along the village streets. '*Schnell, schnell! Vorwärts, vorwärts!*' A terrible fusillade broke out around the houses; and, as our infantrymen, hurriedly wakened, ran to arms, a thick rain of bullets fell upon them. In a few instants, terror was transformed into panic, panic into rout. At this moment the regiment was flying, dispersed in all directions, pursued by the 'hurrahs' of the victorious Germans.

★★★★★★

CHAPTER 2

A Tragedy of Errors

1. THE GERMAN PLAN OF CAMPAIGN

"Errors," "vanities"? These words must be justified, however gently, however briefly. To regard the battle of the Marne without reference to the grievous beginnings that led to and shaped it would be to belittle and falsify a subject peculiarly demanding care for true perspective. The battle may be classed as negatively decisive in that it arrested the invasion long enough to enable the Allies to gain an equality of forces, and so to prevent a final German victory; it was only positively decisive in the larger sense that it recreated on a sounder base the military spirit and power of France, which alone among the Western Allies seriously counted in that emergency, and, by giving the army a new direction, the nation a new inspiration, made it possible for them to sustain the long struggle that was to follow. Perilous illusions, military as well as pacifist, were buried beside the Marne. A fashion of thought, a whole school of teaching was quietly sunk in its waters. The French mind rose to its full stature as the nature of the surprise into which it had fallen broke upon it.

This surprise was threefold. In the first place, the German plan of campaign was misconceived. That plan was grandiose in its simplicity. It rested upon a sound sense of the separation of the Allies: their geographical dispersion, which gave the aggressor the advantages famous in the career of Frederick the Great, as in that of Napoleon; the diversity of character, power, and interest within the Entente, which was, indeed, hardly more than an improvisation, without any sort of common organ, so far; its lack of unity not only in command but in military theory and practice generally. The first of these data indicated to the German Command the Frederician succession of swift offensives; the second narrowed the choice for the first effort, and suggested an after-work of political intrigue; the third had fortified Prussian pride and discipline with a daring strategy and an armament superior, in most respects, to anything the rest of the world had conceived to be possible. Which of the three great States, then, should be first struck down? The wildest Pan-Germanist could not reply "England," in face of her overwhelming sea-power.

So the British Empire, with the North Sea and Channel coasts, were, for the moment, ignored. Its internal problems, its peaceful, almost neutral, temper, its slow-mindedness in European affairs, were more regarded than the trivial military force which alone England could at once offer its friends. For speed was to be of the essence of the plan. Remained France and Russia; and here political as well as military calculations entered. The inchoate Empire of the East would, it was thought, be the slower in getting to its feet. Would a new Moscow expedition break its will for self-defence? The author of the *Willy-Nicky* letters imagined a better way. France would stand by her ally. The "Republic of the Rochettes and Steinheils," however, was not naturally impregnable; when it was finished, would not "dear Nicky" be glad to return to the Drei-Kaiserbund, the old Bismarckian order, and to join in a friendly rearrangement of the world? So the conclusion, with all the neatness of a professorial thesis: Russia was to be held up—actively, on the south, by the Austro-Hungarian armies, passively on the north, by a screen of German troops—while France, as the principal enemy, was swiftly crushed. Thus far, there should have been no surprise.

It was otherwise with the plan of campaign itself, and there are details that will remain in question till all the archives are opened. Yet this now appears the only plan on which Germany could hope to bring an aggressive war to a successful issue. A repetition of the triumph of 1870 would not be enough, for, if France resisted as long this time, everything would be put in doubt. The blow must be still more swift and overwhelming. To be overwhelming, it must at once reach not portions, but the chief mass, of the French armies. But nowhere in the world had military art, working upon a favourable terrain, set up so formidable a series of obstacles to grand-scale manoeuvre as along the line of the Meuse and Moselle Heights and the Vosges. A piercing of this line at the centre, between the fortified systems of Verdun-Toul on the north and Epinal-Belfort on the south, might be an important contributory operation; in itself it could not give a speedy decision. A mere diversion by Belgium, in aid of a main attack in Lorraine, would not materially alter this calculation. The full effects of surprise, most important of all factors in a short struggle, could only be expected where the adversary was least prepared, which was certainly across the north. These offensive considerations would be confirmed by a defensive consideration: German Lorraine, also, was so fortified and garrisoned as to be beyond serious fear of invasion. In neither direction could Alsace provide favourable conditions for a great offensive.

The political objects of the war being granted, these arguments would lead to the strategical conclusion: the strongest possible force will be so deployed, on a vast arc stretching from southern Lorraine to Flanders, that its superiority may at once be brought fully into play. The method was a variant drawn from the teaching of Clausewitz and Schlieffen. The "march on Paris" occupied in the plan no such place as it long held in the popular imagination. The analogy of closing pincers has been used to describe the simultaneous onset of seven German armies ranged in a crescent from the Vosges to Brussels; but it is uncertain whether the southern wing was originally intended to participate immediately in the destructive stroke, or whether this purpose followed upon the collapse of the first French offensives. The latter supposition is the more probable; and we may, therefore, rather picture a titanic bolas ending in five loaded cords, of which the two outer ones are the most heavily weighted. These two outer masses were (a) Kluck's and Bülow's Armies on the west; (b) the Crown Prince of Bavaria's and Heeringen's on the east. Approximately equal, they had very different functions, the road of the one being open, of the other closed; the one, therefore, being essentially offensive, the other provisionally defensive.

Between these two masses, there were three lesser forces under Hansen, the Duke of Würtemberg, and the Imperial Crown Prince. While the eastern armies held the French forces as originally concentrated, the western mass, by an immense envelopment, was to converge, and the three inner bodies were to strike direct, toward the north-centre of France—perhaps toward the upper Seine, but there could hardly be a precise objective till the invasion developed, (see note following)—destroying any resistance in their path. The eastern thrust which actually followed appears, on this hypothesis, as an auxiliary operation rather than part of a double envelopment: we shall see that, delivered at the moment when the Allies in the west were being driven in between Le Cateau and Givet, it failed against a successful defence of the only open road of the eastern frontier, the Gap of

Charmes, and that it again failed a fortnight later. The other German armies went triumphantly forward. In every part of the field is evident the intention to conceal, even to hold back, the movements of approach, and so to articulate and synchronise them that, when the hour of the decisive general action had arrived, there should be delivered a single, sudden, knock-out blow.

★★★★★★

Note:—The question whether the Eastern thrust was integral in the original plan cannot be absolutely determined; but it is significant that at the outset the German forces on the East were inferior to the French.

M. Gabriel Hanotaux (*Revue des Deux Mondes*, November 15, 1916) thinks that the German right, centre, and left were aiming at the region of Troyes, Kluck from the north-west, Prince Ruprecht of Bavaria from the east, and the Imperial Crown Prince from the north.

> The direction of the Prince of Bavaria appears from an order seized on the enemy giving as objective Rozelieures, that is to say, the Gap of Charmes; the direction of the crown prince is revealed by an order of September 6 giving Dijon as objective for his cavalry.

Lt.-General von Freytag-Loringhoven (*Deductions from the World War*) says:

> The intention was to effect an envelopment from two sides. Envelopment by the left wing of the German Army was, however, brought to a standstill before the fortifications of the French eastern frontier.

A German brochure on the Battle of the Marne—*Die Schlachten an der Marne* by a "German Staff Officer" who was evidently an eyewitness, and probably a member of the staff either of General von Kluck, or of General von Moltke, chief of the Grand Staff from the beginning of the war till after the battle, says the plan was to rest on the defensive from the Swiss frontier to the Donon, while the mass of the armies rolled the French up south of the Seine, and Reserve and *Landwehr* Corps advanced to the coast to stop the landing of British troops.

> By all human provisions, this plan might have been carried out by the end of September 1914.

A French translation of this interesting booklet (*Une Version Al-lemande de la Marne*. Brussels et Paris: G. Van Oest et Cie. 1917) includes also a critical study by M. Joseph Reinach, a part of which is given to the results of an examination of the maps taken on German dead, wounded, and prisoners in the beginning of the war. These Staff maps fall into four categories, of which three date from the mobilisation or earlier, and so throw light on the original plan of campaign, while one set was distributed at a later date. The former are: (1) sets of maps of Belgium—the whole country—in seventy sheets, reproducing the Belgian "60,000th" Staff map, and dated 1906, another evidence of premeditation. (2) The north-east of France, from the French "80,000" map, with names in French, but explanations in Italian, dated 1910. These had evidently been printed for the use of Italian troops, but, when Italy declared itself neutral, had been distributed to German officers from motives of economy. (3) The north and north-east of France in 87 sheets, *not including Paris*, dated from 1905 to 1908, and distributed to German officers on the eve of the mobilisation. These are based upon the French "80,000" map, with some variations and special markings. They include the whole of the eastern and northern frontiers from Belfort to Dunkirk; the significant thing is their limits on the west and south.

On the west they include the regions of Dunkirk, St. Omer, Arras, Amiens, Montdidier and Beauvais, but not those of Calais, Boulogne, Abbeville, and Rouen. At 30 or 40 miles north of Paris, they turn eastward, including the sectors of Soissons and Rheims, but excluding those of Paris and Meaux. They then turn south again, including the Chalôns, Arcis, and Troyes sheets; and the southern limit is the regions of Troyes, Chaumont, and Mirécourt. (4) Finally, there is a set of 41 sheets supplementary to the last named, printed in 1914, and either distributed at a later date, or intended for armies other than those of the first invasion. These included Calais and the Channel coast, Rouen, Paris, Meaux, to the south thereof the regions of the Orleanais. Berry, the Nivernais, including the great manufacturing centre of Le Creusot, the north of Burgundy, Franche Comté, the Jura, and the Swiss frontier from Bâle to near the Lake of Geneva.

In his *L'Enigme de Charleroi*, M. Hanotaux expresses the belief that, at the outset, the German Command, regarding England as the chief enemy, intended its armies to cross northern Belgium, "straight to the west and the sea, with Dunkirk and Calais as immediate objective," and that the French resistance diverted them from the coastal region. The evidence of the maps appears to the present writer more convincing than the reasoning of M. Hanotaux.

★★★★★★

2. THE FORCES IN PLAY

In every part the German war-machine was designed and fitted to deliver such a blow. Its effective force was the second great element of surprise for the Entente.

It is now clear that, taking the field as a whole, France was not overwhelmed by superior numbers. True, as a French official report says, "the military effort of Germany at the outset of the war surpassed all anticipations"; but the element of surprise lay not in numbers, but in fighting quality and organisation. Of the whole mass mobilised in August 1914, one quarter was sent to the East. The remainder provided, in the last week of August, for employment against Belgium and France, an effective force of about 80 infantry divisions—45 active, 27 reserve, mixed Ersatz brigades presently grouped in 6 divisions, and 4 *Landwehr* divisions in course of formation,[1] with about 8 divisions of cavalry,—about a million and a half of men, for the most part young, highly trained and disciplined, including 115,000 re-engaged non-commissioned officers (double the strength of the French company cadres). Of the prodigious mass of this west-European force, about a half was directed through Belgium, and—essential fact—nearly a third passed to the west of the Meuse.

The French, on the other hand, admirably served by their railways,[2]

1. It is not necessary here to state the evidence in detail; but these figures may be accepted as substantially correct. I am indebted to a British authority for criticism and information. Besides the 4 *Landwehr* divisions in course of formation during the last days of August, there were a number of *Landwehr* brigades, which, however, had no artillery and were not organised for the field. By the first week of September, the XI Corps and Guard Reserve Corps had gone to the Russian front; but the 4 *Landwehr* divisions named above had come in as effective The "Metz Army Detachment" may be counted as adding a division.

2. The transport of "covering troops" began at 9 p.m. on July 31, and ended at noon on August 3. On the Eastern Railway alone, 538 trains were required. The "transports of concentration," from August 5 to 18, engaged 4300 trains, only a score of which were behind time. After Charleroi, between August 26 and September 3, the removal of three army corps, five infantry divisions, and three cavalry divisions from Lorraine to the Central and Western fronts was effected by 740 trains, while the railways were largely swamped by other military movements and the civilian exodus.

27

put at once into the field 86 divisions (47 active, 25 reserve, 12 Territorial, and 2 Moroccan), of which 66 were at the front, with 7 divisions of cavalry, on the eve of the critical battles of the Sambre and the Gap of Charmes, in the third week of August, Before the Battle of the Marne, all French active troops had been withdrawn from the Italian frontier, only a few Territorials being left there. An exact numerical comparison cannot yet be made. It seems certain, however, that, including five British and six Belgian divisions, in the whole field the Allies were not outnumbered. There was no great difference in cavalry.

But there was a vital difference in the infantry organisation, as to which the French Command had been completely deceived. Not only had it failed to foresee the creation of brigades of Ersatz troops (to say nothing of the *Landwehr* divisions which appeared in September): it had never contemplated the use of reserve formations as troops of shock. In the French Army, the reserve battalions, regiments, and divisions were so many poor relations—inadequate in younger officers and non-coms, insufficiently armed (especially in artillery), insufficiently trained and disciplined, and, accordingly, destined only for lesser tasks. When, as occurred almost at once under pressure of the successful example of the enemy, reserve divisions and groups of divisions had to be thrown into the front line, the homogeneity of the armies and the confidence of their chiefs suffered. Meanwhile, realising a plan initiated in 1913, the German Staff had created 16 army corps of reserves, of which 13 were used on the Western front, where they proved as solid as the regulars, and were given tasks as responsible in all parts of the field. The main mass of attack, therefore, consisted not of 22, but 34, army corps—a difference larger than the strength of the two armies of Kluck and Bülow to which the great enveloping movement was entrusted.[3]

Without this supplementary force—the result not of numbers

3. For fuller explanations on this point, see *Le Revers de 1914 et ses Causes*, by Lt.-Col. de Thomasson. Of the volumes published in France up to this date on the first period of the war, this moderate and closely-reasoned essay by an accomplished officer is one of the most valuable. General Verraux (*L'Oeuvre*, June 1, 1919) refers to this weakness and confirms my general conclusion:"Despite the inferior organisation of reserves, with our 25 Active Corps, the 80 corps battalions of reserves, the Belgians and the British, we had, if not a numerical superiority, almost an equality with the German forces, deducting those on the Russian front." M. Victor Giraud, a competent historical writer, in his *Histoire de la Grande Giteyre* (Part 1 ch. iii.) gives other details, leading to the same conclusion.

available, but of superior training and organisation—the invasion could hardly have been attempted, or would assuredly have failed. On the other hand, as we shall see, had it been anticipated, the French plan of campaign must have been profoundly modified. The balance in armament was not less uneven. The French 3-inch field-gun from the first justified the highest expectations of its rapidity and accuracy of fire. But in pieces of heavier weight and longer range the inferiority was flagrant. While Frenchmen had been counting their "75" against heavier but less handy German guns, while they were throwing all the gravamen of the problem of national defence on three-years' service, the enemy was developing a set of instruments which immensely re-inforced his man-power. Instead of resting content with light guns, he set himself to make heavier types more mobile.

The peace establishment of a German active corps included 160, a French only 120, guns. It was, however, in weight, rather than num-bers, that the difference lay. Every German corps had 16 heavy 5.9-inch mortars. The French had no heavy artillery save a few batteries of Rimailho 6.1-inch rapid-fire pieces, and a few fortress cannon. In addition to 642 six-piece batteries of horse and field artillery (3.1-inch field-gun and 4.1-inch light howitzer), the German armies had, in all, before the mobilisation, 400 four-piece batteries of 5.9-inch howitzers and 8.2-inch mortars. The German artillery alone at the outset had aviators to correct their fire. General Malleterre, speaking from experience in the long retreat,[4] says:—

> Thus is explained the terrible surprise that our troops suffered when they found themselves overwhelmed at the first contact by avalanches of projectiles, fired from invisible positions that our artillery could not reach. For there was this of unexpected in the German attack, that, before the infantry assault, the deployment of units was preceded by showers of shells of all calibres, storms of iron and fire arresting and upsetting our shaken line.

In air services, in petrol transport, and in the art of field defences, also, the French were outmatched. Aviation was essentially their sport and science; but the army had shown little interest in it, and had made only a beginning in its two main functions—general reconnaissance

---

4. *Etudes et Impressions de Guerre*, vol. 1. General Malleterre, commanding the 46th Regiment, 3rd Army, was seriously wounded in the Battle of the Marne. Taking up the pen on his recovery, he became one of the ablest French commentators on the war.

and the ranging of artillery fire.[5] Thus ill-prepared for a modern large-scale offensive, France had not acquired the material or the tactic of a strategical defence. The light and rapid "75" had been thought of almost exclusively as an arm of attack, in which weight and range were now become the master properties. Its remarkable qualities for defence began to appear in the unfortunate actions presently to be traced, and were only fully understood many months later, when "barrage" fire had been elaborated. The *mitrailleuse* was essentially a French invention; but its greatest value—in defence—was not yet appreciated.

The numerical provision of machine-guns was the same as that of the German Army (though differently organised). It was owing to a more considerable difference of tactical ideas that a legend grew up of an actual German superiority in this arm. In the French Army, all defensive methods were prejudiced; in the German, they were not. The deep trenches that might have saved much of Belgium and northern France were scouted, until it was too late, as incompatible with the energy and pride of a great army. The lessons from recent wars drawn,

---

5. "No enterprise, perhaps," says a French military publication, "is as purely French as the conquest of the air. The first free balloon, the first dirigible, the first aeroplane all rose from our soil." However, " the war surprised our aviation in an almost complete state of destitution. Our 200 pilots, almost all sportsmen, possessed between them a total of two machine-guns. A few *squadrillas*, without clearly-defined functions, sought their places on the front." Aerial artillery ranging, photography, and observation had been envisaged, and, more generally, chasing and bombardment; but there was hardly a beginning of preparation. France had at the beginning of the war 24 *squadrillas*, each of five or six machines, all scouts of a speed from 50 to 70 miles an hour. M. Engerand says that "Germany entered the campaign with 1500 aeroplanes; we had on the front only 129." Captive balloons had been abandoned as incapable of following the armies in the war of movement then almost exclusively contemplated. "Events proved our mistake," says the official publication already quoted. "Enemy balloons followed the rapid advance of the armies of invasion. Ascending immediately behind the lines, they rendered the adversary indubitable services at the Battle of the Marne. Then we hurriedly constituted balloon companies; and in 1915 we followed the German model of 'sausage' balloons." *Mons and the Retreat*, by Captain G. S. Gordon, a British Staff officer, contains some information of the Royal Flying Corps in August and September 1914, (published by Leonaur in *The Great Retreat* alongwith *The Fighting Retreat to Paris* by Roger Ingpen). The corps was founded in April 1912, At the beginning of the war, it included six squadrons, only four of which could be immediately mobilised, with a complement of 109 officers and 66 aeroplanes. These, however, did excellent work from the beginning. The writer says: "If we were better scouts and fighters, the Germans were better observers for the guns. The perfect understanding between the Taubes and the German gunners was one of the first surprises of the war."

among others, by the Russian State Councillor, Jean de Bloch, fifteen years before, (see note 1 end of section), went for nothing.

Field-Marshal French writes:—

It is easy to be *'wise after the event,'* but I cannot help wondering, why none of us realised what the most modern rifle, the machine-gun, motor traction, the aeroplane, and wireless telegraphy would bring about. It seems so simple when judged by actual results. . . . I feel sure that, had we realised the true effect of modern appliances of war in August 1914, *there would have been no retreat from Mons.* (See note 2 end of section).

While the German armies were born and bred in the old offensive spirit, their masters had seen the difficulties created by the development of modern gunfire. With a tireless and pitiless concentration of will, the men had been organised, trained, and in every essential way provided, to carry out an aggressive plan of campaign. Yet their generals did not despise scientific field-works, even in the days of their first intoxication, as witness any French story of the Battle of Morhange, or this characteristic note on the fighting in the region of Neufchateau and Palliseul:—

The enemy, whom our aeroplanes and cavalry had not been able to discover, had a powerful defensive organisation: fields of wire entanglement on the ground; wide, deep holes concealing pikes and sword blades; Lines of wire 2 yards high, barbed with nails and hooks. There were also, unfortunately, in certain of our corps, insufficiencies of instruction and execution, imprudences committed under fire, over-bold deployments leading to precipitate retreats, a lack of co-ordination between the infantry and the artillery. The enemy profited by our inexperience of the sort of defence he had organised.[6]

---

6. M. Victor Giraud, in his *Histoire*, writes: "The French troops were neither armed nor equipped as they should have been. . . Neither in the liaison of arms, nor in the role of the artillery, nor in the possibilities of aviation or trenches, had the army very clear ideas; it believed only in the offensive, the war of movement, which precisely, today more than ever, calls for a superiority of armament, if not also of effectives. . . . France could and should have remembered that it was the country of Vauban and de Sère de Rivière. . . . There was no longer any faith in permanent fortification, but only in the offensive, which was confused with the offensive spirit." Pierre Dauzet, *Guerre de 1914. De Liège à la Marne.* "I shall not exaggerate much in saying that in many regiments the recruits incorporated in October 1913 commenced the war next August without ever having .shifted a spadeful of earth or dug the most modest trench."—(Thomasson).

For the German soldiers at the outset of the war, this was only a passing necessity. The principle of the instant strategical offensive well expressed the spirit of an authoritarian Government bent on aggression, of its constituency, at once jealous and servile, and its war-machine, sustained by a feverishly developed industrialism. None of these conditions obtained under the Third Republic. Of the weaknesses of the French Army in tactical science, one result is sufficiently tragic proof; in the first month of the war, 33 army corps and divisional generals were removed from their commands.[7]

★★★★★★

Note 1:—De Bloch, who had been a large railway contractor in the Russo-Turkish War, and a leading Polish banker, published the results of his experiences and researches, in six volumes, under the general title *La Guerre*, during the last years of the nineteenth century, and afterwards established a "Museum of War and Peace" at Lucerne to illustrate the subject. His chief thesis was that, owing to the technical development of military instruments and other factors, an aggressive war between States of nearly equal resources could not now give the results aimed at; and there is no longer any doubt that he foresaw the main track of military development as few soldiers did. The following sentences from a sketch of the writings and conversations of de Bloch, published by the present writer in 1902, will serve to show that he anticipated some of the governing characteristics of the Great War:

> The resisting power of an army standing on the defensive, equipped with long-range, quick-firing rifles and guns, from ten to twenty times more powerful than those of 1870 and 1877, expert in entrenching and the use of barbed wire and other obstacles, and highly mobile, is something quite different from that which Napoleon, or even later aggressors, had to face. Not only is it a much larger force, the manhood of a nation; it is also a body highly educated, an army of engineers. Its infantry lines and battery positions will be invisible. Reconnaissances will be easily prevented by protecting; bands of sharp-

---

7. Two commanders of armies, 7 of corps, 20 infantry *divisionaires*, 4 commanders of cavalry divisions. In some army corps, the commander and his two divisional generals were removed (Thomasson).

shooters; and no object of attack will offer itself to the invader till he has come within a zone of deadly fire. The most heavy and powerful shells, which are alone of use against entrenched positions, cannot be used in great number, or brought easily into action. Artillery shares the advantage of a defensive position. If the attackers have a local superiority, the defenders can delay them long enough to allow of an orderly retirement to other entrenched positions. The attacker will be forced to entrench himself, and so the science of the spade reduces battle to sieges. Battle in the open would mean annihilation; yet it is only by assault that entrenched positions can be carried.

Warfare will drag on more slowly than ever. While an invading army is being decimated by sickness and wounds, and demoralised by the heavy loss of officers and the delay of any glorious victory, the home population will be sunk in misery by the growth of economic burdens, the stoppage of trade and industry. The small, elastic, and manageable army of the past could make quick marches, turning movements, strategical demonstrations in the widest sense. Massed armies of millions, like those of to-day, leaning on long-prepared defences, must renounce all the more delicate manifestations of the military art. Armies as they now stand cannot manoeuvre, and must tight in directions indicated in advance. The losses of to-day would be proportionately greater than in past wars, if it were not for the tactical means adopted to avoid them. But the consequence of distance and dispersion is that victorious war—the obtaining of results by destroying the enemy's principal forces, and thus making him submit to the conqueror's will—can exist no more.

With all its errors of detail, de Bloch's picture, drawn when the aeroplane and the petrol motor-wagon, "wireless" and the field-telephone, poison-gas and barrage fire were unknown, was a true prophecy, and all the belligerents paid dearly for neglecting it.

For somewhat similar prognostications by a French officer, see *Comment on pouvait prévoir l'immobilisation des fronts dans la guerre moderne*, being a summary of the writings of Captain Emile

Mayer, whose first studies date from 1888.

Note 2:—He adds: "and that if, in September, the Germans had learned their lesson, the Allies would never have driven them back to the Aisne." This is a more disputable proposition. On the Sambre, the French were immediately driven back; on the Ourcq, the Germans held out for four days, and retired partly because their supply services had given out. To a very large extent they had certainly learned their lesson; and for nearly four years thereafter they bettered it on the Aisne hills.

The quotations are from the volume *1914*, by Field-Marshal Viscount French of Ypres, an important body of evidence, passages of which, however, must be read critically, (*1914* by Sir John French also republished by Leonaur.) Lord French in his narrative repeatedly insists upon the slowness with which the need of a " transformation of military ideas," owing to the factors named, was recognised. "It required the successive attempts of Maunoury, de Castelnau, Foch, and myself to turn the German flanks in the North in the old approved style, and the practical failure of these attempts, to bring home to our minds the true nature of war as it is today."

Of the end of the Battle of the Marne, he writes (ch. 7.):

> We had not even then grasped the true effect and bearing of the many new elements which had entered into the practice of modern war. We fully believed we were driving the Germans back to the Meuse, if not to the Rhine; and all my communications with Joffre and the French generals most closely associated with me breathed the same spirit. . . . We were destined to undergo another terrible disappointment. The lessons of war, as it is today, had to be rubbed in by another dearly-bought experience, and in a hard and bitter school.

There is both courage and *naïveté* in the following tardy profession of the belief de Bloch had expounded fifteen years before:

> Afterwards, we witnessed the stupendous efforts of de Castelnau and Foch; but all ended in the same trench! trench! trench! I finished my part in the Battle of the Aisne, however, unconverted, and it required the further and more bitter lesson of my own failure in the North

to pass the Lys River, during the last days of October, to bring home to my mind a principle in warfare of today which I have held ever since, namely, that, given forces fairly equally matched, you can ' bend,' but you cannot 'break,' your enemy's trench line. . . . Everything which has happened in the war has borne out the truth of this view; and, from the moment I grasped this great truth, I never failed to proclaim it, although eventually I suffered heavily for holding such opinions.

★★★★★★

3. THE FRENCH WAR DOCTRINE

It was not the fault, but the glory, of France that she lived upon a higher level, to worthier ends, than her old enemy. But if we find reason to suspect that, the nation having accepted the burden of taxation and armed service, its arms and preparation were not the best of their kind, that a superstitious fidelity to conservative sentiments and ideas was allowed to obscure the hard facts of the European situation and the changing nature of modern warfare, the fact that certain critics have plunged rashly into the intricacies of a most difficult problem, or the risk of being corrected when more abundant information appears, must not prevent us from facing a conclusion that is important for our subject. We do not espouse any partisan thesis, or question any individual reputation; we can do no more here than open a line of inquiry, and no less than recall that the men whose responsibility is in cause had suddenly to challenge fate on evidence al many points slighter than now lies before any studious layman.

In every detail, Germany had the benefit of the initiative. The French Staff could not be sure in advance of British and Belgian aid or of Italian neutrality, and it was bound to envisage the possibility of attack by the Jura, as well as by Belgium. It could not be sure that any smaller strength would secure the Lorraine frontier; and it was possibly right in regarding a defeat on the east as more dangerous than a defeat in the north. The distrust of fortification, whether of masonry and steel, or of field-works, may have become exaggerated by a too lively sense of the power of the newer artillery; but it had a certain basis in the fear of immobilising and paralysing the armies. To discover a happy mean between a dangerous obstinacy in defending a frontier, and a dangerous readiness to abandon precious territory and its people in order to preserve freedom of movement, was perhaps beyond any brain of that time.

Nevertheless, when all allowances have been made, it must be said (1) that the importance of gaining time by defensive action was never realised, and this chiefly because of dogmatic prepossessions; (2) that the actual concentration expressed a complete misjudgement of the line of greatest danger; and (3) that these two faults were aggravated by the kind of offensive upon which all hopes were placed. The misapprehension of the German system of reserves, referred to above, and therefore of the total effective strength of the enemy, had led the French Staff to conclude that there was nothing to fear west of the Meuse, and at the same time had confirmed a temperamental belief in the possibility of crippling the attack by a rapid and unrestrained offensive. The whole conception was erroneous.

For Belgium, there was no other hope than a provisional defensive. In any war with Germany, the principal object for France, it now seems evident, must be to stave off the *coup brusqué* till Russia was fully ready, and England could bring more aid. But the traditional dogma was in possession; any doubt was damned as a dangerous heresy. The chief lesson of 1870 was now thought to be the folly of passivity. Looking back upon events, many French soldiers recognise, with General Malleterre, that the French strategy should have been "a waiting disposition behind a powerfully-organised Meuse front, with a mass of manoeuvre ready to be directed against the principal attack." This writer adds:—

> But our minds had been trained in these latter years to the offensive *à outrance*.[8]

They had been trained in part upon German discussions, the deceptive character of which, and the very different facts behind, were not realised. At its best, for instance in Foch's lectures at the Ecole Supérieure de Guerre (1895-1901), there was in this teaching somewhat too much of emotion, too little of cold analysis. The faith in sheer energy and will is placed too high, the calculation of means to

---

8. *Etudes.* And again: "The offensive idea had become very clear and very formal in our minds. It had the place, so to say, of an official war doctrine. The lesson of the Russo-Japanese war and the Balkan wars seemed to have disturbed the teaching of the War School and the governing ideas of our Staff. At the moment when the war opened, there was a sharp discussion between the partisans of the offensive *à outrance* and those who, foreseeing the formidable manoeuvre of Germany, leaned to a more prudent, more reasoned method, which they described *as defensive strategy and offensive tactic.*"

ends too slightly insisted upon. It is true, it is, indeed, a truism, that "the battle must not be purely defensive," that "every defensive battle must be terminated by an offensive action, or it will lead to no result." Foch himself, before he had risen to the supreme direction of the Allied armies, had learned to recognise that, with millions of men in play, no effort of will can suddenly give a decision, that the defensive may have to continue for months, even for years, a new war-machine may have to be built up, ere a victorious reaction becomes possible.

In the General Staff instructions of October 28, 1913, the doctrine had received its extremest expression. The milder instructions of 1895 were condemned as based upon the "most dangerous" idea that a commander might prefer defence on a favourable, to attack on an unfavourable, ground. "In order to avoid all misunderstanding on so important a point of doctrine, the new instructions admit only a single justification for the defensive in combat, that is, the necessity of economising troops on certain points in order to devote more forces to attacks; so understood, the defensive is, properly speaking, no more than an auxiliary of the offensive." "The offensive alone leads to positive results"; this is the sole permissible rule governing the conduct of operations.

Attacks must be pressed to the extremity without *arrière-pensée* or fear of heavy losses: "every other conception must be rejected as contrary to the very nature of war" (art. 5). "A Commander-in-Chief will never leave to his adversary the priority of action on the pretext of waiting for more precise information; he will, from the beginning of the war, stamp it with such a character of violence and determination that the enemy, struck in his morale and paralysed in action, will perhaps find himself compelled to remain on the defensive" (art. 6). "All the decisions of the command must be inspired by the will to seize and keep the initiative"; and they must be pursued "even if the information collected up to then on the forces and dispositions of the enemy be obscure and incomplete." The plan should, indeed, be supple, so that changes can be made according to new information; but "success in war depends more on perseverance and tenacity than on ability in the conception of the manoeuvre ." (art. 15). "The French Army," added the commission which elaborated these rules "returning to its traditions, now admits in the conduct of operations no law other than that of the offensive."

Fortunately, no code can do more than hamper the natural elasticity of the French mind. But the direction of the armies from top to bottom, and even the traditional aim of keeping in hand a mass of manoeuvre, which had figured strongly in the teaching of Foch and other military writers of ten or fifteen years before, were affected by the current prescriptions of the Staff. We cannot here attempt to trace the growth of the perversion. The spirit of the French command on the eve of the war is, however, sufficiently evidenced in its actual dispositions; and we know that it threw its only mass of manoeuvre (the 4th Army) into the Belgian Ardennes in the third week of August, and had to fight the Battle of the Marne without any general reserve. In brief, along with every arm and method of defence, the service of information, the preparation of battle, and the art of manoeuvre—which is irreconcilable with a dogma of universal and unconditional attack—were depreciated and prejudiced. (See note 1 end of section). In the strength and weakness of this creed, France entered the war.

The results in the lesser commands were serious enough. Speaking of the advance into the Ardennes, M. Hanotaux, in general an apologist of the old school, says that it was conducted "in an extremely optimistic mood," that "mad bayonet charges were launched at a mile distance from the enemy without artillery preparation," and that, "doubtless, the spirit of the offensive, ill-regulated and ill-restrained, among officers as well as men, was one of the causes of our reverse," Officers and men took only too literally the rules on which they had been trained. Strengthened by the general belief in a short war, and by an exaggerated idea of the importance of first results, a like infatuation governed the strategy and the tactics of the French armies.

A succession of surprises marks the light regard for information of the enemy's means and movements, as a series of instant reverses measures the scorn for well-pondered manoeuvre. Was France required by her Eastern ally to attack at once? The attack need not have surpassed the proportions of holding actions punctuating a stout defence. Was Belgium closed to the French armies by the old treaty of neutrality? That did not justify a plan of campaign which left the north uncovered to a German aggression. For all that followed from disunity of the Allied commands, England and Belgium share the responsibility. Had they, as well as Russia, been long in alliance, and Italy's neutrality assured in advance, all might have gone otherwise; probably, indeed, there would have been no war. These circumstances do not afford excuse for a radically unsound conception of the danger and the reply.

A German attack through Belgium had been much and long discussed. If few would have said before the event, as the German Chancellor and Foreign Secretary pleaded immediately afterward, that it was "a question step absolutely required," it was at least more than probable; and we have Marshal Joffre's word for it that the contingency was contemplated by the French Staff. (See note 2 end of section). But two doubts remained, even in vigilant minds. Would the invasion by the north be large or small, and would it be more or less extensive, proceeding only by Belgian Luxembourg and the Meuse valley, or also by a more daring sweep across the Flanders plain into the valley of the Oise? Moltke had advocated a march to the North Sea coast, and a descent by the Channel ports, through the *trouée* of the Oise, upon Paris, turning not merely the principal line, but the whole system, of the French fortresses.

Bernhardi had toyed with the idea of an even more extensive movement, violating Dutch territory, but seemed at last to favour the more limited project, "the army of the right wing marching by the line Trêves-Stenay, crossing Luxembourg and southern Belgium." In fact, neither of these ways was taken. The invasion pursued a middle route, Holland being avoided, the descent upon the coast deferred, and armies thrown across both the Flanders plain and the difficult country of the Belgian Ardennes.

Notwithstanding the advertisement of the *Kaiser's* chief ministers in their famous pleas in justification, on the first day of the war, the French Staff do not seem to have anticipated anything more in the north than an attack by Luxembourg and the Ardennes, or to have altered their dispositions to meet it until the middle of August. We do not yet fully know what are the reasons for the arrest of the German offensive after the effective reduction of Liège, until August 19. Instead of six days, with, perhaps, three more for re-concentration, the German right wing took sixteen days in crossing Belgium. As this week of Belgium's vicarious sacrifice saved France, it cannot be supposed to have been a voluntary delay made simply for the purpose of deceiving the Allies, It had that effect, however.

Thwarted at Liège, the German command did everything it could to conceal the true nature of the blow it was about to deliver—by terrorising the population and occupying the mind of the world with its atrocities, by the ubiquitous activity of its cavalry screen, by avoiding Western Flanders and the coast, and by holding up the advance of its first three armies behind the line of the Gette and the Meuse till everything was ready. The Allies altogether failed to pierce the veil of mystery covering the final concentration. They were deceived (1) as to

39

the main direction of the coming onslaught, (2) as to its speed, (3) as to its power in men and armament. General Sordêt's cavalry got little information during their Belgian wanderings; the few French aviators still less. No doubt, the Allies hoped for a longer Belgian resistance, especially at Liège and Namur, as the enemy expected a shorter. The French Staff clung blindly to its belief that it need expect, at most, only an attack by the Meuse valley and the Ardennes. (See note 3 end of chapter). The first French plan of campaign, then, envisaged solely the eastern and north-eastern frontier. The original concentration placed the two strongest armies, the 1st and 2nd (Dubail and Castelnau—each five corps) between Belfort and Toul; the 3rd and 5th (Ruffey and Lanrezac—three and five corps respectively) from Verdun to Givet, where the Meuse enters Belgium; the 4th (de Langle de Cary—three corps) supporting the right, at its rear, between the Argonne and the Meuse.

Of 25 reserve divisions, three were kept in the Alps till Italy declared her neutrality, three garrisoned Verdun, and one Epinal. The remainder were grouped, one group being sent to the region of Hirson, one to the Woevre, and one before Nancy. There was also a Territorial group (d'Amade) about Lille. These dispositions are defended as being supple and lending themselves to a redirection when the enemy's intentions were revealed. (See note 4 end of section). We shall see that, within a fortnight, they had to be fundamentally changed, Lanrezac being sent into the angle of the Sambre and Meuse, de Langle bringing in the sole reserve army in on his right, and Ruffey marching north into the Ardennes—a north-westerly movement involving awkward lateral displacements, the crossing of columns, and oblique marches. Some of the following failure and confusion resulted from the dislocating effect of a conversion so vast.

★★★★★★

Note 1:—In *L'Erreur de 1914. Réponse aux Critiques* (Paris and Brussels: G. van Oest. 1919), General Berthaut is reduced to the suggestion that some of these phrases were intended " to stimulate the ardour of the young officers," but that "the Command was not at all bound to take them literally."

General Berthaut was sub-chief of the French General Staff, and director of the geographical service, from 1903 to 1912; and his defence of the ideas prevailing up to the eve of the war deserves careful reading, unsatisfying as it may be found on many points. It is mainly intended to justify the Eastward concentration, and to controvert those who think the business of an army is to defend the national territory foot by foot. The general appeals to the weight of military authority (which, as we shall see, is less one-sided than he suggests):

> From 1875 to 1914, we had 40 Ministers of War; we changed the Chief of Staff sixteen times; changes were still more numerous among subchiefs of Staff, heads of bureaux and services. Several hundred officers of all arms, returning periodically to their regiments, contributed to the Staff work of the army. Yet the directive idea of our defence never varied. Such as it was in 1876, so it was revealed in 1914.

Throughout this time, concentration was foreseen and prepared behind the upper courses of the Meuse and Moselle with a view to positions being held in the upper valleys of the Marne, Aube, and Seine. The idea that the French eastern frontier was infrangible, General Berthaut considers "extremely exaggerated." If it had not been adequately held, the Germans would have turned thither from the north. The violation of the neutrality either of Switzerland or Belgium was, however, beyond doubt. To cover the whole frontier was impossible; and, "incontestably," the armies had to be turned in one mass toward the east. Trenches are "an effect, not a cause, of the stabilisation of fronts." The general has a very poor opinion of fortresses, the only one to which he attributes great importance being Metz! Liège was "a practically useless sacrifice"; Maubeuge" stopped nothing."

These opinions seem to the present writer untenable; and General Berthaut admits that the reaction against fortification "went too far". He may be said to damn the three French offensives with faint praise. The move into Alsace "could not be of any military interest," and was " a political affair." The Lorraine offensive was "necessarily limited," as a distant objective could not be pursued between Metz and Strasbourg. As to Charleroi, France was bound to make a demonstration on behalf of Belgium and "to satisfy public opinion." Much of General Berthaut's *apologia* is vitiated by his assumption that France had necessarily to face a superiority of force.

One of the critics General Berthaut started out to controvert is M. Fernand Engerand, deputy for Calvados, whose articles (particularly in *Le Correspondant*, December 10, 1917, and subsequent numbers) have been reprinted in a volume of 600 pages: *Le Secret de la Frontière, 1815-1871-1914. Charleroi.* The French plan of campaign, says M. Engerand, was "humanly impossible. Nothing happened as our High Command had foreseen; there was surprise all along the line, and, what is gravest, surprise not only strategic but intellectual, the reversal of a doctrine of war. After the magnificent recovery of the Marne, we may without inconvenience avow that never has there been so complete a self-deception. The error was absolute and, worse, deliberate, for never was an attack more foreseen, more announced, more prophesied than that of August 1914. Strategists of the old school had not only predicted it for forty years. but had given us the means of parrying it; their ideas were scouted and their work was destroyed."

M. Engerand quotes, in particular, Lt.-Colonel Grouard on the impossibility of an immediate French offensive beyond the frontiers (see Grouard, *La Guerre Eventuelle*, 1913; and *L'Art de la Guerre et le Colonel Grouard,* by C. de Bourcet, 1915). Grouard foresaw, among other things, that "the army of the German right, marching by the left bank of the Meuse, would pass the Sambre in the neighbourhood of Charleroi, and direct itself toward the sources of the Oise." M. Engerand's chapters contain a summary of the three French offensives. His general comment is:

> No unity of command, separate and dislocated battles, no notion of information and safeguards before and during the combat, systematic misconception of the ground and defensive means, defective liaison between the corps and between artillery and infantry, no manoeuvre, but only the offensive, blind, systematic, frantic. If we were defeated, is it an exaggeration to say that it was less by the enemy than by a false doctrine?

Lt.-Col. de Thomasson, on these points, quotes warning notes from General Collin's *Transformation de la Guerre*, written in 1911, and refers to the case of Lt.-Col. Berrot, who, in 1902, had exposed "the dangerous theories that had been deduced from the Napoleonic wars," and who "was disgraced pitilessly, and died while yet young."

Note 2:—Early French writers on the war found it difficult to make up their minds whether there had, or had not, been a surprise in the North. See *Histoire de la Guerre de 1914* (ch. "*Septembre*"), by Gabriel Hanotaux. This work, the most ambitious of the kind yet attempted, is being published in fortnightly sections and periodical volumes, of which the first deals with the origins of the war, the next three with the frontier battles, and the following ones with the battles of the retreat and preliminaries of the Battle of the Marne.

M. Hanotaux says:

> The project prepared by the German Staff of an offensive by Belgium was not a secret. All was public and confessed. There was no surprise in the absolute sense of the word. But there remained an unknown quantity: would the probable hypothesis be realised?

> The long-prepared manoeuvre consisted in crushing us by the carefully veiled onslaught not of 12, but of 25, army corps, so that the surprise was double for us: the most eccentric movement and the most unexpected numbers. . . . It was this combination of circumstances, foreseen and unforeseen, that the French Command had to parry: political necessity, surprise, numbers, preparation, munitions.

> The invasion of Belgium *by the left bank of the Meuse* certainly surprised the French High Command ("*La Manoeuvre de la Marne," Rev. des Deux Mondes*, March 15, 1919).

M. Reinach, usually so clear and positive, was also ambiguous on this point (*La Guerre sur le Front Occidental,* vol. 1.). It suffices he says, to glance at the map:

> Nature herself traced this path (Flanders and the Oise). Innumerable armies have followed it, in both directions, for centuries.

Nevertheless, the French Staff, though it had "followed for many years the German preparations for an offensive by Belgium," remained in an "anguish of doubt."

Much evidence with regard to the events of the first phase of the war is contained in the reports of the French "Commission of Inquiry on Metallurgy," 1918-19, the special task of which was to consider why the Briey coalfield was not defended. On May 14, 1919, General Maunoury testified to disaccord existing between commanding officers at the beginning of the campaign, failure to co-ordinate efforts, and ignorance of some generals of the plan of concentration. On the same day. General Michel said that, in 1911, when he was Vice-President of the Superior War Council, that is, *Generalissimo* designate, he submitted a plan of concentration based upon a certitude of the whole German invasion passing by Belgium and of the need of the principal French action being directed to the North. The plan was rejected, after being examined by General Brun, M. Berteaux, and M. Messimy.

General Percin, at the same inquiry (May 24, 1919), spoke of "intrigues" and a "real palace revolution" in 1911 to replace General Michel, as future Commander-in-Chief, by General Pau, the offence of the former being to have foretold that the Germans would advance by the left bank of the Meuse, and that they would at once engage their reserves. According to General Percin, in the spring of 1914 General de Castelnau said:

> If the Germans extend their fighting front as far as Lille, they will thin it so much that we can cut it in two. We can wish for nothing better.

There is other evidence of this idea prevailing in the General Staff: apparently it arose from underestimates of the effective strength of the invasion.

Marshal Joffre gave evidence before the commission on July 5, 1919, but his reported statements do not greatly help us. He defended the concentration under "plan 17," which, he said, was operated much more to the north than in previous plans, nearly all of these foreseeing concentration south of Verdun. The French Staff was chiefly concerned to give battle only when it had its full forces in hand. The 3rd Army had a quite particular function, that of investing Metz. The plan made before the war was not absolute, but was a directive modifiable according to events.

Officially, it stopped short at Hirson; but the Staff had foreseen variants to second the Belgian effort. In March 1914, the Staff had prepared a note in which it had foreseen the invasion by Belgium—a plan providing for eventualities. It was, therefore, absurd to pretend that it had never foreseen the invasion by Belgium. The Briey district was under the cannon of Metz, and could not be included in the region of concentration. The loss of the "Battle of the Frontiers" was due to the fact that the best units of the German Army presented themselves on the feeble point of our front. On the French side there were failings. Generals who had great qualities in peace time failed under stress of war. He had had to take action against some who were his best friends, but believed he had done his duty. Asked by the chairman with how many rifles he commenced the war, Marshal Joffre replied, "with 2,300,000." Lille, he said, could not be defended.

Field-Marshal French (*1914*) says:

> Personally, I had always thought that Germany would violate Belgian neutrality, and in no such half-hearted measure as by a march through the Ardennes.

Note 3. In an article on the second anniversary of the first Battle of the Yser, the *Temps* (Oct. 30, 1916) said that, before the war, Belgium was more suspicious of England and France than of Germany.

> If our Staffs had wished to prepare, for the defence of Belgium, a plan of operations on her territory, these suspicions would have taken body and open conflict occurred. Nothing was foreseen of what happened, and nothing was prepared.

Field-Marshal French says:

> Belgium remained a 'dark horse' to the last, and could never be persuaded to decide upon her attitude in the event of a general war. . . . We were anxious she should assist and co-operate in her own defence.

On August 21, he received a note from the Belgian Government remarking that the Belgian field army had from the commencement of hostilities "been standing by hoping for the active co-operation of the Allied Army," but was now retreating upon Antwerp.

M. Engerand (*Le Drame de Charleroi*) says that on July 29, General Lanrezac had sent to General Joffre a report on the likelihood of an enveloping movement by the left bank of the Meuse; that after the German Chancellor's defence, on August 4, of the violation of Belgian neutrality, the Belgian Government asked France for aid; that the French Minister of War had of his own initiative offered to send five army corps:

> But, on August 5, our Councillor of Embassy at London, M. de Fleurian, informed the Belgian Minister that 'the French *generalissimo* did not intend to change his strategic plan, and only the non-co-operation of the British Army would oblige him to extend the French left.' The Sordêt Cavalry Corps, on and after August 6, reported to the General Staff that 13 German Corps, in two armies, were intended to operate west of the Meuse, and that ten others were ready to advance on the east of the river. On August 7, Lanrezac addressed to the Grand Quartier General another report on the danger to our left; and on the 14th he expressed his conviction that there would be a strong offensive west of the Meuse directly to General Joffre, who did not credit it.

Major Collon, French military *attaché* at Brussels, and afterwards attached to French Headquarters, has published the following facts in a letter to the Swiss Colonel Egli (Temps, September 19, 1918): Although the Army of Hanover (Emmich's Army of the Meuse) was mobilised from July 21 and concentrated in Westphalia from July 26, it was not till August 3, after the publication of the German ultimatum, that France offered Belgium her eventual military aid. This was declined; but on August 4, when the violation of the frontier occurred the offer was accepted in principle. On August 5, General Joffre authorised the Sordêt Cavalry Corps to move to the Semoy. It began its march on the 6th, and on that night Major Collon arrived at Belgian Headquarters with a view to assuring the co-ordination of the French and Belgian operations.

Note 4:—"This plan was at once weak and supple. It was feeble because General Joffre, who established it, 'saw too many things,' in the words of the Napoleonic warning.... He knew as well as any one the feebleness of his plan. It was imposed upon him. He sought at least to make it supple" (Reinach, *op. cit.*).

In an article reviewing this volume (*Petit Parisian*, June 16, 1916), M. Millerand, who became Minister of War a few days after the events in question, endorsed this opinion: The French Staff "had to foresee, did foresee, the two hypotheses—that of Belgium, certainly, but also that of Lorraine. Hence general dispositions whose suppleness did not escape weakness, a concentration for two ends." The word "Belgium" here is ambiguous; it is clear that an attack by Western Belgium was not foreseen. The vice of the concentration was not that it faced two ends, "Belgium
and "Lorraine," but that it essentially faced the end of a Lorraine offensive, whereas what was essentially needed was a northern defensive.

General Bonnal remarks:

> The project of offensive operations conceived by Bernhardi in 1911 in case of a war with France deserved close study by us, which would probably have led to modifications in our plan of concentration while there was yet time (*Les Conditions de la Guerre Moderne*).

General Palat writes:

> The French concentration was vicious. Better conceived, it would have saved hundreds of thousands of our compatriots from the tortures of the invasion and occupation(*La Revue*, Dec. 1, 1917).

Lt.-Col. de Thomasson, says:

> The unknown quantity on the side of Belgium condemned us at the outset to a waiting strategy. The idea of at once taking the offensive madly overpassed the boldest conceptions of Napoleon

> A well-advised command would have understood that it was folly to launch at once all its army to attack troops of the value of the Germans; that the offensive should have been made only on certain points of the front, with a sufficient numerical superiority, and for this purpose the forces must be economised; that, in brief, the beginning of hostilities could only be favourable to us on condition of a superior strategy such as was shown in the preparation for the battle of the Marne, but not in the initial plan or in the first three weeks of the war.

4. The Three French Offensives

Instead of an initial defensive over most of the front, with or without some carefully chosen and strongly provided manoeuvre of offence—as the major conditions of the problem would seem to suggest—the French campaign opened with a general offensive, which for convenience we must divide into three parts, three adventures, all abortive, into Southern Alsace, German Lorraine, and the Belgian Ardennes. The first two of these were predetermined, even before General Joffre was designed for the chief command; the second and third were deliberately launched after the invasion of Belgium was, or should have been, understood. A fourth attack, across the Sambre, was designed, but could not be attempted.

The first movement into Alsace was hardly more than a raid, politically inspired, and its success might have excited suspicions. Advancing from Belfort, the 1st Army under Dubail took Altkirch on August 7, and Mulhouse the following day. Paris rejoiced; General Joffre hailed Dubail's men as "first labourers in the great work of *la revanche*." It was the last flicker of the old Gallic cocksureness. On August 9, the Germans recovered Mulhouse. Next day, an Army of Alsace, consisting of the 7th Corps, the 44th Division, four reserve divisions, five Alpine battalions, and a cavalry division, was organised under General Pau. It gained most of the Vosges passes and the northern buttress of the range, the Donon (August 14). On the 19th, the enemy was defeated at Dornach, losing 3000 prisoners and 24 cannon; and on the following morning Mulhouse was retaken—only to be abandoned a second time on the 25th, with all but the southern passes. The Army of Alsace was then dissolved to free Pau's troops for more urgent service, the defence of Nancy and of Paris,

The Lorraine offensive was a more serious affair, and it was embarked upon after the gravity of the northern menace had been recognised.[9] The main body of the Eastern forces was engaged—nine active corps of the 2nd and 1st Armies, with nine reserve and three cavalry divisions—considerably more than 400,000 men, under some of the most distinguished French generals, including de Castlenau, unsurpassed in repute and experience even by the *generalissimo* himself; Dubail, a younger man, full of energy and quick intelligence; Foch,

---

9. See Hanotaux, *Histoire Generale de la Guerre*; Engerand, "Lorraine-Ardennes" (*Le Correspondant*, April 25, 1918); Paul H. Courrière, "*La Bataille de Sarre-et-Seille*" (*La Revue*, Jan. 1, 1917); Gerald Campbell, *Verdun to the Vosges*—the author was correspondent of *The Times* on the Eastern frontier; Thomasson, *loc. cit.*

under whose iron will the famous 20th Corps of Nancy did much to limit the general misfortune; Pau, who had just missed the chief command; and de Maud'huy, a sturdy leader of men.

As soon as the Vosges passes were secured, after ten days' hard fighting, on August 14, a concerted advance began, Castelnau moving eastward over the frontier into the valley of the Seille and the Gap of Morhange, a narrow corridor flanked by marshes and forests, rising to formidable cliffs; while Dubail, on his right, turned north-eastward into the hardly less difficult country of the Sarre Valley. The French appear to have had a marked superiority of numbers, perhaps as large as 100,000 men; but they were drawn on till they fell into a powerful system, established since the mobilisation, of shrewdly hidden defences, with a large provision of heavy artillery, from Morville, through Morhange, Bensdorf, and Fenetrange, to Phalsburg—the Bavarian Army at the centre, a detachment from the Metz garrison against the French left, the army of Von Heeringen against the right.

The French command can hardly have been ignorant of these defences, but must have supposed they would fall to an impetuous assault. Dubail held his own successfully throughout August 19 and 20 at Sarrebourg and along the Marne-Rhine Canal, though his men were much exhausted, Castelnau was immediately checked, before the natural fortress of Morhange, on August 20. His centre—the famous 20th Corps and a southern corps, the 15th—attacked at 5 a.m.; at 6.30 the latter was in flight, and the former, its impetuosity crushed by numbers and artillery fire, was ordered to desist. The German commanders had concentrated their forces under cover of field-works and heavy batteries. Under the shock of this surprise, at 4 p.m., Castelnau ordered the general retreat. Dubail had to follow suit.

Happily, the German infantry were in no condition for an effective pursuit, and the French retirement was not seriously impeded. The following German advance being directed southward, with the evident intention of forcing the Gap of Charmes, and so taking all the French northern armies in reverse, the defence of Nancy was left to Foch, Castelnau's centre and right were swung round south-westward behind the Meurthe, while Dubail abandoned the Donon, and withdrew to a line which, from near Rozelieures to Badonviller and the northern Vosges, made a right-angle with the line of the 2nd Army, the junction covering the mouth of the threatened *trouée*. In turn, as we shall see (Chap. 3, sec. 3), the German armies here suffered defeat, only five days after their victory.

But such failures and losses do not "cancel out," for France had begun at a disadvantage. Ground was lost that might have been held with smaller forces; forces were wasted that were urgently needed in the chief field of battle. Evidently it was hoped to draw back parts of the northern armies of invasion, to interfere with their communications, and to set up an alarm for Metz and Strasbourg. These aims were not to any sensible extent accomplished.

Despite the improbability of gaining a rapid success in a wild forest region, the French Staff seems to have long cherished the idea of an offensive into the Belgian Ardennes in case of a German invasion of Belgium, the intention being to break the turning movement by a surprise blow at its flank. By August 19, the French were in a measure prepared for action between Verdun and the Belgian Meuse. Ruffey's 3rd Army (including a short-lived "Army of Lorraine" of six reserve divisions under Maunoury), and Langle de Cary's 4th Army, brought northwards into line after three or four days' delay, counted together six active corps and reserve groups making them nearly equal in numbers to the eleven corps of the Imperial Crown Prince and the Duke of Würtemberg.

But, behind the latter, all unknown till it debouched on the Meuse, lay hidden adroitly in Belgian Luxembourg another army, the three corps of the Saxon War Minister, Von Hansen. Farther west, the disparity of force was greater, Lanrezac and Sir John French having only about seven corps (with some help from the Belgians and a few Territorial units) against eleven corps left to Bülow and Kluck after two corps had been detailed to mask the Belgian Army in Antwerp. Neither the Ardennes nor the Sambre armies could be further strengthened because of the engagements in Lorraine and Alsace.

A tactical offensive into the Ardennes, a glorified reconnaissance and raid, strictly limited and controlled, might perhaps be justified. The advance ordered on the evening of the defeat of Morhange, and executed on the two following days, engaging the only general reserve at the outset in a thickly-wooded and most difficult country, was too large for a diversion, and not large enough for the end declared: it failed completely and immediately—in a single day, August 22—with heavy losses, especially in officers.[10] Here, again, there was an approxi-

---

10. See Hanotaux, "*La Bataille des Ardennes, Etude Tactique et Strategique*" (*Revue des Deux Mondes*, Feb. 15, 1917); Engerand, as above; Ernest Renauld, "Charleroi-Dinant-Neufchateau-Virton" (*La Revue*, Oct. 1916—inaccurate as regards the British Army); Malleterre, *Un Peu de Lumière sur les Batailles d'Août-Septembre 1914*.

mate equality of numbers; again, the French were lured on to unfavourable ground, and, before strong entrenchments, crushed with a superiority of fire. Separated and surprised—the left south-west of Palliseul, the centre in the forests of Herbeumont and Luchy, the Colonial Corps before Neufchateau and Rossignol, where it fought literally to the death against two German corps strongly entrenched, the 2nd Corps near Virton—the body of the 4th Army was saved only by a prompt retreat; and the 3rd Army had to follow this movement. True, the German IV Army also was much exhausted; and an important part of the enemy's plan missed fire. It had been soon discovered that the Meuse from Givet to Namur was but lightly held; and the dispatch thither of the Saxon Army, to cut in between the French 4th and 5th Armies, was a shrewd stroke. Hansen was late in reaching the critical point, about Dinant, and, by slowness and timidity, missed the chance of doing serious mischief.

Meanwhile, between the fields of the two French adventures into German Lorraine and Belgian Luxembourg, the enemy had been allowed without serious resistance to occupy the Briey region, and so to carry over from France to Germany an iron- and coal-field of the utmost value. "Briey has saved our life," the ironmasters of the Rhineland declared later on, with some exaggeration. Had it been modernised, the small fortress of Longwy, situated above the River Chiers three miles from the Luxembourg frontier, might have been an important element in a defence of this region. In fact, its works were out of date, and were held at the mobilisation by only two battalions of infantry and a battery and a half of light guns. The Germans summoned Colonel Darche and his handful of men to surrender on August 10; but the place was not invested till the 20th, the day on which the 3rd Army was ordered to advance toward Virton and Arlon, and to disengage Longwy. Next day, Ruffey was north and east of the place, apparently without suspecting that he had the Crown Prince's force besieging it at his mercy. On the 22nd, it was too late; the 3rd and 4th Armies were in retreat; Longwy was left to its fate.[11]

5. THE BATTLE OF CHARLEROI-MONS

The completest surprise naturally fell on the west wing of the Allies; and, had not the small British force been of the hardiest stuff, an irreparable disaster might have occurred. Here, with the heaviest preponderance of the enemy, there had been least preparation for any

---

11 See *L'Illustration*, March 16, 1918: *La Défense de Longwy*, by P. Nicou.

hostilities before the crisis was reached. On or about August 10, we war correspondents received an official map of the "Present Zone of the Armies," which was shown to end, on the north, at Orchies—16 miles S.E. of Lille, and 56 miles inland from Dunkirk. The western half of the northern frontier was practically uncovered. Lille had ceased to be a fortress in 1913, though continuing to be a garrison town; from Maubeuge to the sea, there was no artificial obstacle, and no considerable body of troops.[12]

The position to be taken by the British Expeditionary Force—on the French left near Maubeuge—was only decided, at a Franco-British Conference in London, on August 10.[13] On August 12, the British Press Bureau announced it as "evident" that "the mass of German troops lie between Liège and Luxembourg." Three days later, a Saxon advance guard tried, without success, to force the Meuse at Dinant. Thus warned, the French command began to make the new disposition of its forces which has been alluded to.

Lanrezac had always anticipated the northern attack, and had made representations on the subject without effect.[14] At last, on August 16, General Joffre, from his headquarters at Vitry-le-François, in southern Champagne, agreed to his request that he should move the 5th Army north-westward into the angle of the Sambre and Meuse. At the same time, however, its composition was radically' upset, the 11th Corps and two reserve divisions being sent to the 4th Army, while the 18th

---

12. The military history of Lille, is curious. See *Lille*, by General Percin. M. Engerand, in his chapter on "The Abandonment of Lille," says that a third of the cannon had been removed earlier in the year, but that on August 21 , when General Herment took command, there remained 446 pieces with enough ammunition and 25,000 men, not counting the neighbouring Territorial divisions of General d'Amade. Though Lille had been virtually declassed on the eve of the war. General Percin, the governor (afterwards cruelly traduced on the subject) and General Herment were anxious, and had begun preparations, to defend it. The municipal and other local authorities protested to the Government against any such effort being made; and at the last moment, on the afternoon of August 24, when the retreat from the Sambre had begun, the Minister of War ordered the abandonment of the town and the evacuation of the region. German patrols entered the city two days later, but it was only occupied at the beginning of October. It has been argued that, with Lille and Maubeuge held on their flanks, and the Scarpe, Scheldt, and Rhonelle valleys flooded, the Allied forces might have delayed the enemy long enough to permit of a definite stand on the line Amiens-La Fère-Laon-Rheims. General Berthaut rejects any such idea, and says that inundations would have required forty days.
13. French's *1914*.
14. See *La Grande Guerre sur le Front Occidental*, especially vol. iv., by General Palat.

Corps and the Algerian divisions were received in compensation. On August 16, the British commander-in-chief, after seeing President Poincaré and the Ministers in Paris, visited the *generalissimo* at Vitry; and it was arranged that the Expeditionary Force, which was then gathering south of Maubeuge, should move north to the Sambre, and thence to the region of Mons.

On the same day. General d'Amade was instructed to proceed from Lyons to Arras, there to gather together three Territorial divisions of the north which, reinforced by another on the 21st and by two reserve divisions on the 25th, ultimately became part of the Army of the Somme. Had there been, on the French side, any proper appreciation of the value of field-works, it might, perhaps, not have been too late to defend the line of the Sambre and Meuse. It was four or five days too late to attempt a Franco-British offensive beyond the Sambre.

To do justice to the Allied commanders, it must be kept clearly in mind that they had (albeit largely by their own fault) but the vaguest notion of what was impending. Would the mass of the enemy come by the east or the west of the Meuse, by the Ardennes or by Flanders, and in what strength? Still sceptical as to a wide enveloping movement, Joffre was reluctant to adventure too far north with his unready left wing; but it seemed to him that, in either case, the intended offensive of the French central armies (the 3rd and 4th) across the Ardennes and Luxembourg frontier might be supported by an attack by Lanrezac and the British upon the flank of the German western armies—the right flank, if they passed by the Ardennes only; the left, if they attempted to cross the Flanders plain toward the Channel.

Thus, it was provisionally arranged with the British Commander that, when the concentration of the Expeditionary Force was complete, which would not be before the evening of August 21, it should advance north of the Sambre in the general direction of Nivelles (20 miles north-east of Mons, and halfway between Charleroi and Brussels). If the common movement were directed due north, the British would advance on the left of the 5th Army; if to the north-east or east, they would be in echelon on its left rear. General Joffre recognised that the plan was only provisional, it being impossible to define the projected manoeuvre more precisely till all was ready on August 21, or till the enemy revealed his intentions.

It was only on the 20th that two corps of the French 5th Army reached the south bank of the Sambre—one day before Bülow came up on the north, with his VII Corps on his right (west), the X Reserve and X Active Corps as centre, the Guard Active Corps on his left, and the VII Reserve (before Namur) and Guard Reserve Corps in support. In this posture, on the evening of August 20, Lanrezac received General Joffre's order to strike across the Sambre. Namur was then garrisoned by the Belgian 4th Division, to which was added, on the 22nd, part of the French 8th Brigade under General Mangin. Lanrezac had not even been able to get all his strength aligned on the Sambre when the shock came.[15]

On the 21st, his five corps were grouped as follows: The 1st Corps (Franchet d'Espérey) was facing east toward the Meuse north of Dinant, pending the arrival, on the evening of the 22nd, of the Bouttegourd Reserve Division; the 10th Corps (Defforges), with the 37th (African) Division, on the heights of Fosse and Arsimont, faced the Sambre crossings at Tamines and Auvelais; the 3rd Corps (Sauret) stood before Charleroi, with the 38th (African) Division in reserve; the 18th Corps (de Mas-Latrie) was behind the left, south of Thuin. Of General Valabrègue's group of reserve divisions, one was yet to come into line on the right and one on the left.

Could Lanrezac have accomplished anything by pressing forward into the unknown with tired troops? The question might be debatable had the Allies had only Bülow to deal with; but, as we shall see, this was by no means the case. Meanwhile, the British made a day's march beyond the Sambre. On the 22nd they continued the French line west-north-westward, still without an enemy before them, and entrenched themselves, the 5th Cavalry Brigade occupying the right, the 1st Corps (Haig) from Binche to Mons, and the 2nd Corps (Smith-Dorrien) along the canal to Condé-on-Scheldt. West and south-west of this point, there was nothing but the aforesaid groups of French Territorials. The I German Army not yet having revealed itself, the general idea of the French command, to attack across the Sambre with its centre, and then, if successful, to swing round the Allied left in a north-easterly direction against what was supposed to be the German right flank, still seemed feasible. But, in fact, Kluck's Army lay beyond Bülow's to the north-west, on the line Brussels-Valenciennes;

---

15. For details, see Hanotaux, *Histoire General* and *L'Enigme de Charleroi*; Maurice, Thomasson, Engerand, *loc. cit.*; Sir John French's *Dispatches* and *1914*; Lord Ernest Hamilton, *The First Seven Divisions; La Campagne de l'Armée Belge,* from official documents; *L'Action de l'Armée Belge,* also official; Van der Essen, *L'Invasion Allemande.* For some information in this chapter and the subsequent note with regard to the British Army, I am indebted to the military authorities.

it is quite possible, therefore, that a preliminary success by Lanrezac would have aggravated the later defeat.

However that may be, the programme was at once stultified by the unexpected speed and force of the German approach. The bombardment of the nine forts of Namur had begun on August 20. Bülow's Army reached the Sambre on the following day, and held the passages at night. Lanrezac's orders had become plainly impossible, and he did not attempt to fulfil them. Early on the afternoon of the 21st, while Kluck approached on one hand and Hausen on the other. Bülow's X Corps and Guard Corps attacked the 3rd and 10th Corps forming the apex of the French triangle. These, not having entrenched themselves, and having, against Lanrezac's express orders, advanced to the crossings between Charleroi and Namur, there fell upon strong defences flanked by machine-guns, and were driven back and separated. Despite repeated counter-attacks, the town of Chatelet was lost.

On the 22nd, these two French corps, with a little help from the 18th, had again to bear the full weight of the enemy. Their artillery preparation was inadequate, and charges of a reckless bravery did not improve their situation.[16] Most desperate fighting took place in and around Charleroi. The town was repeatedly lost and won back by the French during the day and the following morning; in course of these assaults, the Turcos inflicted heavy losses on the Prussian Guard. While the 10th Corps, cruelly punished at Tamines and Arsimont, fell back on Mettet, the 3rd found itself threatened with envelopment on the west by Bülow's X Reserve and VII Corps, debouching from Chatelet and Charleroi.

That evening, the 22nd, Lanrezac thought there was still a chance of recovery. He wrote:—

The enemy does not yet show any numerical superiority, and the 5th Army, though shaken, is intact.

---

16. Speaking of the attack of the 20th Division (10th Corps) at Tamines, M. Hanotaux (*Histoire*, vol. v.) says it advanced with feverish ardour only to fall upon solidly held defences. " Our officers had always been told that, on condition of attacking resolutely and without hesitation, they would surprise the enemy and easily dispose of them. But the Germans everywhere awaited them firmly on solid positions flanked with innumerable machine-guns, before which most of our men fell." Of the "insensate immolation" of the 3rd Corps at Chatelet, M. Engerand says: "Without artillery preparation, and knowing that they were going to a certain death, these picked troops threw themselves on the enemy infantry, solidly entrenched on the edge of the town; in a quarter of an hour a half of their effectives had fallen." He adds that the upper command of the corps was relieved the same evening.

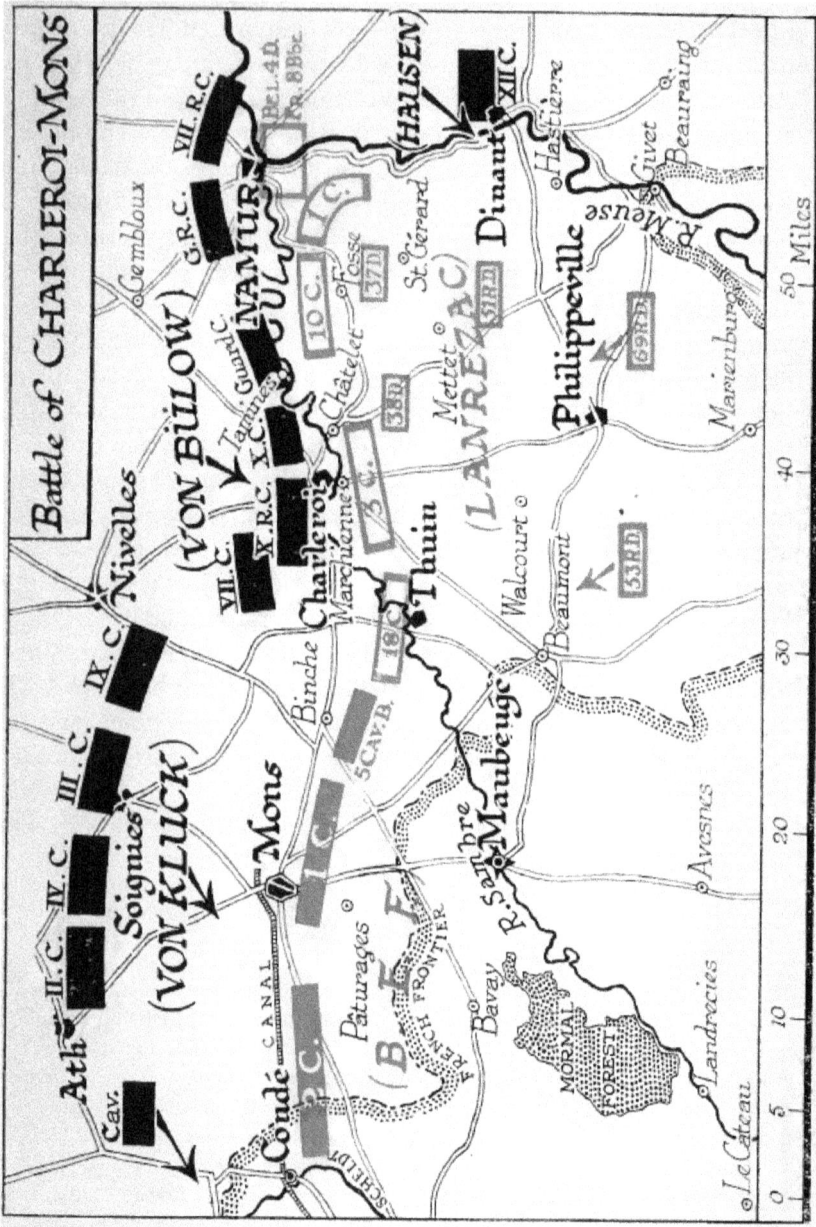

Battle of CHARLEROI-MONS

Cav.
Ath.
II.C.
IV.C.
III.C.
IX.C.
Soignies
(VON KLUCK)
Nivelles
VII.C.
X.R.C. X.C.
Tarin Guard C.
VII.C. (VON BÜLOW)
G.R.C.
VII.R.C.
Fr.L.4.D.
Fr.8.Bde.
NAMUR
GUARD
(HAUSEN)
Gembloux
10 C.
Fosse
37D.
St. Gerard
XII.C.
Hastière
Givet
Beauraing
R. Meuse
Charleroi
Marchienne
Chatelet
38.D.
3 C.
Metter
Dinant
51.R.D.
LANREZAC
Walcourt
Philippeville
69.R.D.
Marienburg
Binche
Mons
Thuin
18.C.
5 CAV. B.
I.C.
Beaumont
53.R.D.
Maubeuge
Walcourt
Avesnes
Condé
CANAL
Pâturages
FRENCH FRONTIER
(B.E.F.)
9 C.
Bavay
R. Sambre
MORNAL
FOREST
Landrecies
Le Câteau
SCHELDT

0   5   10   20   30   40   50 Miles

The 1st Corps was at length free, having been relieved in the river angle south of Namur by the 51st Reserve Division; the 18th Corps had arrived and was in full action on the left about Thuin; farther west, other reserves were coming up, and the British Army had not been seriously engaged. The French commander therefore asked his British *confrère* to strike north-eastward at Bülow's flank. The field-marshal found this request "quite impracticable" and scarcely comprehensible. He had conceived, rightly or wrongly, a very unfavourable idea of Lanrezac 's qualities; and the sight of infantry and artillery columns of the 5th Army in retreat southward that morning, before the two British corps had reached their positions on either side of Mons, had been a painful surprise. He was already in advance of the shaken line of the 5th Army; and news was arriving which indicated a grave threat of envelopment by the north-west. French had come out from England with clear warning that, owing to the impossibility of rapid or considerable reinforcement, he must husband his forces, and that he would "in no case come in any sense under the orders of any Allied general." He now, therefore, replied to Lanrezac that all he could promise was to hold the Condé Canal position for twenty-four hours; thereafter, retreat might be necessary.

On the morning of the 23rd, Bouttegourd and D'Espérey opened an attack on the left flank of the Prussian Guard, while the British were receiving the first serious shock of the enemy. The French centre, however, was in a very bad way. During the afternoon the 3rd Corps gave ground, retreating in some disorder to Walcourt; the 18th was also driven back. About the same time, four surprises fell crushingly upon the French command. The first was the fall of Namur, which had been looked to as pivot of the French right. Although the VII Reserve Corps did not enter the town till 8 p.m., its resistance was virtually broken in the morning. Most of the forts had been crushed by the German 11- and 16-inch howitzers; it was with great difficulty that 12,000 men, a half of the garrison, escaped, ultimately to join the Belgian Army at Antwerp. Secondly, the Saxon Army, hitherto hidden in the Ardennes and practically unknown to the French Command, suddenly made an appearance on Lanrezac 's right flank.

On the 23rd, the XII Corps captured Dinant, forced the passages of the Meuse there and at Hastière, drove in the Bouttegourd Division (51st Reserve), and reached Onhaye. The 1st Corps, thus threatened in its rear, had to break its well-designed attack on the Prussian Guard, and face about eastward. It successfully attacked the Saxons at Onhaye, and prevented them from getting more than one division across the river that night, so that the retreat of the French Army from the Sambre toward Beaumont and Philippeville, ordered by Lanrezac on his own responsibility at 9 p.m., was not impeded. Thirdly, news arrived of the failure of the French offensive in the Ardennes.

The fourth surprise lay in the discovery that the British Army had before it not one or two corps, as was supposed until the afternoon of August 23, but three or four active corps and two cavalry divisions of Kluck's force, a part of which was already engaged in an attempt to envelop the extreme left of the Allies. Only at 5 p.m.—both the intelligence and the liaison services seem to have failed—did the British commander, who had been holding pretty well since noon against attacks that did not yet reveal the enemy's full strength, learn from Joffre that this force was twice as large as had been reported in the morning, that his west flank was in danger, and that "the two French reserve divisions and the 5th French Army on my right were retiring." About midnight the fall of Namur and the defeat of the French 3rd and 4th Armies were also known. In face of this "most unexpected "news," a 15-miles withdrawal to the line Maubeuge-Jenlain was planned; and it began at dawn on the 24th, fighting having continued through the previous night.

Some French writers have audaciously sought to throw a part, at least, of the responsibility for the French defeat on the Sambre upon the small British Expeditionary Force. An historian so authorised as M. Gabriel Hanotaux, in particular, has stated that it was in line, instead of the 20th, as had been arranged, only on the 23rd, when the battle on the Sambre was compromised and the turning movement northeastward from Mons which had been projected could no longer save the situation; and that Sir John French, instead of destroying Kluck's corps one by one as they arrived, "retreated after three hours' contact with the enemy," hours before Lanrezac ordered the general retreat of the 5th Army.(See note 1 end of chapter). It is the barest justice to the first British continental Army, its commander, officers, and men, professional soldiers of the highest quality few of whom now survive, to say that these statements, made, no doubt, in good faith, are inaccurate, and the deductions from them untenable.

It was not, and could not have been, arranged between the Allied commands that French's two corps should be in line west and east of Mons, ready for offensive action, on August 20, when Lanrezac's fore guards were only just reaching the Sambre. General Joffre knew from

Sir John, at their meeting on August 16, that the British force could not be ready till the 21st; and it was then arranged that it should advance that day from the Sambre to the Mons Canal (13 miles farther north). This was done. Bülow had then already seized the initiative. If the British could have arrived sooner, and the projected north-easterly advance had been attempted, Bülow's right flank might have been troubled; but the way would have been left clear for Kluck's enveloping movement, with disastrous consequences for the whole left of the Allies. It is not true that the British retreat preceded the French, or that it occurred after "three hours' contact with the enemy." Lanrezac's order for the general retreat was given only at 9 p.m.; but his corps had been falling back all afternoon. Kluck's attack began at 11 a.m. on the 23rd, and became severe about 3 p.m. An hour later, Bülow's right struck in between Lanrezac's 3rd and 18th Corps, compelling them to a retreat that left a dangerous gap between the British and French Armies. From this time the British were isolated and continuously engaged. The British commander, (in his dispatch of September 7, 1914), says:—

When the news of the retirement of the French and the heavy German threatening on my front reached me, I endeavoured to confirm it by aeroplane reconnaissance; and, as a result of this, I determined to effect a retirement to the Maubeuge position at daybreak on the 24th. A certain amount of fighting continued along the whole line throughout the night; and, at daybreak on the 24th, the 2nd Division made a powerful demonstration as if to retake Binche, to enable the 2nd Corps to withdraw.

The disengagement was only procured with difficulty and considerable loss. Had it been further delayed, the two corps would have been surrounded and wiped out. They were saved by courage and skill, and by the mistakes of Kluck, who failed to get some of his forces up in time, and spent others in an enveloping movement when a direct attack was called for.

Such, in brief, is the deplorable story of the breakdown of the first French plan of campaign. By August 25, the local panics of the preceding days were arrested; but from the North Sea to the Swiss Alps the Allied armies were beaten back, and their chief mass was in full retreat. King Albert had shepherded his sorely stricken regiments into the entrenched camp of Antwerp, where, and in West Flanders, they were to drag upon the invader for nearly two months to come.

For the rest, Belgium was conquered, much of it ravaged. The forces to which it had looked for aid were disappearing southward, outnumbered, outweighed in material of war, and severely shaken. But the heroic Belgians never thought of yielding. On August 25, they made a valuable diversion, striking out from Antwerp, and forcing the small German watching force to retire to near Brussels. This and the landing of 2000 British Marines at Ostend sobered the enemy, and caused the detention of two corps (the III and IX Reserve) before the Scheldt fortress.

The short-lived victories of Rennenkampf and Samsonov at Gumbinnen and in the Masurian Lake region, threatening a greater invasion of East Prussia, also affected slightly the distribution of German troops, though it probably stimulated the urgency of the Western invasion. The French eastern armies were to keep inviolate the pivot of Verdun, the crescent of the Nancy hills, and the line of Epinal-Belfort . The tiny garrison of Longwy resisted till August 26, that of Montmédy till the 30th. Maubeuge held out from August 25 to September 7, (See note 2 end of chapter). and might be expected to hold longer. The front of the retreating armies was never broken; but at what a price was their cohesion purchased—the abandonment of a wide, rich tract of the national territory, with much of its hapless population.

Enough has been said to show that the reverses of the beginning of the war which led to the long retreat were due not only to the brutal strength of the German invasion, but to bad information, bad judgment, bad organisation, an ill-conceived strategy and reckless tactics, on the side of the Allies. The impact on the north and north-west (including now the Crown Prince's Army) of some 28 army corps—considerably over a million men—provided with heavy artillery, machine-guns, transport, and material on a prodigious scale, had never been dreamed of, and proved irresistible.

We shall now have the happier task of following the marvellous rally of will and genius by which these errors were redeemed.

★★★★★★

Note 1:—"It was expected that the British Army would take its place on the 20th, But it arrived only on the 22nd. On the 20th, it was still far behind in the region of Le Nouvion-Wassigny-Le Cateau. If it had been in place on the 20th, the Allied Army would have found itself constituted at the very moment when the Germans entered Brussels." This last phrase is at least singularly ambiguous: Von Bülow was not in Brussels, but only a day's march from the Sambre, on the 20th. But, if the British had then been at Mons, the Allied Army would not have been "constituted," for Lanrezac's forces were far from being all in place on that day. "It is true," said M. Hanotaux a little later, "that the French Army was not all in place on the 22nd, and that the Territorial divisions were in rather mediocre conditions as to armament and *encadrement*" (*L'Enigme de Charleroi*). It is Bülow's appearance on the Sambre a day before Lanrezac was ready that makes the French historian credit the enemy with "the principal advantage, the initiative."

After the reference to Brussels, M. Hanotaux continues: "The role reserved to the British Army was to execute a turning movement of the left wing, advancing north of the Sambre toward Mons, in the direction of Soignies-Nivelles; it was thought it would be there before Kluck." It was there a day before Kluck. "Unfortunately, as the *Exposé de Six Mois de Guerre* recognises, it did not arrive on the 20th, as the French Command expected. . . . In fact, it was only in line on the 23rd." M. Hanotaux repeats himself with variations. The Allied Armies suffered, he says, not only from lateness and fatigue, but from lack of co-ordination in the High Command.

> It is permissible today to say that the Belgian Command, in deciding to withdraw its army into the entrenched camp of Antwerp, obeyed a political and military conception which no longer conformed to the necessities of the moment. Again, the British Army appeared in the region only on the 23rd, although the battle had been engaged for two days and was already compromised between Namur and Charleroi. The role of turning wing which the British Army was to fulfil thus failed at the decisive hour.

M. Hanotaux mentions the receipt by Sir John French, at 5 p.m. on August 23, of "a telegraphic message qualified as 'unexpected,'" announcing the weight of Kluck's force and the French retirement, but omits to say that this message came from the French *generalissimo*. He adds that the British commander gave the order to retreat at 5 p.m., Lanrezac only at 9 p.m., omitting to explain that the French retreat was, in fact, in operation at the former hour, while the British retreat only began at dawn on the 24th, after a night of fighting. "By 5 p.m., on Sunday the 23rd, when Joffre's message was received at British Headquarters"—says Captain Gordon, on the authority of the British War Office (*Mons and the Retreat*—published by Leonaur alongwith *The Fighting Retreat to Paris by Roger Ingpen* in the double edition *The Great Retreat*.)—

> The French had been retiring for ten or twelve hours. The British Army was isolated. Standing forward a day's march from the French on its right, faced by three German Corps with a fourth on its left, it seemed marked out for destruction.

In strong contrast with M. Hanotaux's comments—repeated, despite public correction, in his article of March 1919 cited above—are M. Engerand's references to the part played by the British Expeditionary' Force. First, to its:

> Calm and tenacious defensive about Mons, a truly admirable defence that has not been made known among us, and that has perhaps not been understood as it should be. It was the first manifestation of the form the war was to take; the English, having nothing to unlearn, and instructed by their experiences in the South African war, had from the outset seized its character. . . . It shows us Frenchmen, to our grief, how we might have stopped the enemy if we had practised, instead of the infatuated offensive, this British defensive 'borrowed from Brother Boer.' (Then as to the retreat:) The retreat of the British followed ours, and did not precede it. It is a duty of loyalty to say so, as also to recognise that, in these battles beyond the frontiers, the British Army, put by its chief on the defensive, was the only one, with the 1st French Army, which could contain the enemy.

M. Engerand, who is evidently well informed, and who strongly defends General Lanrezac, says that Sir John French told this officer on August 17, at Rethel, that he could hardly be ready to take part in the battle till August 24.

Lt.-Col. de Thomasson, while regretting that the British did not try to help Lanrezac on the 23rd, admits that an offensive from Mons would have been fruitless and might have been disastrous.

M. Hanotaux' faulty account of the matter appears to be inspired by a desire to redistribute responsibilities, and to prove that, if the British had attacked Bülow's right flank, the whole battle would have been won. This idea will not bear serious examination. The French Command cannot have entertained this design on August 20, for it must have known that the British force was two days behind the necessary positions. When it came into line before Mons, on the evening of the 22nd, it was certainly too late for so small a body of troops to make an offensive movement north-eastward with any prospect of success. Had it been possible at either date, the manoeuvre which M. Hanotaux favours might conceivably have helped Lanrezac against Bülow; but it would have left Kluck free to encircle the Allies on the west, and so prejudiced, at least, the withdrawal and the subsequent successful reaction. It might well have created a second and greater Sedan.

In dealing with these events, M. Hanotaux, by adding the strength of Lanrezac's army, d'Amade's Territorial divisions, the British Army, and the garrisons of Namur (General Michel, 25,000 men), Maubeuge (General Fournier, 35,000 men), and Lille (General Herment, 18,000 men), arrives at the remarkable conclusion that "the Allied armies, between August 22 and 25, opposed to the 545,000 men of the German armies a total figure of 536,000 men." This figure is deceptive, and useless except to emphasise the elements of Allied weakness other than numbers. So far as the later date is intended, it has no relation to the battle of Charleroi-Mons. At both these dates, and later, when the Allies were in full retreat, and both sides had suffered heavy losses, the Allied units named were so widely scattered and so disparate in quality that it is impossible to regard them as a single force "opposed" to the three compact masses of Kluck, Bülow, and Hansen. The deduction that General Joffre had on the Sambre "Allied forces sufficient to keep the mastery of the operations" is, therefore, most questionable.

The actual opposition of forces on the morning of August 23 was as follows: Lanrezac's Army and the Namur garrison, amounting to an equivalent of five army corps, or about 200,000 men, had upon their front and flank six corps of Bülow and two corps of Hansen, about 320,000 men. The little British Army, of 2½ corps, had immediately before it three of Kluck's corps, with two more behind these.

General Lanrezac published in the *New York Herald* (Paris edition) of May 17 and 18, and in *L'Oeuvre* of May 18 and 22, 1919, dignified replies to certain statements of Field-Marshal French. To the latter's remark that the B.E.F. at Mons found itself in "an advanced position," he answers that the battle shifted from east to west, and "on the evening of the 23rd, the 5th Army had been fighting for forty-eight hours, while the British were scarcely engaged." Doubtless owing to Lord Kitchener's original instruction that it would not be reinforced, the B.E.F. kept, during the later part of the retreat, "two days' march ahead of the 5th Army, and obstinately maintained this distance, stopping only on the Seine." "It was rather French who uncovered my left than I who uncovered his right." General Lanrezac disowns any critical intent in saying this:

> In my opinion, in the tragic period from August 22 to September 4, 1914, the British did all they could, and showed a magnificent heroism. It was not their fault if the strategic situation forbade our doing more.

In regard to the original French plan of campaign. General Lanrezac refused to put himself in the position of being both judge and party, but added:

> The Commander-in-Chief had a plan; he had elaborated it with the collaboration of officers of his Staff, men incontestably intelligent and instructed, General Berthelot among others. Nevertheless, this plan, as I came to know it in course of events, appeared to me to present a fundamental error. It counted too much on the French centre, 3rd and 4th Armies, launched into Belgian Luxembourg and Ardennes, scoring a prompt and decisive victory which would make us masters of the situation on the rest of the front.
>
> So it was that General Berthelot, on August 19, told M. Messimy that, if the Germans went in large numbers west of the Meuse, it was so much the better, as it would be easier to beat them on the east.

Note 2:—Four years passed ere a detailed account of the defence and fall of Maubeuge was published (*La Verité sur le Siege*

de Maubeuge, by Commandant Paul Cassou, of the 4th *Zouaves*).
There are, in the case of this fortress, points of likeness to and
of difference from that of Lille. In June 1910 the Ministry of
War had decided that Maubeuge should be regarded as only
a position of arrest, not capable of sustaining a long siege; and
in 1913 the Superior War Council decreed that it should be
considered only as a support to a neighbouring field army. It
then consisted of an enceinte dating from Vauban, dominated
by an outer belt of six main forts and six intermediate works
about twenty years old, furnished with 335 cannon, none of
which carried more than 6 miles. The garrison consisted of an
infantry regiment, three reserve and six Territorial regiments. In
the three weeks before the siege began, 30,000 men were engaged in digging trenches, laying down barbed wire, and making other defences.

The siege was begun by the VII Reserve Corps, a cavalry brigade, and a division from another corps, about 60,000 men,
on August 25. On that and two following days effective sorties
were made. On the 20th the bombardment began. One by one
the forts were smashed by heavy guns and mortars, including
420 mm. pieces throwing shells of nearly a ton weight, firing
from the safe distance of 9 or 10 miles. On September 1, all the
troops available made a sortie, and a regular battle was fought.
Some detachments reached within 250 yards of the German
batteries, only to be mown down by machine-gun fire. After
this two German attacks were repulsed.

On September 5, however, the enemy got within the French
lines, and on the 7th the place had become indefensible. At
6 p.m. the capitulation was signified, and on September 8, at
noon, the garrison surrendered. General von Zwehl saying to
General Fournier: "You have defended the place with a rare
vigour and much resolution, but the war has turned against
you." The German Command afterward claimed to have taken
at Maubeuge 40,000 prisoners, 400 guns, and a large quantity
of war material.

★★★★★★

CHAPTER 3

Joffre Starts Afresh

1. ECCE HOMO!

France, land of swift action and swifter wit, was the last one would expect to take kindly to the new warfare. She looked then, as her elders had always looked, for a man. And she found one; but he was far from being of the traditional type.

Joseph Cesaire Joffre was at this time sixty-two years old, a burly figure, with large head upheld, grey hair, thick moustache and brows, clear blue eyes, and a kindly, reflective manner. His great-grandfather, a political refugee from Spain, named Gouffre, had settled in Rivesaltes, on the French side of the eastern Pyrenees, where his grandfather remained as a trader, and his father lived as a simple workman till his marriage, which brought him into easier circumstances. One of eleven children, Joffre proved an industrious pupil at Perpignon, entered the Ecole Polytechnique in 1869, advanced slowly, by general intelligence rather than any special capacity, entered the Engineers after the War of 1870, and during the 'eighties commenced a long colonial career. His report on the Timbuctoo Expedition of 1893-4, where he first won distinction, is the longest of his very few printed writings. It shows a prudent, methodical, lucid, and energetic mind, with particular aptitude for engineering and administration.

After an interval in Paris as secretary of the Inventions Commission, the then Colonel Joffre went out to direct the establishment of defence works in Madagascar. In 1900, promoted general, he commanded an artillery brigade, in 1905 an infantry division. After other experience at the Ministry of War and in local commands, he became a member of the Higher War Council in 1910, and in July 1911 Vice-President of that body, and thus Commander-in-Chief designate.

This heavy responsibility fell to him almost by accident. It was the time of the Agadir crisis; France and Germany were upon the verge of war. M, Caillaux was Prime Minister, M. Messimy Minister of War, General Michel Vice-President of the Council, a position, at the end of a long period of peace, of little power, especially as the Council had only a formal existence. The Government recognised its weakness, but feared to establish a Grand Staff which might obtain a danger-ous authority. Moreover, General Michel was not "well seen" by the majority of his colleagues. Messimy thought him lacking in spirit and ability.[1] There were also differences of opinion; Michel thought the reserves should be organised to be thrown into line directly upon the outbreak of hostilities, and he believed in the probability of an inva-sion by way of Belgium.

Generals Pau and Gallieni were the first favourites for the succes-sion. Both, however, would attain the age limit at the end of 1912. Gallieni declined on the further ground that his experience had been almost wholly colonial, and that he would not be welcomed by the metropolitan army. Michel's ideas having been formally rejected at a meeting of the Higher War Council on July 19, 1911, the post was of-fered to Pau, a universally esteemed officer. The Ministry had decided to strengthen the post of Vice-President of the Council by adding to it the functions of Chief-of-Staff; . but when Pau demanded the right to nominate all superior officers, Messimy hesitated, and turned to Jof-fre, the member of the Council having the longest period—over five years—of service before him.

Joffre was little known outside army circles; and he had none of the qualities that most easily bring popularity. Southerners would recog-nise his rich accent, but little else in this silent, though genial, figure. His profound steadiness, a balance of mind that was to carry him

---

1. Statement of M. Messimy before the Commission of Inquiry on Metallurgy, May 30, 191 9, reported in the Paris Press the following day. In his evidence, M. Messimy blamed Joffre for not having been willing, in August 1914, to recognise the danger on the side of Belgium. Undoubtedly, he added, it was a fault of the French Com-mand in 1912 and 1913 not to contemplate the prompt use of reserves, and to fall back on the Three Years' Service law, "which no one would defend today." M. Mes-simy argued that the doctrine of the offensive à outrance was common to the French and German Armies, and was at that time universal in military circles. *Joffre, Première Crise du Commandement*, by Mermeix, is a careful and unprejudiced study of the changes, ideas, and personal antagonisms in the French Army Commands during the first period of the war. It concludes with a section in which "Attacks upon Joffre" and "Explanations collected at the G.Q.G.," are set forth on opposite pages.

through the worst of storms, a cool reflectiveness almost suggesting insensibility, were qualities strange in a French military leader. He was understood to be faithful Republican; but, unlike some high officers, he had never trafficked with party, sect, or clique, and he showed his impartiality in retiring the freethinker Sarrail and the Catholic de Langle de Cary, as in supporting Sir John, French and in advancing Foch. When I looked at him, I was reminded of Campbell-Bannerman; there was the same pawkiness, the same unspoiled simplicity, the same courage and bonhomie. Before the phrase was coined or the fact accomplished, he prefigured to his countrymen the *"union sacrée"* which was the first condition of success; and to the end his solid character was an important factor in the larger concert of the Allies.

While there appears in Joffre a magnanimity above the average of great commanders, it is, perhaps, not yet possible to say that, through this crisis, his sense of justice was equal to every strain. There are friends of General Gallieni who would question it. The case of General Lanrezac is less personal, and more to our purpose. An officer of decided views and temper, who had been professor at St. Cyr in 1880, and had risen to be director of studies in the Staff College, he became a member of the War Council only six months before the outbreak of war, when the opinions formerly represented by General Michel, and partially and more softly by Castlenau, were definitely discredited.[2] Always sceptical of the orthodox doctrine of the general offensive, Lanrezac was convinced by information obtained at the beginning of the campaign that the great danger had to be met in the north, and that the armies should be shifted immediately to meet it. We have seen that Joffre would not accept this view till the third week in August, and still pursued an offensive plan which now appears to have been foredoomed to failure.

Nevertheless, Lanrezac was punished for the defeat on the Sambre, by being removed from the command of the 5th Army; and, to the end of the war, the *generalissimo* persisted in attributing the frontier repulses to subordinate blundering. Joffre's action in the height of the crisis, his wholesale purge of the army commands, may be justified; it is too late to shelter the Staff of those days from their major share in the responsibility. It must remain to his biographers to explain more precisely the extraordinary contrast between the errors we have indicated and the recovery we have now to trace. This much may here be said: Joffre was hardly the man, in days of peace, to grapple with a dif-

2. See Note 2 end of Section 3, chapter 2.

ficult parliament, or to conceive a new military doctrine. He was not, like his neighbour of the South, Foch, an intellectual, a bold speculator, a specialist in strategy, but an organiser, a general manager.

The first French plan of campaign, for which he had such share of responsibility as attaches to three years in charge of the military machine, was the expression of a firmly established teaching, which only a few pioneers in his own world had consciously outgrown. It did not reflect his own temperament; but he could not have successfully challenged it, in the time at his disposal, against prejudices so inveterate, even if he had had the mind to do so. It was the first time all the services concerned in war preparations, including the War Council, the General Staff, the Staff Committee, the Higher War School, had come under a single control; and, even had there been no arrears, no financial difficulties, a greater permanence of Ministries, the task would have called for all one man's powers of labour and judgment. Joffre was surrounded during that period by men more positive, in certain directions, than himself, more ambitious, men whose abilities could no more be defied than their influence. One of his eulogists, who compares him with Turenne, citing Bossuet on that great soldier says:—

> He had more character than personality. He was used to fighting without anger, winning without ambition, and triumphing without vanity.[3]

It was as though Nature, seeing the approach of a supreme calamity, had prepared against it, out of the spirit of the age—an age by no means Napoleonic—an adequate counter-surprise.

The slow growth and cumulation of his career are characteristic. It is all steady, scrupulous industry. It smacks of an increasingly civilian world. There is no exterior romance in the figure of Joffre, nothing mediaeval, nothing meretricious. He is a glorified *bourgeois*, with the sane vigour and solidity of his race, and none of its more showy qualities. There is extant a lecture which he delivered in 1913 to the old scholars of the Ecole Polyteclmique. He presented the Balkan wars for consideration as a case in which two factors were sharply opposed—numbers, and preparation. Setting aside high strategy and abstract teaching, he preached the virtue of all-round preparation— in the moral and intellectual factors, first of which a sane patriotism and a worthy command, as well as in the material factors of numbers,

---

3. G. Blanchon, *Le General Joffre,* Pages Actuelles, 1914-5, No. 11.

armament, supplies, and so on. He says:—

> *To be ready* in our days carries a meaning it would have been
> difficult for those who formerly prepared and conducted war
> to grasp. . . . To be ready today, all the resources of the country,
> all the intelligence of its children, all their moral energy, must
> be directed in advance toward a single aim—victory. Every-
> thing must have been organised, everything foreseen. Once
> hostilities are commenced, no improvisation will be of any use.
> What lacks then will lack definitively. And the least omission
> may cause a disaster.

That he and his Staff were caught both unprepared and ill-prepared
gives an impish touch of satire to this passage. That it is, nevertheless,
the authentic voice of Joffre is confirmed by one of his rare personal declarations in the course of the war. This statement was made
in February 1915—when many of the commanders referred to had
been removed, and the officership of the French Army considerably
rejuvenated—to an old friend [4] who asked him whether Charleroi
was lost under pressure of overwhelming numbers.

Joffre replied:—

> That is absolutely wrong. We ought to have won the Battle of
> Charleroi; we ought to have won ten times out of eleven. We
> lost it through our own faults. Faults of command. Before the
> war broke out, I had already noted that, among our generals,
> many were worn out. Some had appeared to me to be incapa-
> ble, not good enough for their work. Some inspired me with
> doubt, others with disquietude. I had made up my mind to
> rejuvenate our chief commands; and I should have done so in
> spite of all the commentaries and against any malevolence. But
> the war came too soon. And, besides, there were other generals
> in whom I had faith, and who have not responded to my hopes.
> The man of war reveals himself more in war than in studies,
> and the quickest intelligence and the most complete knowl-
> edge are of little avail if they are unaccompanied by qualities
> of action. The responsibilities of war are such that, even in the
> men of merit, their best faculties may be paralysed. That is what
> happened to some of my chiefs. Their worth turned out to be
> below the mark. I had to remedy these defects. Some of these

---

4. M. Arthur Hue, editor of the *Dépeche de Toulouse*, in which journal the interview
was printed, March 1915.

generals were my best comrades. But, if I love my friends much, I love France more. I relieved them of their posts. I did this in the same way as I ought to be treated myself, if it be thought I am not good enough. I did not do this to punish them, but simply as a measure of public safety. I did it with a heavy heart.

Such were the character and record of the man upon whom, at the darkest moment in modem history, fell the burden of the destinies of liberal Europe; who was called upon to prove, against his own words, that a great leader must and can improvise something essential of what has not been prepared; who, between August 23 and 25, 1914, in a maze of preoccupations, had to provide the Western Allies with a second new plan of campaign. Some day his officers will tell the story of how he did it, of the outer scene at his shifting headquarters during those alarming hours, as the emperor's marshals portrayed their chief pacing like a caged tiger by candlelight in a Polish hut, or gazing gloomily from the Kremlin battlements upon the flames that were turning his ambition to ashes.

Joffre will not help us to such pictures; and in this, too, he shows himself to be representative of the modern process, which is anything but picturesque. If he had none of the romance of the stark adventurer about him, he had a cool head and a stout heart; and we may imagine that, out of the depths of a secretive nature, there surged up spontaneously in this crisis all that was worthiest in it, the stored strength of a Spartan life, the will of a deep patriotism, the lessons of a long, varied, pondered experience. So far from dire peril paralysing his faculties, it was now that they first shone to the full. Calm, confident, clear, prompt, he set himself to correct the most glaring errors, and to create the conditions of an equal struggle. We know from his published Army Orders what resulted. Castlenau, Pau, Foch were far away on the east, or at the centre. There were other advisers; but, in the main, this was Joffre's own plan.

Before we state it, and trace its later modification, it will be well to recall the main features of the problem to be solved.

2. The Second New Plan

The first fact which had to be reckoned with was that the main weight of the enemy was bearing down across the north and northeast, and was, for the moment, irresistible. Retreat, at the outset, was not, then, within the plan, but a condition of it. There was no choice; contact with the invader must be broken if any liberty of action was to be won back. Defeat and confusion had been suffered at so many points, the force of the German offensive was so markedly superior, that an unprepared arrest on the Belgian frontier would have risked the armies being divided, enveloped, and destroyed piecemeal.

If the first stage of the retreat was enforced, its extension was in some measure willed and constantly controlled. For all the decisions taken, Joffre must have the chief credit, as he had the whole responsibility. The abandonment of large tracts of national territory to a ruthless enemy cannot be an easy choice, especially when the inhabitants are unwarned, and the mind of the nation is wholly unprepared (the defeats on the Sambre and the Meuse were not known for several days to the civil public, and then only very vaguely). A less cool mind might have fallen into temporising expedients. Maubeuge was to hold out for a fortnight more; the 4th Army had checked the enemy, and Ruffey had repulsed several attacks; Longwy had not yet capitulated. But the commander-in-chief was not deceived. He had no sooner learned the weight of Kluck's flying wing than he realised that the only hope now lay in a rapid retirement. The fact that the British force, holding the west flank, depended upon coast communications for its munitions, supplies, and reinforcements, was an element to be counted. In every respect, unreadiness in the north dominated the situation.

Evidently the retreat must be stayed, and the reaction begun, at the earliest possible moment. Not only were large communities and territories being abandoned: the chief German line of attack seemed to be aimed direct at the capital, which was in a peculiar degree the centre of the national life. This consideration, which no commander-in-chief could have forgotten, was emphasised in a letter addressed at 5 a.m. on August 25 by the Minister of War, M. Messimy, to General Joffre. It contained a specific order from the government—probably the only ministerial interference with the operations in this period—thus phrased: "If victory does not crown a success of our armies, and if the armies are compelled to retreat, an army of at least three active corps must be directed to the entrenched camp of Paris to assure its protection." In an accompanying letter, the minister added:

> It goes without saying that the line of retreat should be quite other, and should cover the centre and the south of France. We are resolved to struggle to the last and without mercy.[5]

---

5. Statement by General Messimy at the Commission of Inquiry on Metallurgy, April 28, 1919.

No doubt, these measures would, to Joffre, seem to "go without saying."

The retreat, so long as necessary, must be directed toward the centre of the country, and at the same time the capital must be protected.

There was another necessity of no less importance. The retreat must be covered on the east. After the reverse of Morhange-Sarrebourg, this was a continual source of anxiety. On August 25, the German Armies of Lorraine, now reinforced, were hammering at the circle of hills called the Grand Couronné of Nancy, and were upon the Moselle before the Gap of Charmes. Belfort and Epinal were safe, and Verdun was not yet directly threatened. Very little consideration of the rectangular battle front—the main masses ranged along the north, while a line of positions naturally and artificially strong favoured the French on the east—would lead to the further conclusion: to stand fast along the east, as cover for the retreat from the north. Castelnau and Dubail, therefore, were asked to hold their critical positions at any cost. At the same time, Mulhouse and the northern Vosges passes were abandoned; Belfort, Epinal, and even Verdun were deprived of every superfluous man, in order to meet the main flood of invasion. The evacuation of Verdun and Nancy was envisaged as a possibility. The line Toul-Epinal-Belfort could not be lost without disaster.

Such were the three chief conditions affecting the extent of the strategic retreat. Conditions are, however, to be made, not only suffered; and General Joffre had no sooner got the retreat in hand than he set himself to the constitution of a new mass of manoeuvre by means of which, when a favourable conjuncture of circumstances should be obtained, the movement could be reversed. The simultaneous disengagement and parallel withdrawal of four armies, with various minor forces, over a field 120 miles wide and of a like depth, was an operation unprecedented in the history of war. The pains and difficulties of such a retreat, the danger of dislocation and demoralisation, are evident. Its great compensation was to bring the defence nearer to its reserves and bases of supply, while constantly stretching the enemy's line, and so weakening his striking force.

This could not, of course, be pure gain: the French and British Armies lost heavily on the road south by the capture of laggards, sick, wounded, and groups gone astray, as well as in killed and men taken in action. The Germans lost more heavily in several, perhaps in most, of the important engagements, and they were much exhausted when the crucial moment came. On the other hand, the Allies were constantly picking up reinforcements; while the enemy had to leave behind an army of occupation in Belgium, and large numbers of men to reduce Maubeuge, to garrison towns like Lille, Valenciennes, Amiens, St. Quentin, Cambrai, Laon, Rethel, Rheims, to terrorise scores of smaller places, and to provide guards and transport for ever-lengthening lines of communication.

Upon these chief elements Joffre constructed his new plan of campaign. It was first mooted, a few hours after the issue of the order for the general retreat, in the tactical "Note for All the Armies" of August 24, and in the strategical "General Instruction" of August 25. General Headquarters were then housed in the old college, in the small country town of Vitry-le-François. Here, far behind the French centre, undisturbed by the turmoil of the front and the capital, the commander-in-chief, aided by such men as General Belin (a great organiser particularly of railway services). General Berthelot and Colonel Pont, grappled with the dire problem and, in the shadow of defeat, imperturbably drafted the design of the ultimate victory.

The tactical note gathered such of the more urgent lessons of the preceding actions as were capable of immediate application: the importance of close co-operation of infantry and artillery in attack; of artillery preparation of the assault, destruction of enemy machine-guns, immediate entrenchment of a position won, organisation for prolonged resistance, as contrasted with "the enthusiastic offensive"; extended formation in assault; the German method of cavalry patrols immediately supported by infantry, and the need of care not to exhaust the horses.

"When a position has been won, the troops should organise it immediately, entrench themselves, and bring up artillery to prevent any new attack by the enemy. The infantry seem to ignore the necessity of organising for a prolonged combat. Throwing forthwith into line numerous and dense units, they expose them immediately to the fire of the enemy, which decimates them, stops short their offensive, and often leaves them at the mercy of a counter-attack."

The *generalissimo* offered his lieutenants no rhetorical comfort, but the purge of simple truth. He knew, and insisted on their understanding, that the shrewdest of strategy was useless if faults such as these were to remain uncorrected.

The "General Instruction No. 2," issued to the Army Commanders at 10 p.m. :on August 25, consisted of twelve articles, which—omitting for the moment the detailed dispositions—contain the following

74

orders:

1. The projected offensive manoeuvre being impossible of execution, the ulterior operations will be regulated with a view to the reconstitution on our left, by the junction of the 4th and 5th Armies, the British Army, and new forces drawn from the region of the east, of a mass capable of resuming the offensive, while the other armies contain for the necessary time the efforts of the enemy.

2. In its retirement, each of the 3rd, 4th, and 5th Armies will take account of the movements of the neighbouring armies, with which it must keep in touch. The movement will be covered by rearguards left in favourable irregularities of the ground, so as to utilise all the obstacles to stop, or at least delay, the march of the enemy by short and violent counter-attacks, of which the artillery will contribute the chief element.

6. In advance of Amiens, a new group of forces, constituted by elements brought up by railway (7th Corps, four divisions of reserve, and perhaps another active army-corps), will be gathered from August 27 to September 2. It will be ready to pass to the offensive in the general direction St. Pol-Arras, or Arras-Bapaume.

8. The 5th Army will have the main body of its forces in the region of Vermand-St. Quentin-Moy, in order to debouch in the general direction of Bohain, its right holding the line La Fère-Laon-Craonne-St. Erme.

11. All the positions indicated must be organised with the greatest care, so as to make it possible to offer the maximum of resistance to the enemy.

12. The 1st and 2nd Armies will continue to hold the enemy forces which are opposed to them."

Articles 3, 4, and 5 specified the lines of retreat and zones of action of each of the Western forces. Articles 7, 9, and 10, like articles 6 and 8 quoted above, indicate the positions from which the projected offensive movement was to be made. The whole disposition may be summarised as follows:—On the extreme left, from the coast to near Amiens, the northern Territorial Divisions were to hold the line of the Somme, with the Cavalry Corps in advance, and the 61st and 62nd Reserve Divisions in support. Next eastward, either north or south of the Somme, was to come the new, or 6th Army, which was to strike north or north-east, on one side or the other of Arras, according to circumstances. Beside it, the British Army, from behind the Somme between Bray and Ham, would advance to the north or north-east. The 5th Army (article 8 above) had an exceedingly strong position and role.

With the Oise valley before it, and the St. Gobain and Laon hills behind, it was to attack due northward between St. Quentin and Guise. The 4th Army was to reach across Champagne from Craonne to the Argonne either by the Aisne valley or by Rheims; while the 3rd hung around Verdun, touching the Argonne either at Grandpré or Ste. Menehould.

The great military interest of these arrangements must not detain us. Their publication reveals the fact, long unknown save to a few, that Joffre not merely hoped for, but definitely planned, a resumption of the offensive from a line midway between the Sambre and the Marne, that is, from the natural barrier of the Somme and the St. Gobain-Laon hills. We shall see that an effort was made to carry out these dispositions, and that it failed. The failure was lamentable, inasmuch as it doomed another large tract of country to the penalties of inva-sion. But, because the dispositions ordered on August 25 were only provisional details, not essentials, of the new plan, the military result was in no way compromised. While dealing with local emergencies or opportunities, Joffre envisaged steadily the whole national situation.

The essentials of the "General Instruction" of August 25 were four in number: (a) a defensive stand by the armies of Alsace and Lorraine, and a provisional defensive by the two armies next westward, the 3rd and 4th; (b) a strictly controlled continuation of the northern retreat while reorganisation took place and forces were transferred from the east to the north-west; (c) an ultimate offensive initiated by the west-ern and central armies, of which one additional, to be called the 9th, under General Foch, about to be interjected between the 4th and 5th, is not yet mentioned; (d) the constitution of a new left wing, to meet the extraordinary strength of the German right, and to attempt a counter-envelopment. The Amiens-Laon line fell out of the plan; the plan itself remained, and it is fully true to say that in it lies the germ of the Battle of the Marne.

3. BATTLE OF THE GAP OF CHARMES

Everything was conditional upon the defence of the eastern frontier, now at its most critical phase. [6]

On the morning of August 24, Lunéville having been occupied on the previous day, the hosts of Prince Ruprecht and General Heeringen were reported to be advancing rapidly toward the entry of the Gap of Charmes by converging roads—the former, on the north, passing before the Nancy hills, southward; the latter, coming westward from around the Donon, by Baccarat. We have seen that, on the other hand, the 2nd and 1st French armies, in preparation for a decisive action, were ranged in the shape of a right angle—that of Castelnau (based on Toul) from the foothills north-eastward of Nancy, southward, to Rozelieures and Borville; that of Dubail (based on Epinal) from the northern end of the Vosges, westward, to the same point. How far these positions, with the prospect of being able to close in upon the flanks of the enemy, arose from necessary directions of the retreat, and how far from strategical design, whether of one or both of the army commanders, or of the commander-in-chief, does not here concern us; suffice it to say that the two generals won equal honour, and that the Grand Quartier effectively supervised this and subsequent developments of the situation. The opposed forces were now about equal in strength—nine corps on either side.

A space had been left at the point of the angle, north of the Forest of Charmes, west of Rozelieures; and this may have tempted the Germans forward. The 16th Corps of the French 2nd Army, the 8th and 13th of the 1st, with three divisions of cavalry under General Conneau masking them, were ready to fill this space, and, as soon as Lunéville had been lost, proceeded to do so, artillery being massed particularly on Borville plateau. On the afternoon of August 24, the pincers began to close, Dubail holding the imperilled angle and Heeringen's left, while Castelnau beat upon the enemy's northern flank. On the morning of the 25th, the Germans took Rozelieures; at 2 p.m. they abandoned it; at 3 p.m., Castelnau issued the order: "*En avant, partout, à fond!*"

Foch's 20th Corps, aiming at the main line of enemy communications, the Arracourt-Lunéville road, took Ràméreville and Erbevillier, east of Nancy, and struck hard, farther south, at Maixe, Crevic, Flainval, and Hudviller, toward Lunéville, which was at the same time threat-

---

6. For details, see Hanotaux, "*La Bataille de la Trouée de Charmes*," *Rev. des Deux Mondes*, November 15, 1916; Engerand, *loc. cit.*; a vindication of General Dubail, by "Cdt. G.V.": "*La Ire Armée et la Bataille de la Trouée de Charmes*," *La Revue*, January 1, 1917; Barrés: "*Comment la Lorraine fut Sauvée*," *Echo de Paris*, September 1917.

ened on the south-west by the 15th Corps, reaching the Meurthe and Mortagne at Lamath and Blainville. By night, the enemy was conscious of his danger, and escaped constriction by a general withdrawal. On the 26th, further hard fighting confirmed the French victory. Positions were occupied at the foot of the Grand Couronné, on the north, and near St, Dié on the south, which were to save the situation a fortnight later. The Gap of Charmes was definitely closed. The German armies had suffered their first great defeat in the war; and, although little known to the outer world, it did much for the moral of the French ranks. On August 27, General Joffre issued an order praising this "example of tenacity and courage," and expressing his confidence that the other armies would "have it at heart to follow it."

Towards the north end of the Franco-German frontier, another check was administered at the same time to the Crown Prince's Army, near Etain, halfway between Verdun and Metz. General Maunoury, with an ephemeral "Army of Lorraine," consisting of three reserve divisions, formed part of the 3rd Army of General Ruffey, but was given by the G.Q.G. the special task of watching for any threat on the side of Metz. He could do little, therefore, to help Ruffey in the Battle of Virton,[7] On August 24, however, a German postal van was captured with orders showing that the crown prince intended to attack in the belief that the French had engaged all their troops. Generals Ruffey, Paul Durand, Grossetti, and Maunoury held a hurried conference; and, the G.Q.G. having given permission, on the following day Maunoury struck out suddenly at the crown prince's left, which was thrown back in disorder.

This victory might have been followed up. But General Joffre did not mistake the real centre of gravity of the situation, and would not change the basis of his new plan. He now considered the eastern front sufficiently secure to justify a transfer of certain units to meet the emergency in the western field. Thither, our attention may return.

4. BATTLES OF LE CATEAU, GUISE, AND LAUNOIS

During the night of August 25—while Smith-Dorrien's men were defending themselves at Solesmes and Haig's at Landrecies—General Maunoury received the order to disengage his divisions, and to hurry across country to Montdidier with his Staff, there to complete the formation and undertake the command of the new 6th Army. This

---

7. See chapter 2, section 5. The mismanagement of this battle was the subject of evidence at the Metallurgical Commission of Inquiry on May 15, 1919.

distinguished soldier was sixty-seven years of age. Wounded in the war of 1870, he had taken a leading part in the development of the French artillery, directed the Ecole de Guerre, and restored a strict discipline in the garrison of the capital as Governor of Paris. Two of his phrases will help to characterise this gallant officer. The first was that in which, in the moment of victory, he spoke of himself as having for forty-four years directed all his energies toward "*la revanche de 1870.*" The other was addressed to a group of fellow-officers who were discussing certain German brutalities. He could not understand such things, he said, and added: "When we are in their country, we will give them a terrible lesson in humaneness."[8]

The Army of the Somme consisted at the outset of the 7th Corps, taken from Alsace (*minus* its 13th Division, left in Lorraine; *plus* the 63rd Reserve Division and a Moroccan Brigade from the Châlons camp); the 55th and 56th Divisions of Reserve, taken from the Verdun-Toul region; the 61st and 62nd Divisions of Reserve, detached from the Paris garrison to Arras, under General d'Amade, and brought back from Arras to Amiens. It was constituted in the most unfavourable circumstances; and the idea of a flank attack from the Arras-Amiens region, in support of an offensive from the old line of secondary fortresses La Fère-Laon-Rheims, was no sooner conceived than it had to be abandoned. Maunoury was compelled to send his divisions off piecemeal from railhead to the battlefield. The chief body of them had had such rest as a long journey in goods-vans permits; d'Amade's reservists had been routed in the north, and had lost heavily. If Kluck had not been absorbed in the effort to destroy Sir John French's little band of heroes, Maunoury's task could never have been fulfilled.

The debt was quickly repaid. The moment had come when the British must be relieved, or exterminated. Between Le Cateau and Cambrai, on August 26, the three infantry divisions and two cavalry brigades of the 2nd Corps, although worn by long marches, checked the onrush of seven German divisions and three mounted divisions, including some of the best Prussian troops, supported by at least a hundred batteries. Again trusting to his guns while he planned a double envelopment, Kluck allowed his enemy to escape. While this first experience of massed artillery fire revealed the fine quality of our "Old Contemptibles," it is a debated question whether General Smith-Dorrien's temerity was justified. He had been expressly or-

---

8. Miles, *Le General Maunoury*, Pages Actuelles, No. 49.

dered to continue the retreat, and General Allenby had warned him of the risk he ran. A sharp blow upon the German right flank by Sordêt's cavalry and some of d'Amade's battalions relieved the perilous situation. But the British losses were heavy after as well as during the battle. At night, during the disengagement, the 1st Gordons marched into the camp of a German division, and were taken prisoner almost to a man. The following is the judgment of the British commander-in-chief upon this affair:

"The magnificent fight put up by these glorious troops saved disaster, but the actual result was a total loss of at least 14,000 officers and men, about 80 guns, numbers of machine-guns as well as quantities of ammunition, war material and baggage, whilst the enemy gained time to close up his infantry columns marching down from the northeast. . . . The hope of making a stand behind the Somme or the Oise, or any other favourable position north of the Marne, had now to be abandoned, owing to the shattered condition of the army, and the far-reaching effect of our losses at the battle of Le Cateau was felt seriously even throughout the subsequent Battle of the Marne, and during the early operations on the Aisne. It was not possible to replace our lost guns and machine-guns until nearly the end of September."[9]

At this time Bülow was pursuing Sir Douglas Haig along the Guise road. On the 27th, the 2nd Munster Fusiliers were cut off, and killed or captured, except a handful saved by the 15th Hussars. On the 28th, the weary remnant of an army which had marched 90 miles in four days, fighting continually, tramped down the Oise valley, from La Fère to Noyon. That evening, Gough's cavalry, at the south of the Somme near Ham, and Chetwode's a little farther east, in covering the retreat, had to bear two severe attacks, which they effectually broke. On August 26, Sir John French had met Generals Joffre and Lanrezac at St. Quentin, and had again found the attitude of the latter officer unsatisfactory. On August 29, at 1 p.m., General Joffre visited the British commander at the latter's headquarters in the *château* of Compiègne. "I strongly represented my position," Sir John reported to Lord Kitchener, "to the French commander-in-chief, who was most kind, cordial, and sympathetic, as he has always been." The field-marshal was persuaded from this time on that "our stand should be made on some

---

9. French, *1914*, (also published by Leonaur),ch. 4. The Hon. J. W. Fortescue (*Quarterly Review*, Oct. 1919), defending Smith-Dorrien, charges Lord French with "clumsy and ludicrous misstatements," and questions the figures in the text.

line between the Marne and the Seine."

The needed relief had already been arranged when the conference took place, by a movement which we may summarise as an inclination of the 6th and 5th French Armies toward each other across the British rear. Sordêt's three cavalry divisions had already passed from the right to the left of the British Army. D'Amade's divisions had done something to check Von Kluck's advance by the Bapaume-Amiens and Peronne-Roye highroads. Nevertheless, Von der Marwitz's cavalry was on the Somme on August 28. That day Lanrezac's Army, which had retired from the line Avesnes-Chimay west -south-westward, took positions south of the Oise between La Fère and Guise. On the following day, August 29, while Joffre had gone from Lanrezac's headquarters at Laon to consult Sir John French at Compiègne, Maunoury and Lanrezac struck two hard blows, the one eastward from the Santerre plateau toward Peronne, the other northwest from the Oise toward St. Quentin, against the two flanks of Kluck.

In the former action, between the villages of Villers, Bretonneaux and Proyart, 15,000 French *chasseurs* and troops of the line arrested a larger German force for a day and a night, then falling back toward Roye. Lanrezac was more successful in the simultaneous Battle of Guise (extending to Ribémont on the west, and eastward to Vervins), although its original aim was not carried out. This was to wheel about, and to strike westward. The delicate manoeuvre might have ended disastrously, for Bülow was closer than was thought, but for a rapid return to the old front. The left of the 5th Army (18th and 3rd Corps) crossed the Oise toward St. Quentin in the morning of the 29th, but was stopped in view of the arrest of the right (1st and 10th Corps) by heavy German attacks. The 3rd Corps was then transferred to the right; and, to the east of Guise, a serious repulse was inflicted on the German X Corps and the Guard.

This seems to have been the strongest of several factors which now produced a deep disturbance of the German plans. On August 28, according to Bülow's war-diary,[10] the High Command, probably under the impression of Le Cateau, had ordered the I Army to continue south-westward to the Seine below Paris, and the II Army to

---

10. *Meine Bericht zur Marneschlacht*, notes, written in December 1914, on the operations of the II Army to the end of the Battle of the Aisne. Bülow charges Kluck with not having informed German G.H.Q. of the gathering of Maunoury's forces and the action of Proyart. For the Battle of Guise, see Hanotaux, "*La Bataille de Guise-St. Quentin*," *Rev. des Deux Mondes*, September 1, 1918.

make straight for the capital. Guise altered the whole prospect. Bülow had had to ask aid from Kluck (who, till August 27 subject to Bülow, was then given an independence of command which continued till September 10). Kluck, evidently the more forceful personality, and opposed to an immediate descent on Paris, then proceeded south-east to the Oise about Compiègne. The new direction was at once accepted by General Headquarters—a momentous change which will be discussed presently. Other important results were attained by these actions. The British Force was freed, and retired to the north bank of the Aisne, between Compiègne and Soissons, there to reorganise. At the same time, the neighbouring French armies, albeit outnumbered, were so ranged as to close the breach thus left against Kluck and Bülow. Field-Marshal French, not having received reinforcements, had rejected Joffre's request to "stand and fight," and refused to budge when it was repeated by President Poincaré and Lord Kitchener.[11]

Dislocation became apparent on both sides at this juncture. Kluck's liaison with Bülow was not very good, or the movements just described would not have been possible. A considerable gap had also developed between Hansen and Bülow. True, there was a corresponding void between the French 5th and 4th Armies, a distance of 25 miles held only by a few flying columns. But behind this breach, a few miles to the south (between Soissons and Château Porcien), the new so-called 9th Army had begun to form on August 27, under General Foch, fresh from his failure and success in Lorraine.

It is difficult now not to regard this appointment in the light of later fame.[12] But the commander of the 20th Corps was already distinguished. It is noteworthy that Ferdinand Foch was born within 4 miles and four months of Joffre—at Tarbes in the Upper Pyrenees, on October 2, 1851. Of a solid and comfortable middle-class family, he is said to have called the *generalissimo's* attention, when he was offered the army command, to the fact that he had a brother who was a Jesuit priest. Joffre swept the hinted objection aside. Foch, who had served as subaltern in the 1870 war, had risen to be brigadier-general when he

---

11. For his report of a stormy interview with Lord Kitchener at the Embassy in Paris on September 1 see *1914*, ch. v. This account has, however, been strongly questioned by Mr. Asquith (speech at Newcastle, May 16, 1919), who says that Lord Kitchener did but convey the conclusions of the Cabinet, which had been "seriously disquieted" by Sir John French's communications.
12. See *Foch*, by Réné Puaux, and, above all, Foch's own works, *De la Conduite de la Guerre*, and *Les Principes de la Guerre*.

was made director of the Ecole de Guerre. Later, he commanded successively the 13th Division, the 8th Corps, and the 20th, of Nancy.

The new force he was now called upon to lead—consisting of the 42nd Division of the 6th Corps, taken from the 3rd Army, the 9th and 11th Corps, taken from the 4th Army, the 1st Moroccan Division, and two reserve divisions from the 4th Army—was not yet ready to enter into action. Joffre's purpose in creating and placing it was not only to strengthen his centre, but to preserve the offensive force of the 5th Army. The German Staff probably did not know of the existence of Foch's "detachment." It did know that, farther east, its central armies, those of Duke Albrecht of Würtemberg and the Prussian Crown Prince, were not doing as well as had been expected.

On August 28, de Langle, having obtained the *generalissimo's* leave to suspend the retreat of the 4th Army for a day, and a day only,[13] drove the German IV Army back across the Meuse between Sedan and Stenay with his right, while, with his left, he struck at the Saxons between Signy-l'Abbaye and Novion-Porcien (sometimes called the Battle of Launois), where, in particular, the 1st Moroccan Division dealt faithfully with the I Saxon (XII German) Corps. The 3rd French Army was also deliberate in its retirement toward and around the northern limits of the entrenched camp of Verdun, and, on the 29th, near Dun-sur-Meuse, almost completely destroyed one of the Crown Prince's regiments which tried to cross the river.

5. End of the Long Retreat

The position along the French front on this day was, therefore, more favourable than it had been. In Lorraine, there was a slackening of the German attacks, pending the arrival of fresh forces; and Castelnau, his weakened army fully rallied, was more confident of the issue. In the west, one new army had come, and another was coming, into line. At the right-centre and left-centre, the enemy had suffered checks which must have disturbed his arrogance, and caused hesitation and divided counsels that were presently to contribute to his undoing. They were checks only, however. A superiority of power remained; and Kluck's right wing, doing forced marches of 25 to 30 miles a day, although the Allies broke most of the bridges behind them, was a very serious menace. Foch was not ready for a decisive engagement; and

---

13. "I see no inconvenience," Joffre replied, "in your turning back tomorrow, 28th, in order to affirm your success, and to show that the retreat is purely strategic; but on the 29th everyone must be in retreat."

the commander-in-chief never wavered in his view that the general reaction must commence from the left.

So the offensive must be postponed, the subsidiary scheme of August 25 cancelled, the retreat prolonged. General Joffre had left Lanrezac, at noon on the 29th, with the knowledge that an offensive toward St. Quentin was impossible, and during the afternoon had listened to the representations of the British commander, who was accompanied by his three corps commanders and General Allenby. In his report of the interview, French says:—

A general retirement on the line of the Marne was ordered, to which the French forces in the more eastern theatre of war were directed to conform.

Whilst closely adhering to his strategic conception, to draw the enemy on at all points until a favourable situation was created from which to assume the offensive, General Joffre found it necessary to modify from day to day the methods by which he sought to attain this object, owing to the development of the enemy's plans and changes of the general situation.

It was a hard decision to retreat to the Marne, so abandoning the second great defence line established after the war of 1870, including the forts of La Fère, Laon, and Rheims. This new objective emphasised the dangerous unevenness of the front, for, on the 29th, de Langle's army was 40 miles north of the Marne (beyond Rethel), Lanrezac was 50 miles to the north (near Guise), Maunoury and the British were about 30 miles to the north (between Clermont and Compiègne). It was a bold decision. But there was something still more heroic to follow.

Retreat and pursuit now attained their maximum speed, the greatest pressure being always on the west. The city and important railway centre of Amiens was evacuated by d'Amade, and occupied by Kluck's extreme right, on August 30 (the British base had already been moved to St. Nazaire). On that memorable Sunday, all the roads converging towards Paris were crowded with fugitives, whose panic-haste was only too well justified by the barbarities that marked the progress of the invasion. On the 31st, while the 5th Army was still north of Laon, Kluck was driving across the rearguards of Maunoury and of the British (restored to the general line, after a day's rest) in the Clermont-Compiègne region. The curvature of the Allied line, and the threat of envelopment on the left, or division of the left from the centre, were acute. As we shall see, however, the enemy had fallen into a more perilous predicament. Paris had begun to be a major factor in the situation. The railways running southward from the capital were overwhelmed with multitudes of flying civilians; so that the detrainment of some of the reinforcements from the east had to be made at a point more distant than had been intended.[14]

The British commander-in-chief, conscious of the weakness of his means, but sensible also of what might happen to the great city, now expressed his readiness to take part in a general battle before Paris, provided that his flanks could be covered.[15] But neither of Joffre's two new armies, the 6th and 9th, was ready for a decisive test. Kluck was hard upon the heels of d'Amade, Maunoury, and the British; and even on the Marne they might not be able to make a stand. Weighing up the possibilities from hour to hour, the *generalissimo* concluded that he was not yet justified in risking everything. On September 1, from his headquarters, which were moved on that day from Vitry to a quiet *château* at Bar-sur-Aube, orders were issued to extend the retreat by another 30 miles to the south banks of the Aube and the Seine. He wrote:—

Despite the tactical successes obtained by the 3rd, 4th, and 5th

---

14. For details of the last stages of the retreat and pursuit, see *La Marche sur Paris de l'Aile Droite Allemande*, by Count de Caix de Saint Aymour; Gordon and Hamilton, *op. cit.*: and *La Retraite de l'Armée Anglaise du 23 Août 1914*, by Ernest Renauld, *Renaissance*, November 25, 1916. On September 3, General Lanrezac was removed from the command of the French 5th Army—"because his views were contrary to a complete liaison with the British Army," says M. Hanotaux (*Rev. des Deux Mondes*, March 1919); but this is a partial and inadequate statement. As we have seen, Lanrezac had been at issue with G.Q.G. from the beginning of the campaign. M. Hanotaux quotes a note sent to the Minister of War. M. Millerand, on September 3, by General Joffre, who, "finding that the rapid recoil of the British Army, effected too soon and too quickly, had prevented Maunoury's Army from coming into action in good conditions, and had compromised Lanrezac's left flank," described his intention thus: "To prepare a new offensive in liaison with the British and with the garrison of Paris, and to choose the battlefield in such a way that, by utilising on certain parts of the front prepared defensive organisations, a numerical superiority could be assured in the zone chosen for the principal effort."

15. An anonymous writer, "*ZZZ*," in the *Revue de Paris*, September 15, 1917, says that Field-Marshal French's communication was made on September 1 to the French Government—probably it was a result of the Kitchener interview—and was transmitted to Joffre by the Minister of War, who, subject to the full liberty and responsibility of the *generalissimo*, favoured the idea of resistance on the north and north-east of Paris.

Armies on the Meuse and at Guise, the enveloping movement of the left of the 5th Army, insufficiently arrested by the British troops and the 6th Army, obliges the whole of our formation to pivot upon its right. As soon as the 5th Army has escaped the enveloping manoeuvre against its left, the mass of the 3rd, 4th, and 5th Armies will resume the offensive.

This order marks the moment at which Verdun became a pivot for the remaining portion of the western retreat.

The *generalissimo* added (September 2):—

We shall reach this line only if we are constrained. We shall attack, before reaching it, if we can realise a disposition permitting the co-operation of the whole of the forces.

The "General Instruction No. 4" of September 1 indicated, as the turning-point, the line Bray-sur-Seine-Nogent-sur-Seine-Arcis-sur-Aube-Camp-de-Mailly-Bar-le-Duc. By the supplementary note of the following day, this line of arrest was pushed back a little farther still, from Pont-sur-Yonne (south-east of Fontainebleau), through Brienne-le-Château, to Joinville, 25 miles south of Bar-le-Duc. These positions were never reached; but the orders are of great interest, anticipating, as they did, the possibility of a movement that might well have involved the abandonment of Verdun and the creation of a new pivot at Toul-Nancy. Joffre's public words are so few and sententious that the "General Order No. 11" may be given in full:

Part of our armies are falling back to re-establish their front, recomplete their effectives, and prepare, with every chance of success, for the general offensive that I shall order to be resumed in a few days. The safety of the country depends upon the success of this offensive, which, in accord with the pressure of our Russian Allies, must break the German armies, that we have already seriously damaged at several points.

Every man must be made aware of this situation, and strain all his energies for the final victory. The most minute precautions, as well as the most draconian measures, will be taken that the retirement be effected in complete order, so as to avoid useless fatigue. Fugitives, if found, will be pursued and executed. Army commanders will give orders to the depots so that these shall send promptly to the corps the full number of men necessary to compensate for losses sustained and to be foreseen in the next few days.

The effectives must be as complete as possible, the cadres re-constituted by promotion, and the moral of all up to the level of the new tasks for the coming resumption of the forward movement which will give us the definitive success.

At General Headquarters, September 2, 1914.

The General Commanding-in-Chief,

Joffre

CHAPTER 4

The Great Dilemma, Paris–Verdun

1. THE GOVERNMENT LEAVES THE CAPITAL

Retreat to the Somme was much, to the Marne so much more as was to be appreciated only in the after-years of the war. Retreat to the Seine, besides endangering the venerable fortress and pivotal place of Verdun, left in peril of capture, perhaps of destruction, Paris, the richest and most beautiful city of Continental Europe, the seat of a strongly centralised system of government and many industries, the home of two millions of people, the converging point of the chief national roads and railways. That Government and people accepted such a risk speaks eloquently for the mind that imposed it upon them.

The passionate strain of those few days will ever rest in the memories of those who experienced it. News, vague and unexplained, of the northern invasion had faUen upon us with avalanche swiftness. Paris was almost universally regarded as its immediate objective. On August 27, the Viviani Ministry was reconstructed as an enlarged Government of National Defence, with M, Millerand in M. Messimy's place at the Ministry of War, M. Delcassé at the Quai d'Orsay, M. Briand at the Ministry of Justice, and the Socialist M. Sembat at the Public Works. The same evening M. Millerand visited the Grand Quartier General at Vitry-le-Francois. He afterwards wrote:—

> On the staircase I shook hands with General Maunoury, who was leaving for the north to take command of his new army. The Staff officers were working in tranquillity, silence, and order. The brains of the army functioned freely. General Joffre kept me long in conference. I never found him more calm, more master of himself, more sure of the future. I left him full of respect, admiration, and confidence. (*Petit Parisien*, June 16, 1916.)

On the same day, General Gallieni was appointed military governor of Paris. Amongst the people of the capital, at least, this step excited keener interest, since it bore directly upon the question that was beginning to be asked on all hands—must we leave, or stay? Gallieni, who, long years before, had been Joffre's chief in the military organisation of the colony of Madagascar, was, like him, of the type of soldier-administrator. But his temperament spoke of his Corsican origin; and he had asked for, and Joffre had refused him, an army command—circumstances to be remembered when we see him in action. A man of impeccable honesty, emphatic will, and few words, he immediately won the confidence of his men and the population at large, and in the height of the crisis presented a worthy, if somewhat stiff, personification of the new spirit which France began to exhibit before her armies had scored any victory.

On August 29, the French official bulletin (communicated to an anxiously waiting crowd of journalists in a stable-like building beside the Ministry of War, thereafter to be scanned greedily as the *pièce de résistance* of the world's press) contained a partial revelation of the whereabouts of the enemy: "The situation *from the Somme to the Vosges* remains as yesterday." At the same time, the new government, in a manifesto to the nation, declared that "our duty is tragic, but simple: to repel the invader, to hold out to the end, to remain masters of our destinies." This phrase *"jusqu'au bout,"* repeated by Gallieni a few days later—with its homologues, *"jusqu'auboutist," "jusqu' auboutisme"*—was to become for years afterwards a catchword of the general resolve to fight to a victorious finish.

Refugees and wounded soldiers were now streaming into the city from the north, and families from the holiday resorts of the west and south. More than 30,000 fugitives from Belgium and the north of France reached the Nord Station on the 29th. A considerable current had begun to flow outwards, and during the next few days the railways were overwhelmed; but there was at no time real panic among the people of the great city. On Sunday the 30th, the first of a series of aeroplane raids provided a novel boulevard entertainment; the president of the City Council, M. Mithouard, advised residents to send their women and children into the country; and an edict was issued forbidding the papers to publish more than one edition daily. Railways, posts, and telegraphs were working subject to many hours' delay. The city hospitals were being cleared. Thousands of civilians were helping the garrison to dig trenches, and clear fields of fire. The *bois* and neighbouring lands were turned into a vast cattle and sheep farm; and large quantities of wheat were stored against the possibility of a siege.

On the night of the 31st, I received privately the alarming news—only made public on September 3—that the government had that afternoon decided to abandon the capital. The staffs and papers of the Ministries were already being removed; Ministers themselves, with the President of the Republic, and the ambassadors, except those of Spain and the United States, started for Bordeaux during the night of September 2. Many of the treasures of the Louvre and other museums and galleries were carried away at the same time. M. Poincaré and all the ministers signed a lengthy manifesto declaring that they were departing "on the demand of the military authority," in order to keep in touch with the whole country, after assuring the defence of the city "by all means in their power."

A quarter of the inhabitants of Paris had by now left, or v/ere endeavouring to leave, the city. The remainder, very anxious—for the red-handed enemy was only a day's march away—but still outwardly calm, preferred to any eloquence of political personages the terse promise of General Gallieni: "I have received the mandate to defend Paris against the invader. This mandate I shall fulfil to the end." Certainly, the government was in duty bound to see that it did not fall into the hands of Von Kluck. The utmost that can be said for the popular sentiment of the day is that, having prepared for departure, the chief magistrates of the Republic might perhaps have remained a few hours longer, when they would have discovered that there was no need to move after all.

2. KLUCK PLUNGES SOUTH-EASTWARD

The German Staff had, in fact, no immediate intention of attacking Paris; and Kluck, passing beyond gun-range of the outer forts of the entrenched camp, was racing south-east toward Meaux and Château-Thierry after the British and the French 5th Armies. This unexpected change of direction was only discovered on the afternoon of September 2, and confirmed during the next twenty-four hours by successive cavalry and aviation reports brought in to the headquarters of the British Army, Maunoury's Army, and the Paris garrison. It had, in fact, begun two days before, though it could not then be considered decisive. No sooner had he occupied Amiens, and crossed the Somme and Avre, than Kluck began to alter his course from south-west to south-east, while Maunoury and the British continued due south (the former two days behind the latter).

Thus, while conducting foreguard actions with the British, Kluck increasingly left aside Maunoury, and came into contact with the 5th Army. Under Joffre's orders, Maunoury continued his direct march on Paris, his last units not leaving Clermont till early on the morning of September 2, whereas the Expeditionary Force had crossed the Aisne on August 30, and traversed Senlis, Crépy, and Villers-Cotterets on the following day, to pass the Marne at and near Meaux. It is true that detachments of the German extreme right got as far afield as Creil, on the evening of September 2, and Chantilly on the following morning, but they were no more than a flank guard. Senlis, on September 2, was the last place occupied in any force, the last scene of fighting, and of assassination, pillage, and incendiarism, on the main road to Paris, 23 miles away. Immediately in front lay the forests of Ermenonville and Chantilly, an uncomfortable country for what had become a mere wing-tip of the invasion.

While Maunoury's exhausted troops were thus left liberty, behind these woods, to re-form and rest across the north-eastern suburbs of Paris (from Dammartin to the Marne), Kluck's main body was making south-eastward after the British at a hot pace, at the same time closing up on its left with other forces coming due south from Soissons through Villers-Cotterets. Crépy-en-Valois was occupied by the Germans on September 1, 120,000 troops passing through toward Nanteuil-le-Haudouin and Betz, which were reached on September 3. By the time Gallieni got wind of the new direction, in fact, nearly the whole of Kluck's Army and Bülow's right wing were nearing Meaux and Château-Thierry (27 and 54 miles east of Paris). On September 3, the British blew up the Marne bridges behind them, and altered their line of retreat to south-west, reaching .quietude and reinforcements on the Seine on September 4. Kluck pursued his south-eastward course, and, having crossed the Marne, Petit Morin, and Grand Morin, established himself, on September 5, with his Staff, in the house of a Dr. Alleaume in the little country town of Coulommiers. "This is the last stage," he is reported as saying; "the day after tomorrow, we shall leave Coulommiers to enter Paris."[1] That programme could not be carried out. Three days later, the boaster had fled, and Sir John French was ensconced in Coulommiers Town Hall.

Before we go on to trace the advantage the Allied commanders took of this situation, we may pause to consider two questions which

1. *Le Livre du Souvenir*, by Paul Ginisty and Arsène Alexandre.

have been, and may yet be, keenly discussed: (1) How came Kluck, reputedly one of the best of living German officers, to perform this evolution across Maunoury's front, and so to reach a position that was to prove fatal to the whole enterprise? (2) Was the German Staff right in deciding to postpone the attack upon Paris?

It was natural that the problem should at first be posed in this double form, because, when information is scanty, it is easier to criticise an individual commander than a Grand Staff, and because the fate of a capital is more generally interesting than a strategical hypothesis. The most usual reply to the two questions was that, while the commander had made an evident blunder, the Command had only followed the orthodox military rule that no lesser objective should be allowed to interfere with that of breaking the enemy's main armies, and, the French and British armies being unbroken, it was right not to adventure upon another task, the reduction of a great city which might be obstinately defended, till this was accomplished. That Berlin understood the importance of taking the French capital, and hoped to take it quickly, may be assumed.[2] Among other detailed evidence, the tardiness of a message from Berlin to the Ambassador of the Unit-

2. Major-General Sir F. Maurice, in his brilliant study, *Forty Days in 1914*, speaks, however, of the German Staff assuming "that Paris had only a moral and not a military value." General Maurice refers to the city as being "at the mercy of the enemy," and emphatically condemns Kluck for failing to occupy it, and so "sacrificing substantial gains in favour of a grandiose and ambitious scheme which, as events proved, could not be realised. Despite General Maurice's great authority, I see no reason to change the conclusions in the text with regard to the points here discussed. There are several important factors which he does not mention, particularly the influence of the appearance of the new 9th Army, under Foch, at the French centre, and the equalisation at this time of the German and Allied forces. Kluck was the victim of necessity rather than of any grandiose ambition; and as for the Staffs, it was more Joffre's strategy than "Prussian conceit and self-sufficiency" that "marred the execution of a well-laid plan." Says Mr. Joseph Reinach (*La Guerre sur le Front Occidental, 1914-1915*, ch. v. sec. 7): "Bernhardi has classed the capitals of Europe in two categories: those whose capture has a decisive importance from the military point of view, like Paris and Vienna, and those whose importance is much smaller. To take Paris, what glory! to enter Paris, what a gage! But the same Bernhardi, the master of all the German generals, and before him all the greatest captains, all the oracles of the military art, Moltke, Jomini, insist that the aim of war must be fixed as high as possible, and this aim is the complete ruin of the enemy State by the destruction, the putting out of action, of its armies. Only an enemy completely disarmed will bow to the will of the conqueror. . . . The opinion that prevailed with the German Staff is that to attack Paris before having finished with the Allied Armies would be a fault entailing very serious consequences. . . . The event does not prove that this opinion was mistaken."

ed States (then still neutral) in Paris warning him to prepare for this event,[3] and the fact that the German armies were not at first provided with maps of the region of the capital reinforce the probability that this aim was originally, as after August 29, subordinated to that of a decisive battle.

But the wisdom of the decision has been strongly questioned. General Cherfils says:—

> First to beat the enemy army is a means to an end, and generally the best. But this means is only a rule generally justified, not at all a principle. The principle of war is higher, and, like other principles, immutable—it is that the aim of war is to impose peace, and to this end to produce on the enemy government or command an effect of decisive demoralisation. We all know that Paris was not defended, and that, if the Germans had pushed right on to the capital with their I Army, nothing would have prevented them from destroying two of the forts, bombarding Paris, and entering the city. I ask if, at that hour, such a disaster would not have produced an effect of demoralisation equal to the finest victory. The Germans neglected to put in play the terrifying surprise of such a catastrophe. I am sure the Grand Staff must have regretted it.[4]

3. This message, first published by *Le Matin*, February 27, 1918, was dispatched by Mr. Gerard, United States Ambassador in Berlin, on the morning of September 8, to his colleague in Paris, Mr. Myron Herrick, who received it late on the same evening. It read as follows: "Extremely urgent. September 8. The German General Staff recommends that all Americans leave Paris *via* Rouen and Le Havre. They will have to leave soon if they wish to go.—Gerard." It is added that the message was sent on the pressing wish of the German Staff, and that it was doubled, one copy going *via* Switzerland, and the other *via* Rome. When this document was penned, the struggle had been proceeding on the Ourcq for two days and a half; Kluck had withdrawn nearly all his forces from the Marne; and the British and d'Espérey's Armies were advancing rapidly northward. How, in these circumstances, could the German General Staff imagine that they could arrange "soon" a triumphant entry into Paris? There is one, and only one, fact in the military situation that they could build upon. At 5 a.m. on September 8, the right wing of Foch's Army had broken down, and was in full retreat toward Fère Champènoise. If they really accepted this as such a promise of victory as to justify the warning to the Americans of Paris, the German Staff must have been in an infatuated state of mind. It is possible, however, that the message was only a reckless piece of propaganda on their part, intended, at a critical moment, to awe the neutrals of America, Switzerland, and Italy, and to frighten some good Americans out of Paris. In no case can a warning conveyed on September 8 countenance the idea that the entry into Paris was originally intended to occur before a decisive victory' had been won.

4. In the *Gaulois*, "*Une Cause do la Defaite Allemande sur la Marne.*"

More convincing reasons than this may be found for the fact that Kluck was afterwards relegated, first to a lesser command, in which he was wounded, and then to the retired list. It is an exaggeration to speak of the city as "not defended." The garrison consisted of four Territorial divisions, to which Maunoury could have added on September 5 the nine divisions of his new army. The ring of outer forts, with a circumference of nearly a hundred miles, was too long to be held by such a force; but it was also too long for investment or general attack by the ten or eleven divisions Kluck might have brought up. The German commander would, doubtless, have struck at a short sector; and the question, probably unanswerable, is whether the defenders, in their inadequate trenches connecting the old-fashioned forts, could have prevented him from breaking through, at least until the general battle on the Marne was won. It is highly probable they could have done so. It is certain that Gallieni would have made a spirited and obstinate defence; he had received specific permission to blow up the Seine bridges within the city, if he found it necessary to retire to the south bank.

We know, also, that Kluck would have had to wait several days before his heavy artillery could be brought into position. Although the shortest distance between the outer forts and the boundaries of the city is about eight miles, much of Paris might then have been destroyed. But, the government having gone south, would there have been any "decisive demoralisation"? And what, meanwhile, would have happened to the remaining armies? Assuming that the 6th French Army would have been wholly occupied with Kluck in the Paris area, instead of on the Ourcq, could Bülow, the Saxons, and the Duke of Würtemberg have fulfilled their task on the Marne? Would there not have been a dangerous gap on their right? Kluck would then have found it much more difficult to disentangle himself, and perhaps impossible, in case of a general retreat, to keep touch with his colleagues.

It has been stated, not very convincingly, that, in daring to pronounce against such an adventure, Kluck encountered the opposition of the emperor and part of the Imperial Staff.[5] Von Bülow testifies that

5. M. Reinach states this, adding: "There was, it seems, an exchange of messages between the Staff and Kluck. Finally, theory prevailed" (La Guerre; Commentaires de Polybe, vol. iv.). According to an article in the Renaissance, September 2, 1916, Kluck had previously favoured the advance on Paris, quoting a reply of Blücher to Schwartzenberg in 1814: "It is better to go to Paris; when one has Paris, one has France." At a council held at German Headquarters after the battle of Guise and St. Quentin, says the writer, Kluck went over to the advice of Moltke.

the Staff abandoned the advance on Paris directly after the order was given. The problem which had arisen was of a larger and graver character than that which has excited so much ingenious speculation.

3. JOFFRE'S OPPORTUNITY

For it was no exaggeration to say that a rapid victory was an *essential* condition of the German plan. The envelopment of the west wing of the Allies might succeed if it were effected by the time they reached the Somme, or a little beyond, but not later, and that for three main reasons. In the first place, there was, south of the Somme, Maunoury's force, not large at first, but constantly growing, a grave threat to Kluck's west flank, whether realised or not. In the second place, there was Foch's new army forming at the centre; and, between Lanrezac and Foch, Bülow's advance was so compromised that it had become necessary for Kluck to move eastward in order to relieve his comrade. Thirdly, Paris stood across the path of a more directly southward movement, with the certainty of delaying, and the probability of dislocating, an immediate attack. The design of envelopment by the west was, therefore, necessarily abandoned.

Between August 29 and September 1, when he had passed the Somme, Kluck ceased his south-westerly course, which no longer had any important purpose, and came in touch with Bülow, to support his blow at the strongest of the French Armies, the 5th. It was probably thought, on the following days, that Maunoury would be locked up in Paris by a distraught Government, and that the British Army, virtually disabled, would not require very serious attention. Personal ambition, fear of being late for the action that was to give a dramatic victory, may have spurred on the commander of the I Army.[6]

---

6. M. Hanotaux (*Histoire Illustrie*, especially ch. xxxvii., and in the Rev. des Deux Mondes, March 1919) has his own picturesque theory of these events, supported by rather frail evidence. It is, briefly, that there was an antagonism between Kluck, who wished to complete his enveloping movement, and Bülow, who after Guise had persuaded the Grand Staff to renounce it in favour of a frontal action against the French centre in which he would be the chief actor. After Charleroi and after Guise, Bülow had had to call Kluck to his aid. They were natural antagonists, the junker and the popular soldier. Moltke and the Staff hesitated between them, and then decided for Bülow. Bülow was to lead the attack; Kluck was ordered to remain between the Oise and the Marne to watch the region of Paris. But he refused to be thus thwarted of his victory, and rode impetuously on toward Provins, overrunning Bülow's slower approach. Maunoury's attack caught him *in flagrante delicto*. All this is plausible enough except the statement that Kluck was ordered to remain north of the Marne. Had he done so, the same result, (continued next page),

So Kluck continued his course till his advance guards had reached a point on the Brie plateau 50 miles south-east of Paris. His first purpose was fulfilled. The space between the central lines of the German I and II Armies on September 4 may be roughly measured by the distance between Crépy-en-Valois and Fismes—no less than 50 miles. Next day, this space was bridged. It could not have been otherwise closed, except by arresting one or both forces, that is to say by suspending the whole enterprise. Paris had been covered as well as was possible with the forces in hand, the IV Reserve Corps, with a cavalry division, being left north of the Marne, while the II Corps was to turn from Coulommiers facing the southeast of the capital. It is uncertain how far Kluck knew of the strength or position of the French 6th Army.[7] As it afterwards came into action on the Ourcq, he could not know of it, for it was not yet fully constituted; but he had been repeatedly in conflict with some of its elements, from Baupaume to Senlis. The German Command can hardly have supposed that Paris would be left without a respectable garrison, especially as they were certainly cognisant of Gallieni's proclamation. Whether they under- or over-estimated the strength Gallieni and Maunoury could put forth, the result would be much the same. In any case, Kluck must close up toward Bülow and cover his flank; new lines of communication must be organised; if the French should attempt a serious flank attack, it could be delayed till the main battle had been won.

It was, doubtless, a risky disposition, made more than risky by Kluck's headstrong determination to have his full share in the decisive shock. British critics, with his failings in the north in mind, have dealt very severely with this 'commander; French writers, better acquainted with the fighting on the Ourcq, are more respectful. Kluck's movement, like the advance of Prince Ruprecht and Heeringen across the

would have been produced two or three days sooner.
M. Hanotaux also states that Marwitz's three cavalry divisions had been ordered on September 1 to carry out a raid to the gates of Paris, destroying railways as they went, but that "Kluck had other views" (*La Manoeuvre de la Marne*).
8. The author of *Die Schlachten an der Marne* says: "Kluck knew there were troops to the left of the British, but did not know their exact strength."
In his book *Comment fut sauvé Paris,* M. P. H. Courrière cites the following order issued by General von Schwerin at dawn on September 5, and afterwards found on the battlefield: "The IV Reserve Corps continues today the forward march, and charges itself, north of the Marne, with the covering of the north front of Paris; the IV Cavalry Division will be added to it. The II Corps advances by the Grand Morin Valley below Coulommiers, and directs itself against the east front of Paris."

face of Castelnau's Army toward the Gap of Charmes, may have contained a large element of recklessness, born of foolish contempt for the retiring forces. But he was not responsible for the dilemma in which he was involved. The error was that of the German Grand Staff rather than of any particular commander. We shall see that, if Kluck was gambling, he had not lost his head. Had the Allied retreat been less prolonged, had he been able to come up with the French 5th and British Armies sooner, he might have won, or at least have stopped on the Marne, instead of the Aisne. He had no longer a free choice of his movements.

To have stayed between Aisne and Marne would not have solved the problem; it would have eased the British advance. Every man was needed on the extreme front, if the whole aim of the invasion was not to be missed. Bülow had had to leave one corps behind at Maubeuge, and was just losing the support, on his left, of one of Hausen's Saxon corps (the XI), ordered off to the Russian front, Foch's new army of the centre had, doubtless, been discovered before this time, though its numbers would not yet be known. Kluck had to throw forward every regiment not demonstrably needed elsewhere. All the German commands were now engaged in a reckless gamble; but, where his masters lost their nerve, Kluck did not. To this complexion had the great enveloping movement come under pressure of the Joffrean dilemma. With all his anxieties, the French *generalissimo* may well have smiled blandly as he saw the enemy enter between the horns of Paris and Verdun.

It is important to realise that the consequences we have to trace arose, not chiefly from individual blundering, but from the nature of the invasion, from a plan of campaign resting upon the need and expectation of a rapid victory, and the French manner of meeting it. To this need every lesser aim, however promising in itself, had been sacrificed. King Albert was allowed to carry his army into the shelter of Antwerp, there to prepare for the Battle of the Yser. Ostend, Dunkirk, Calais, Boulogne, all the coast of Flanders and the Channel, with its hinterland, and with them the sea communications of England, were ignored in obedience to the strategical doctrine of the major objective, and in the sure belief that if this were attained, the rest would follow easily. The watching world was staggered by the immense boldness of these criminals. Joffre was in no wise intimidated, never thought of temporising, immediately saw that a most daring crime can only be overcome by a still more daring virtue, and set all his mind to the task of gathering the utmost force in the best position for the decisive test. That meant abandoning the north; so be it—he, too, must stake all on a blow.

After rescuing the armies from a deadly constraint on the frontier, after preparing a mass of manoeuvre which would restore to him the initiative, after so lengthening the retreat that a virtual equality of forces was obtained, Joffre's aim was to reach a level front whence, his flanks being safe, he could swing round the whole line in a sudden riposte. His wings were now, in a measure, protected; and the same process which had brought the Allied forces near their reserves, their supplies and their most favourable battleground had attenuated the enemy's columns, dislocated their line, and prejudiced their power of manoeuvre. The dilemma which Paris presented in the west, Verdun repeated at the other end of the line, 170 miles away. There, too, the beginnings of a modern defensive system were being extemporised.

Sarrail had just succeeded Ruffey in command of the 4th Army; he would have defended, did, indeed, afterwards defend, his circle of forts and hill-trenches as Gallieni would have defended the capital. The Imperial Crown Prince was faced by a replica of Kluck's problem—to attack the fortress of the Meuse Heights, and to that extent to neglect the French field armies; or to neglect the fortress, and risk all that might, and did, happen. Either the invaders must entangle themselves upon these protruding points, and so weaken the intermediate forces, or they must go forward to the crucial encounter leaving a peril un-reduced upon either flank. That the Crown Prince's answer was the same as Kluck's indicates that it was not their individual answer only, but the decision of the Grand Staff,

On the west, there are, before the Battle of the Marne, three main stages in the development of this result: the loss of a week at the outset in Belgium, which enabled the French command to shift its forces north-westward, and the British Army to assemble; the failure of the surprise on the Sambre and Meuse to produce a decision; and the failure, on or south of the Somme, either to envelop or to break the retreating masses. On the east, where there was less possibility of surprise or manoeuvre, a like inability to pierce or envelop appeared in five successive failures: that of the Gap of Charmes on August 25; the battle of the Mortagne, at the beginning of September; the Battle of the Grand Couronné of Nancy on September 4-11; that of Fort Troyon on September 8-13; and that of the Crown Prince's Army in course of the main battle of the Marne. To the German marching wing the most important mission had been entrusted; and its failure must be adjudged the most grave.

Its greatest exponents have admitted that the danger of dislocation is inherent in the tactic of envelopment; Clausewitz himself laid it down that the manoeuvre should only be attempted when the force attacked is wholly engaged with the assailant's centre.[8] After the Sambre, the German armies never had this opportunity; and ere they could change a plan that had governed all their dispositions, it had aggravated the disorder natural in so violent a pursuit. What at first sight looks like a sudden change of fickle fortune is, in fact, the logical end of an immense strategical deception, of weaknesses in an imposing organism discovered by a higher intelligence, and exploited by a higher prudence and courage.

However the lesser questions we have touched be answered in the light of fuller knowledge, it seems sure that history will pronounce Joffre's master idea one of the boldest and soundest conceptions to be found in military annals. It dominated the ensuing battle, which thus yielded an essentially strategic victory. Gallieni has been justly praised for the promptitude with which he took advantage of Kluck's "adventurous situation." The only alternative for the latter, however, was another situation hardly, if at all, less adventurous; and the choice was imposed upon him—as, at the other end of the line, upon the crown prince—by the French commander-in-chief. The manoeuvrer had become the manoeuvred before the battle began.

---

8. General von Freytag-Loringhoven says: "It was proved on the Marne that the age of armies numbering millions, with their improved armament and widely extended fronts, engenders very special conditions. . . . The envelopment of the whole host of the enemy is a very difficult matter" (*Deductions*).

CHAPTER 5

The Order of Battle

1. GALLIENI'S INITIATIVE

It was in the early hours of September 3 that the first definite evidence of Kluck's divergence south-eastward was reported to the Military Government of Paris; but the officers in charge did not venture to disturb their weary chief, who received the news only when he rose in the morning.[1] At noon, he issued to the garrison the following note:—

A German army corps, probably the Second, has passed from Senlis southward, but has not pursued its movement toward Paris, and seems to have diverged to the south-east. In a general way, the German forces which were in face of the 6th Army appear to be oriented toward the south-east. On our side, the 6th Army is established to the north-east of the entrenched camp on the front Mareil-en-France-Dammartin-Montgé. The British Army is in the region south of the Marne and the Petit Morin, from Courtevroult (west) to beyond La Ferté-sous-Jouarre (east).

During the day, the news, the importance of which Gallieni immediately realised, was confirmed; the evening bulletin issued in Bordeaux announced that "the enveloping march of the enemy seems definitely conjured."

Perceiving the opportunity of striking a hard, perhaps a decisive, blow at the enemy's flank, the governor appears to have resolved at

---

1. M. Maurice Barrés, *Echo de Paris*, June 1, 1916. But General Maunoury had telegraphed at midnight on August 31 to General Joffre reporting that Kluck seemed to be leaving the direction of Paris.

once to set Maunoury's army in movement,[2] and then to have proceeded to urge the commander-in-chief to make this the commencement of the general offensive which was to have taken place some days later, when the armies had re-formed behind the Seine. "If they do not come to us, we will go to them," said Gallieni to his chief of staff, General Clergerie;[3] and at about 9 a.m. on September 4, he issued to the 6th Army the following order:—

In consequence of the movement of the German armies, which appear to be slipping across our front in a south-easterly direction, I intend to send your army forward against their flank, that is to say in an eastward direction, in touch with the British troops. I will indicate your direction of march when I know that of the British Army; but take forthwith your dispositions so that your troops may be ready to march this afternoon, and to launch tomorrow (September 5) a general movement to the east of the entrenched camp.

In course of the morning and forenoon of the same day (Septem-

---

2. General Cherfils describes the extent of Gallieni's authority as being in a state of "nebulous imprecision." The position appears to have been this: The entrenched camp of Paris, under the old regulations, was under the control of the Minister of War, not the *generalissimo*, who could claim the services of a part of the garrison if he left enough men to assure the safety of the city, subject to a protest by the governor, but could not touch its munitions or supplies. On his appointment as Military Governor of Paris (August 26), Gallieni had asked that the garrison, then consisting of four divisions of Territorials, should be reinforced. The 6th Army was accordingly placed under his orders. On the same day, the entrenched camp was placed, by the Minister, M. Millerand, under the superior orders of General Joffre. There was thus a threefold command, Maunoury being under Gallieni, and Gallieni under Joffre. General Bonnal (*Les Conditions de la Guerre Moderne*) says that it was "in virtue of his own initiative, based on the powers of the governor of a place left to its own forces," that Gallieni ordered Maunoury, on the morning of September 4, to prepare to take the offensive. For particulars of Gallieni's communications with General Joffre and Sir John French, see the work named, the same author's long article in the *Renaissance*, September 4, 1915, and an article in that review on September 2, 1916. According to the last named, it was at 2.50 p.m. on September 4 that the commander-in-chief authorised the advance of Maunoury's Army; and Gallieni's orders were that it was to bring its front up to Meaux on the next day, and to "attack" on the morning of the 6th. Gallieni's control over Maunoury's Army ceased when, by the development of the battle of the Ourcq, it passed out of the region of the entrenched camp of Paris. In August 1915, the old rules on the "*Service de Place*" were altered to give the French commander-in-chief absolute authority over fortresses and their governors, and full power to dispose of their resources.

3 "*La Bataille de l'Ourcq*"; Paul H. Courrière, in the *Renaissance*, September 1, 1917.

ber 4), Gallieni had three telephonic conversations with the *generalis-simo*. Before the last of these communications, between noon and 1 p.m., the governor, with General Maunoury, went by automobile to British headquarters at Melun. Sir John French was not there; but, during the evening, probably after hearing from General Joffre, he replied to Gallieni that the British Army would turn about on the morrow, with a view to the resumption of the offensive on September 6.[4] After reflection, in fact, the *generalissimo* had accepted Gallieni's view of the opportunity, and had issued during the evening orders to the three armies of the left to get into positions of attack on the 5th, and to commence the battle on the morning of the 6th. On the 5th, Sir John French visited General Joffre, who had now come over to Claye, on the road from Paris to Meaux, Maunoury's headquarters. After the interview, there should have been no misunderstandings.

At the end of August, the French General Staff had moved from Vitry-le-François 40 miles farther south to Bar-sur-Aube, where, on the outskirts of the quiet little town, at the large country house called "*Le Jard*" (29 Faubourg de Paris), which had sheltered a century before the Tsar Alexander I and King Frederick William II of Prussia, the commander-in-chief was the guest of M. Tassin, a member of the Paris bar. Refusing all ceremony, General Joffre occupied a large first-floor room looking by two windows upon the gateway and the Paris highroad. But it was in a neighbouring schoolroom where the Staff bureaux were established, and to which the telegraph wires—nerves of the battle—were attached, that the historic orders for the great encounter were composed. On the evening of September 5, another southward move was made to Chatillon-sur-Seine, where, for three weeks, the Staff occupied the chateau of Colonel Maitre, once belonging to Marshal Marmont. It was from the "*Chambre de l'Empereur*" in this old house, so called after a visit of Napoleon in 1814, that General Joffre issued his final summons to the troops on the morning of the battle.

The text of the General Instructions of September 4 and 5 is of great importance, for they determined at least the first shape of the

---

4. In his dispatch of September 17, 1914, Sir John French does not mention any visit or message from General Gallieni, and only speaks of receiving General Joffre's request to turn about, made during their interview on Saturday, September 5. In his volume *1914*, he does mention the visit, but attributes to Gallieni the statement that Maunoury would move east toward the Ourcq "on Sunday the 6th." This suggests that the move actually made on the 5th was not at the time known at British Headquarters.

ensuing struggle, and we will have to recall them in dealing with one of its most critical phases. For the moment, it will suffice to point out this apparent ambiguity, that, while the general offensive was to commence only on September 6, Maunoury's Army was to discover itself on September 5, in a movement that would necessarily provoke strong resistance.

2. GENERAL OFFENSIVE OF THE ALLIES

General Joffre's programme was embodied in the following series of army orders:

General Headquarters, September 4

1. Advantage must be taken of the adventurous situation of the I German Army (right wing) to concentrate upon it the efforts of the Allied armies of the extreme left. All dispositions will be taken during the 5th of September with a view to commencing the attack on the 6th.

2. The dispositions to be realised by the evening of September 5 will be:

(a) All the available forces of the 6th Army, to the north-east, ready to cross the Ourcq between Lizy-sur-Ourcq and May-en-Multien, in the general direction of Château-Thierry (the last phrase was telephonically corrected at 10 p.m. to the following: "in a manner to attain the meridian of Meaux"). The available elements of the 1st Cavalry Corps that are in the vicinity will be put under the orders of General Maunoury for this operation.

(b) The British Army, established on the front Changis-Coulommiers, facing east, ready to attack in the general direction of Montmirail.

(c) The 5th Army, closing up slightly to the left, will establish itself on the general front Courtacon-Esternay-Sézanne, ready to attack in the general direction south to north, the 2nd Cavalry Corps assuring connection between the British and 5th Armies.

(d) The 9th Army will cover the right of the 5th Army, holding the southern end of the Marshes of St. Gond, and carrying a part of its forces on to the plateau to the north of Sézanne.

3. The offensive will be begun by these different armies in the morning of September 6.

(e) To the 4th Army: Tomorrow, September 6, our armies of the left will attack in front and flank the I and II German armies. The 4th Army, stopping its southward movement, will oppose the enemy, combining its movement with that of the 3rd Army, which, debouching to the north of Revigny, will assume the offensive, moving westward.

(f) To the 3rd Army: The 3rd Army, covering itself on the northeast, will debouch westward to attack the left flank of the enemy forces, which are marching west of the Argonne, It will combine its action with that of the 4th Army, which has orders to attack the enemy."

We are now in a position, before entering upon the particulars of the battle, to measure in its chief elements the very marked change in the balance and relation of forces which the French High Command had obtained by and in course of the retreat from Belgium. The most important of these elements are numbers and positions. Both are shown in detail in the following tabular pages, setting forth in parallel columns the dispositions of the opposed armies immediately before the action commenced.

STRENGTH AND POSITION OF THE ARMIES

(On September 5-6, except where otherwise indicated, in order from West to East)

ALLIED	GERMAN
6th ARMY (General MAUNOURY), (H.Q., Claye). Under the direction of General Gallieni till September 10.	I ARMY (General von KLÜCK), (H.Q., Coulommiers).

7th Corps (General Vautier).
   Brought from Lorraine to the Amiens region, thence to east of Paris. Consisting of 14th Division Active (General Villaret) and 63rd Division of Reserve (General Lombard)—the latter in lieu of the 13th Division, left in the Vosges.
   Came into action on September 6, and then formed the left.
	IV Cavalry Division.
	
	IV Corps of Reserve (General von Schwerin).
	   Consisting of the VII and

5th Group of Reserve Divisions (General Lamaze). Also from Lorraine and Amiens, after hard fighting and heavy losses. Consisting of 55th Divi-	XXII Reserve Divisions. At the commencement of the battle, stood, as rearguard on the west of the

sion Reserve (General Leguay), 56th Division Reserve (General de Dartein), and a brigade of Moroccan Infantry (General Ditte).

This group came into action on the afternoon of September 5, and afterwards formed the centre.

45th Division (General Drude).
From Algeria.

A Cavalry Brigade (General Gillet), much fatigued in the retreat from Belgium.

The above units were wholly north of the Marne, save for a thin connection with the British Army.

They were reinforced during the battle by the following :

4th Corps (General Boëlle).
7th and 8th Divisions, brought from the 3rd Army (embarked at Ste. Menehould, September 2). Some regiments had lost heavily on the Meuse. The 8th Division (de Lartigues) was sent across the Marne on September 6 to link Maunoury's and the British Armies ; the 7th Division (General de Trentinian), on September 8, to Maunoury's left, where it was afterwards joined by the 8th Division.

6th Group of Reserve Divisions (General Ebener).
Much reduced by fighting near Cambrai, and exhausted in the retreat. Consisting of 61st Reserve Division (General Deprez) and 62nd Reserve Division (General Ganeval). Engaged September 7 and 9.

1st Cavalry Corps (General Sordet. Succeeded at 9 a.m. on September 8 by General Bridoux).

1st, 3rd, and 5th Divisions : much fatigued in the retreat. Ordered from south of the Seine to Nanteuil-le-Haudouin, September 7.

2½ Battalions of Zouaves were sent on September 9 to the aid of the left wing. A brigade of Spahis, detrained on September 10, took part in the pursuit to the Aisne. Three groups of garrison batteries were sent, on September 6, to support Lamaze, who had no

Ourcq, about Marcilly, Barcy, and Penchard, in face of the French 6th Army. It had nothing behind to call upon, save

A Brigade of Landwehr,
which was brought to the north of the battlefield from the Oise on September 8.

The following units were at first all south of the Marne, facing the British Expeditionary Force and the French 5th Army :

II Corps (General von Linsingen).
Of Stettin. III and IV Divisions, one north and one south of the Grand Morin, between Crécy-en-Brie and Coulommiers, facing the British. Withdrawn to the Ourcq on September 6.

IV Corps (General von Armin).
Of Magdeburg. VII and VIII Divisions; south of the Grand Morin from Coulom-

105

corps artillery. 4 divisions of Territorials (83, 85, 89, and 92) of the Paris garrison did rear duty, but were not engaged in the battle. Admiral Ronar'ch's Brigade of Marines, afterwards famous at Dixmude, was not engaged, being insufficiently trained.

BRITISH EXPEDITIONARY FORCE (General Sir John FRENCH), (H.Q., Melun).

3rd Corps (General Pulteney).

Consisting of the 4th Division (Major-General Snow, 10th, 11th, 12th Brigades, and 5th Cavalry Brigade), and the 19th Brigade. The 4th Division joined before the battle of Le Cateau. This formed the British left, south of Crécy-en-Brie.

2nd Corps (General Sir H. Smith-Dorrien).

Comprising the 3rd Division (Hamilton—7th, 8th, and 9th Brigades, and 2nd Cavalry Brigade); and 5th Division (Ferguson—13th, 14th, and 15th Brigades, and 3rd Cavalry Brigade). This corps had borne the heaviest fighting in the 150 miles' retreat from Mons, its casualties numbering 350 officers and 9200 men. These losses had been partly made good.

1st Corps (General Sir D. Haig).

1st Division (Lomax—1st, 2nd, 3rd Brigades, and 1st Cavalry

Brigade); 2nd Division (Murray—4th, 5th, 6th Brigades, and 4th Cavalry Brigade). This made the British right, east of Rozoy.

All these troops consisted of home regiments of the old regular army.

5th ARMY (General Franchet D'ESPEREY), (H.Q., Romilly-sur-Seine).

2nd Cavalry Corps (General Conneau).

Brought from the Lorraine front.

Comprising the 4th, 8th, and 10th Divisions (Generals Abonneau, Baratier, and Gendron). Arriving from the 2nd Army at the beginning of September, it kept contact with the British Army on the left, northwest of Provins.

miers to Chevru, facing the British. Withdrawn to the Ourcq on September 7.

III Corps (General von Lochow).

Of Berlin. V and VI Divisions, across the highroad from Montmirail to Provins, midway between these towns.

IX Corps (General von Quast).

Of Altona. Two divisions, one north of Esternay, and one at the right of this, near Morsains.

(The III Reserve and IX Reserve Corps of Von Klück's Army had been left behind—partly before Antwerp, partly before Maubeuge.)

Cavalry Corps.

Consisting of the II and IX Cavalry Divisions (General von der Marwitz) facing the left and centre of the British Army, and the V Division and Guard Cavalry Division (General von Richt-

106

18th Corps (General de Maud'huy).

35th, 36th, and 38th Divisions (Generals Marjoulat, Jouannic, and Muteau). Before and behind Provins. There was thus fully 10 miles between it and Sir Douglas Haig's Corps.

3rd Corps (General Hache).

5th, 6th, and 37th Divisions (Generals Mangin, Petain, and Comby), south-west of Esternay.

1st Corps (General Deligny, succeeding General Franchet d'Espérey).

1st and 2nd Divisions (Generals Gallet and Duplessis). Across the Grand Morin at Esternay.

The above three corps faced the left of the German I Army.

10th Corps (General Defforges).

19th and 20th Divisions (Generals Bonnier and Rogerie) east of Esternay. Sent to aid of 9th Army from September 9 to 11.

The above four corps extended over the plateaux from the British right to the Paris-Nancy highroad, midway between Esternay and Sézanne, their right being advanced.

4th Group of Reserve Divisions (General Valabrègue).

Consisting of the 51st, 53rd, and 69th Divisions of Reserve (Generals Bouttegourd, Perruchon, and Legros). In support and reserve : much fatigued after the battle of Guise and the retreat.

Light Brigade of 2nd Division Infantry. in reserve.

9th ARMY (General FOCH), (H.Q., Pleurs).

42nd Division (General Grossetti).

From the 6th Corps of the Army of Verdun. North of Sézanne across the Epernay road, in touch with d'Espérey's right.

9th Corps (General Dubois).

From Nancy ; afterwards part of the 4th Army. Consisting of the 1st Moroccan Division (General Humbert), replacing all but one battalion of the 18th Division (see below) and the 17th Division (General Moussy). On both sides of Fère Champènoise, with advance guards north of the St. Gond

hofen) placed between and before the German IV and III Corps, south of the Grand Morin, at La Ferté Gaucher, facing the junction of the French 5th and British Armies. The Guard C.D. was particularly strong, having 3 Jäger battalions and 6 machine-gun companies attached.

II ARMY (General von BÜLOW),(H.Q., Montmirail).

VII Corps Active (General von Einem), (XIII and XIV Divisions).

This had come on tardily, and was in the rear, between Château-Thierry and Montmirail, when the battle opened. Being behind Klück's left, it has sometimes been counted as part of the I Army and the IX as part of Bülow's. The VII Reserve Corps was detained before Maubeuge, and only reached the Aisne on September 13.

X Corps Reserve (General von Hülsen).

Consisting of the XIX Reserve Division and the II Guard Division. Southeast of Montmirail. It was engaged on the 5th in collecting its wounded and burying its dead.

X Corps Active (General von Eben).

Of Hanover. Facing Foch's left, about Villeneuve-lès-Charleville and St. Prix, at the west end of the Marshes of St. Gond.

Guard Corps (General von Plattenberg).

North and north-east of St. Gond Marshes, from

Marshes.

11th Corps (General Eydoux).

From the 4th Army. The 18th Division (General Lefebvre), from Lorraine, came into line on the evening of September 7 between Connantre and Normée. The 21st Division (General Radiguet) and the 22nd Division (General Pembet) were, at the beginning of the battle, about Lenharrée and the important cross-roads of Sommesous, facing the junction of Von Bülow's and the Saxon Armies, with reserves north of the River Aube.

52nd and 60th Reserve Divisions (Generals Battesti and Joppé).

From the 4th Army. The former was affected to the 9th and the latter to the 11th Corps.

9th Cavalry Division (General de l'Espée).

In the rear at the Camp de Mailly, keeping connection with the 4th Army across a gap of about 12 miles.

4th ARMY (General de LANGLE DE CARY), (H.Q., Brienne).

21st Corps (General Legrand).

13th and 43rd Divisions (Generals Baquet and Lanquetot). From the Vosges. Detrained on the evening of September 8, and engaged September 9 on the left, east of the Camp de Mailly.

17th Corps (General J. B. Dumas).

33rd and 34th Divisions (Generals Guillaumat and Alby). From Courdemanges to Sompuis.

12th Corps (General Roques).

23rd and 24th Divisions (Generals Masnon and Descoings), reduced by previous casualties to about 6 effective battalions. At Vitry and Courdemange. The 23rd Division was lent to the 17th Corps till after the passage of the Marne.

Colonial Corps (General Lefebvre).

2nd and 3rd Colonial Divisions (Generals Leblois and Leblond). Experienced troops, largely re-enlisted from the general army. They had suffered heavily in the Belgian Ardennes, losing many

Etoges to Morains, facing Foch's right-centre. Placed here, without doubt, for the honour of breaking the French centre.

IV Cavalry Corps (General von Falkenhayn).

After the battle of Guise, Bülow's Army had come south through Laon, crossing the Marne between Dormans and Epernay.

III ARMY (General von HAUSEN).

XII Corps Active (I Saxon), (General von Elsa).

North of Normée and Lenharrée. It came abreast of the Guard only on the morning of the 7th.

XII Corps Reserve (General von Kirchbach).

The XXIV and XXIII Divisions; across the Châlons highroad north of Sommesous. The former, which had been besieging Givet, could only join on September 7. It was turned south-west against Foch, the XXIII south-east against de Langle.

XIX Corps (General von Laffert).

On September 6, was south of Châlons, west and north-west of Vitry, facing de Langle's left.

IV ARMY (DUKE Albrecht of WÜRTEMBERG), (H.Q., Triaucourt).

VIII Corps Active (General Tulffe v. Tscheppe u. Weidenbach).

Of Coblenz. North-east of Vitry.

VIII Corps Reserve (General von Egloffstein).

About Ponthion.

XVIII Corps Active (General von Tchenk).

Having lost heavily, was replaced during the battle by the

officers. At Blesmes and Dompremy.

2nd Corps (General Gerard).
3rd and 4th Divisions, less a brigade (Generals Cordonnier and Rabier). At Maurupt and Sermaize.

A division of each of the last two corps was shifted from de Langle's right to his left on September 8. De Langle's Army extended along the railway from Sompius, by Blesmes Junction, to Sermaize.

3rd ARMY (General SARRAIL), (H Q., Ligny-en-Barrois).

15th Corps (General Espinasse).
29th and 30th Divisions (Generals Carbillet and Colle). From the 2nd Army; detrained, September 7. A brigade was diverted, September 8, to the aid of the 4th Army. Near Revigny. Part of the corps was afterwards sent east to defend the passages of the Meuse.

5th Corps (General Micheler).
9th and 10th Divisions (Generals Martin and Gossart). North of Revigny, about Laimont and Villotte. General Gossart replaced General Roques, killed on September 6.

7th Cavalry Division (General d'Urbal).
About Isle-en-Barrois. Sent on September 11 to the Heights of the Meuse.

6th Corps (General Verraux).
12th and 40th Divisions (General Souchier, succeeded by General Herr, and General Leconte) and 107th Brigade of the 54th D.R. (General Estève). South of the Argonne, about Beauzée-sur-Aire.

3rd Group of Reserve Divisions (General Paul Durand).
65th (General Bigot); 67th (General Marabail); 75th (General Vimard). Behind and extending the 6th Corps on the Aire.

72nd Division of Reserve (General Heymann).
Sent from the garrison of Verdun by the Governor, General Coutanceau, to Souhesme-la-Grande, in support.

XVIII Corps Reserve.
Both had come down the west side of the Argonne and the Ste. Menehould highroad. About Somme-Yevre and Possesse.

A Cavalry Division.

V ARMY (The Imperial CROWN PRINCE).

VI Corps (General von Prictt-witz).
Of Breslau. Had come south by Les Islettes, and was now south of the Argonne, striking toward Revigny.

VI Corps Reserve.
A brigade only on the front, at Passavant and Charmontois. The rest west of the Meuse, near Montfaucon, facing Verdun.

Landwehr Division of the same, before Verdun.

XIII Corps (General von Dürach).
Of Stuttgart. Coming by Ste. Menehould, it had reached Triaucourt.

XVI Corps (General von Mudra).
Of Metz. Coming down the east side of the Argonne, it had reached Froidos-sur-Aire, aiming at Bar-le-Duc.

V Corps Reserve (General Count Solms).
Was still on the east bank of the Meuse about Consenvoye, north of Verdun.

A Division of the IV Cavalry Corps.

———

V Active Corps.
Sent from Metz on September 6 to the Meuse Heights the force which attacked Fort Troyon and neighbouring points.

> When the battle was engaged there remained only a few battalions in and before Verdun and on the Heights of the Meuse. Sarrail's Army was deployed south-westward from near Souilly to Revigny.

The composition of the 1st and 2nd Armies of Generals Dubail and de Castelnau, and of the German armies facing them, is given in the chapter dealing with the defence of the eastern frontier.

With so much accuracy as is yet possible, the relative strength of the opposed forces at the maximum was as follows:

SUMMARY OF STRENGTH

ALLIES			GERMANS		
DIVISIONS.			DIVISIONS.		
	Infantry.	Cavalry.		Infantry.	Cavalry.
French 6th Army	9½	3½	German I Army	11	5
British Army	5½		,, II ,,	8	2
French 5th Army	13½	3	,, III ,,	6	...
,, 9th ,,	8	1	,, IV ,,	8	1
,, 4th ,,	10	...	,, V ,,	11	1
,, 3rd ,,	10½	1	From Metz	1	...
	57	9		45 (? 48)	9
(of which 41 Active)			(of which 31 Active)		
(The B.E.F. included 5 Cavalry Brigades)					

French 2nd and 1st Armies (approx.) .	22 Divs	German VI and VII Armies (approx.) . .	24 Divs.	
(of which 11 Active)		(till Sept. 7, of which 12 Active)		

This comparison of totals is of only limited value, for two main reasons: (1) As has been explained, the German reserve divisions were markedly stronger than the French, and the German corps generally were more homogeneous. (2) The table shows only the maximum development of each army. Light artillery was probably in about the same proportion as the infantry, with a marked advantage of quality on the side of the Allies; it had not been possible to bring the full German superiority in heavy guns to bear on the new front. It will be safe to say that between the regions of Paris and Verdun the Allies had obtained a distinct superiority in active formations, and one more marked at the height of the battle in the area of decision. Antwerp and Maubeuge held before them bodies of German troops that might have turned the balance in the south; the occupation of towns and the guarding of communications retained others; whether from nervousness or over-confidence, Berlin had called two corps (11th and Guard R.C.) from France for the Russian frontier—a "fateful" step for which Ludendorff disclaims responsibility.

On the other hand, two new French armies had been created, chiefly at the cost of the eastern border; many units had been re-formed; the upper commands had been strengthened; and the whole line had been brought near to its bases. "The farther the Germans advanced, the French and British adroitly evading a decisive action, the more the initial advantage passed from the former to the latter," says a German writer already cited.[5] "The Germans left their bases farther and farther behind, and exhausted themselves by fatiguing marches. They consumed munitions and food with a fearful rapidity, and the least trouble in the supply services might become fatal to masses so large. Meanwhile, the French were daily receiving fresh troops, daily approaching their stores of munitions and food."

This great overturn of material strength was the first advantage the French Command had worked for and obtained. It is to be noted that on neither side was any mass held as a general reserve. Joffre had hoped to keep back the 21st Corps, but even this proved impossible. He telegraphed to M. Millerand on September 5:—

> The strategic situation is excellent, and we cannot count on better conditions for our offensive. The struggle about to begin may have decisive results, but may also have for the country, in case of check, the gravest consequences. I have decided to engage our troops to the utmost and without reserve to obtain a victory.

3. Features of the Battlefield

The second advantage gained has already been indicated; it consisted in the attainment of a concave front resting upon the entrenched camps of Paris and Verdun, and by them guarded against any sudden manoeuvre of envelopment. Intermediately, this front lay across the heights between the Marne and the Seine, along the chief system of main lines and highroads running eastward from the capital, those of Paris-Nancy. This 200-miles stretch of country, so typically French in character and history, loosely united by the Marne and the tributaries it carries into the Seine on the threshold of the capital—an agricultural country whose only large cities, Rheims and Châlons, were in

5. *Die Schlachten an der Marne.*

the enemy's hands—falls into four natural divisions, corresponding with the Allied left (west), left-centre, right-centre, and right (east).

The western region, between the suburbs of Paris and the gully holding the little River Ourcq and its canal, is the Ile-de-France and the Valois, rolling farmlands of beet and corn, with some parks, bordered on the north by the forests of Chantilly and Villers-Cotterets, and on the south by the broad valley of the Marne. A landscape most intimately French in its rich, spacious quietude, in the old-time solidity of its villages and their people, in the gracious dignity of its *châteaux* and ruined abbeys, with Meaux bells pealing across the brown slopes to the sister cathedral of Senlis, and both looking east to the giant *donjon* of La Ferté-Milon. This is the battlefield of the Ourcq, where Kluck was rounded up by Maunoury and the British. The ancient cathedral and market-town of Meaux marks its limit near the junction of the lesser and greater rivers.

East of the Ourcq this district becomes more crumpled in its rise towards the Montague de Rheims; while, south of the Marne, extends the larger and richer country of Brie, famous for its cheeses, its *fertés*, erstwhile baronial strongholds, and for the scenes of some of Napoleon's greatest victories. In structure, this is a broken triangular plateau, cut by westward-flowing streams (the Marne, Petit Morin, and Grand Morin), bounded on the south by the Seine and Aube, and rising eastward to the Montague de Reims and the Falaises de Champagne, where it falls abruptly. Coulommiers, Château-Thierry, and Provins are substantial market-towns, and La Ferté-sous-Jouarre, Montmirail, and Sézanne smaller centres of rural life. This wide plateau of Brie, the Allied left-centre, was the starting-point of the British recoil, and the field contested by d'Espérey's army against Von Bülow.

Beyond the Rheims-Epernay wine district and the St. Gond Marshes (source of the Petit Morin), we pass into the great expanse of the Champagne moorlands, poor and thinly populated, where large tracts of chalk soil carry nothing but plantations of stunted pines and firs. Châlons-sur-Marne, its capital, has a large permanent garrison, with fixed camps and manoeuvre grounds hard by. Vitry-le-François, at the junction of the Saulx and Ornain with the Marne, and of the Paris-Nancy and Châlons-Rheims railways, is the only other considerable town. On the west of this region, Foch held against Bülow and the Saxons; on the east occurred the shock of de Langle's army with that of the Duke of Würtemberg.

Finally, beyond Revigny, the forces of General Sarrail and the Imperial Crown Prince fought across a more composite region, consisting, in the south, of the Barrois—the district of Bar-le-Duc—and, to the north of this, the near part of the thickly-wooded Argonne hills, the Verdun Heights, and the plain between. Verdun was and remained a defensive position worthy of its ancient renown; and the Argonne, with Valmy on one flank and Varennes on the other (to cite only two historic names), has always been a barrier against invasion secondary to the Heights of the Meuse. These latter are continued with only small breaks by the Heights of the Moselle, where, especially on the hills near Nancy, took place the coincident struggle by which the eastern defence line was preserved. While this must be borne in mind, as an essential part of the general French victory, it seems legitimate and convenient to treat it separately; a brief recital of what there occurred is, accordingly, postponed to the end of our narrative.

The military geographer will have much to add to this note of the he of the land. He will be able to show that all the natural features of the country affected the result; the rivers of the western area inconveniencing both sides, but especially the invader; the patches of forest and the direction of highroads limiting their movements; the French gaining from a virtual monopoly of railway services a power of rapid transfer of troops that was one of the decisive factors of the battle. Everywhere, hill positions proved to be of great tactical value; and this is supremely true of the eastern ranges. The Argonne block delayed and split the crown prince's columns, and so greatly helped Sarrail to maintain his line. The Upper Meuse and its earthy rampart were a still more precious protection.

Between Verdun and Nancy, a distance of 60 miles, only one point was attacked, in the crisis, and this was held by a single fort, that of Troyon. Yet another hill range as signally aided the enemy in the end of the battle, when the victorious Allies were brought up sharp against the Laon Mountains, north of the Aisne. Throughout the field, superior knowledge of the ground must be counted among the advantages of the French. The most important of these natural features, however, is of less consequence than the strategical gain of a front whereon the French wings were both safe, while the German wings were both threatened. Gallieni, in throwing the 6th Army upon Kluck's flank, did but anticipate the inevitable by one or two days. What happened arose necessarily out of the strategy of the retreat, in the direction and form of which Joffre never lost his initiative.

It is possible that, had he retired farther, the victory might have been more complete. Actually, the five German armies were drawn within a hemicycle 200 miles wide and 30 miles deep. Their right could not help passing before Maunoury, or their left before Sarrail, except by refusing battle. They dare not turn aside; but the penalty of going on was to offer two cheeks to the smiter. There is, however, no trace of hesitation. The common soldiers still thought they were advancing "*Nach* Paris." At headquarters, the tactic of envelopment having failed, everything was risked on a converging attack upon the French centre.

4. THE LAST SUMMONS

We can now enter upon the details of the titanic encounter with a clear impression of its general character. As soon as the relation of forces was realised, the tactical purposes dictated by the circumstances to either side were these, and could not be other: for the French, to attack on the wings, especially the western, where there was a promise of surprise, while holding firm at the centre till the pressure there was relieved; for the Germans, to procure a swift decision at the centre, while sufficiently guarding the threatened flanks. But their initiative gave the Allies the benefit of the move: precious hours elapsed ere Kluck could adequately reply. Thus, the disposition of forces governs the whole story of the battle, and gives it a natural unity. It began on the west and developed eastward, as it were, by a series of reverberations, until the shock was returned by Sarrail. In this direction, therefore, we must follow its successive phases. If we speak of a Battle of the Ourcq, a Battle of St. Gond, and so on, it is only to make what can but be a bird's-eye view clearer by a just emphasis. These are so many acts in the Battle of the Marne, one and indivisible.

We have referred above solely to the measurable factors; the moral of the armies will best be seen in the process and the result. But there is a prevision of it in the evenness of the alignment reached on September 5th—much superior to that of the enemy, for some units of the German centre were crowded together, while the crown prince's troops were scattered—and in the readiness of these defeated and weary men for an instant recoil. On the morning of the 6th, the words of the *generalissimo* rang out like a bugle-call along the front:

G.H.Q. (Chatillon-sur-Seine), September 6, 7.30 a.m.
(telegram 3948).

At the moment when a battle is engaged on which depends the salvation of the country, every one must he reminded that the time has gone for looking backward. All efforts must be employed to attack and repel the enemy. Any troop which can no longer advance must at any cost hold the ground won, and be slain rather than give way. In the present circumstances, no failure can be tolerated."

Sir John French struck a more conventionally cheerful note:—

I call upon the British Army in France to show now to the enemy its power, and to push on vigorously to the attack beside the 6th French Army. I am sure I shall not call upon them in vain, but that, on the contrary, by another manifestation of the magnificent spirit which they have shown in the past fortnight, they will fall on the enemy's flank with all their strength, and in unison with their Allies drive them back.

No such general orders on the German side have been made public; but the following summons to the Coblentz Corps of the IV Army, signed by General Tulffe von Tscheppe u. Weidenbach, was afterward found at Vitry-le-François:

The aim of our long and arduous marches has been achieved. The principal French forces have been compelled to accept battle after being continuously driven back. The great decision is now at hand. For the welfare and honour of Germany, I expect every officer and man, despite the hard and heroic fighting of the last few days, to do his duty unfailingly and to his last breath. Everything depends upon the result of tomorrow.

CHAPTER 6

Battle of the Ourcq

1. A PREMATURE ENGAGEMENT

Exactly at noon on Saturday, September 5, the divisions of General Lamaze. constituting the right (save for elements connecting it with the British) of the French 6th Army, came under fire from advanced posts of General Schwerin's IV Corps of Reserve, hidden on the wooded hills just beyond the highroad from Dammartin to Meaux. A surprise for both sides; and with this began the battle of the Ourcq.

The battlefield—a rough quadrilateral, extending from the Dammartin road eastward to the deep ditch occupied by the Ourcq and its canal, and bounded on the north by the Nanteuil-Betz highway, on the south by the looping course of the Marne—consists of open, rolling beet and cornfields where some part of the crops were still standing. A soldier would call it an ideal battlefield, its many and good roads helping the movement of troops, its wooded bottoms and the stone walls of its farmsteads and hamlets giving sufficient cover, its hills good artillery emplacements. The eastern and higher part of the plateau is crossed from south-east to north-west by three ridges, against which the French offensive beat in successive waves.

The northernmost rises to 300 feet above the Ourcq, from near May-en-Multien, along the little River Gergoyne, by Etavigny and Acy, to Bouillancy; the central ridge, that of the Therouanne, runs from opposite Lizy-sur-Ourcq, by Trocy and Etrepilly, to Marcilly; the southernmost from Penchard, through Monthyon and Montgé, to Dammartin. The combat, as we shall see, began in the last-named area, its centre of gravity then moving northward. The Germans had the better of the hill positions, with forward parties well spread out; and, as in Lorraine and the Ardennes, directly they were threatened they

116

entrenched themselves, though not continuously or deeply. Caught in full movement toward the Marne, Kluck's rearguard at once protected itself as it had been taught to do. The position was an awkward one, in the angle of two river-courses. But the German communications necessarily traversed the Ourcq, and hereabouts the west bank rises high above the eastern, covering the passage and commanding the country for miles around.

Starting out in the morning from the hamlet of Thieux, 3 miles south of Dammartin, Lamaze's columns were directed as follows: de Dartein's Division, the 56th Reserve, on the left, toward St. Soupplets, by way of Juilly and Montgé; the 55th, under General Leguay, toward Monthyon, by Nantouillet; the Moroccan Infantry Brigade of General Ditte, toward Neufmontiers. After tramping nearly a hundred miles in three days and nights, with scanty food and sleep, and frequent rear actions, Lamaze's Corps had spent a whole day at rest, and, though far from its full strength, was a little recovered from the pains of the retreat. The sight of Paris near at hand, and the feeling that the supreme crisis was reached, set up a higher spirit, and prepared the men for the stirring appeal of the *generalissimo*. They were now to need all their recovered confidence and courage.

The 5th battalion (276th regiment) of the 55th Division was settling down to its midday meal in face of the hamlet of Villeroy, when it was surprised by a storm of shells from three of Schwerin's batteries, masked by the trees on the heights of Monthyon and Penchard. A French 3-inch battery in front of the battalion, and another brought up toward Plessy-l'Eveque, at once returned this fire, as it was afterward found, with good effect. But the heavier German field-guns, stationed 8 or 9 miles away in the loop of the Marne, at Germigny and Gué-à-Tresmes, and farther north behind Trocy, were far out of range of the French pieces, and were worked with impunity until near the end of the battle. Between Monthyon and Penchard, the enemy had three groups of machineguns, which kept up a deadly rain of bullets. In two and a half hours, the 5th battalion, just referred to, lost 250 men out of a short thousand; in course of the day, there fell of the 19th company all the chief officers, including the brilliant young writer, Lieut. Charles Peguy, and 100 men.[1]

Nevertheless, the line jerked itself forward by short bounds past

---

1. Avec Charles Péguy de la Lorraine à la Marne, by Victor Boudon. Peguy, a sort of mystical Tory-Socialist, or, as M. *Lavisse* says, "Catholic-Anarchist," was author-editor of *Les Cahiers de la Quinzaine.*

Plessis and Iverny toward the Montgé-Penchard ridge. Neufmontiers was the first village carried by assault; and, generally, the Moroccan *chasseurs* made the most rapid progress—their officers, with swords uplifted in gloved hands, leading them through the cornfields and orchards—until they reached the stronghold of Telegraph Hill, by Penchard, where they were thrice repulsed during the afternoon. By 6 p.m., the enemy being reinforced, all the captured ground was lost.

The 55th Division, before Monthyon, and the 56th, on its left, were also at once arrested; but, having administered this check, Von Schwerin proceeded to abandon his advanced position, from Neufmontiers northward. On the left, a patrol of the 56th Division found St. Soupplets evacuated, at 9 p.m. In the evening, while the 7th Corps was coming in on its left, from the highroad between Plessis Belleville and Nanteuil-le-Haudouin, Lamaze's front was drawn back lightly to the line Montgé-Cuisy-Plessy l'Eveque-Iverny-Charny. Night brought a lull in the battle, a snatch of broken sleep for some of the rank and file at least. A harvest moon shone red through the smoke of flaming hayricks and farmhouses.

This was far from being what General Joffre had counted upon in ordering the 6th Army to be in a position on the morning of the 6th, as an essential part of the general offensive, to pass the Ourcq and march upon Château-Thierry. Maunoury was still 9 miles from the Ourcq at Lizy, with no prospect of an easy passage. "Someone had blundered." It is clear that Maunoury's reconnaissance service was gravely at fault. But there is more than that. In determining to precipitate the intended movement of the 6th Army, the *generalissimo* depended upon the telephonic representations made to him by Gallieni. Knowing that, from his starting points on the morning of the 5th, Maunoury had 12 or 14 miles to make to reach the Ourcq, the Governor of Paris must have assumed that no opposition would be encountered—a rash conclusion in face of a commander like Kluck.[2] Lamaze's force was too small to sweep aside any substantial rearguard, too large to come into action without giving the alarm. Why was the 7th Corps not in line with it? Everything must depend upon the efficacy of this flank blow. When the enemy was discovered on the hills

---

2. M. Hanotaux says that Gallieni's order of September 4 was "an order for deployment, not for the offensive," and he adds that the governor intended that the cavalry should feel the way. There is no evidence of cavalry activity on the 5th; and it is manifest that the encounter before St. Soupplets was a complete surprise for the 6th Army.

of Monthyon and Penchard, should contact have been broken till the attack could be made in full force? Suppose that it did not then succeed, after the loss of precious hours? Cruel dilemma! The decision was to go ahead; and the result came near being the abortion of the whole plan of battle.

The morning of September 6 gave Lamaze an easy success on his left, offset by grievous difficulties on his right. The 56th Division, having occupied St. Soupplets at daybreak, rapidly reached the Therouanne at Gesvres, Forfry, and Oissery; and Marcilly was taken in the afternoon. The 55th, checked for a time at the central height of Monthyon, next met a more determined resistance before Barcy and Chambry. The former village was lost twice, and taken a third time, at the cost of many lives. Ditte's brigade, strengthened by Zouaves from the 45th Division, reoccupied Neufmontiers, and took Penchard and Chambry, but failed before the Vareddes ridge. Everywhere it was the same tale; though served with the utmost courage, the bayonet is no match for the machine-gun. Before retreating toward the loop of the Marne, the Germans burned down, by means of hand grenades, the village of Chauconin, with its household goods and farm implements. It is curious that the large town of Meaux altogether escaped damage during the battle.

All possibility of surprise was now past; and an average gain of about 5 miles had been dearly bought. Kluck, just installed at Coulommiers, 14 miles away, had been instantly sobered by the news from his rear, and with a speed and judgment worthy of his repute had taken measures to meet the danger. [3] The French left, the 7th Corps, had no sooner come into action on this morning of the 6th than two enemy columns were signalled as having reached the Ourcq about Vareddes and Lizy. By the middle of the afternoon, when Lamaze was

---

3. Sir John French, in his dispatch, says: "I should conceive it to have been about noon on the 6th September, after the British Forces had changed their front to the right, and occupied the line Jouy le Chatel-Faremoutiers-Villeneuve le Comte, . . . that the enemy realised the powerful threat that was being made against the flank of his columns moving south-east, and began the great retreat which opened the battle." This is a significant mistake. We now know that Bülow sent a first warning of an Allied concentration towards the west on the afternoon of September 5 to Kluck, who by then had his own information from the IV Reserve Corps. A few hours later Kluck was fully aware of his danger; and, as he has since stated to an interviewer, decided " in five minutes" how to meet it. Field-Marshal French (*1914*, ch. 5), wrongly, I think, considers that Kluck "manifested considerable hesitation and want of energy."

facing the hills beside Etrepilly, and General Vautier's two divisions, which had easily attained the line Villers St. Genest-Brégy, were striking out from the first to the second line of heights, from Bouillancy to Puisieux, with the prospect of turning the right of the German IV Reserve Corps, they found this new adversary before them. It was a part of the II Corps, withdrawn from the British front by a hard night march, and now thrown adroitly against Maunoury's left wing.

2. THE BRITISH MANOEUVRE

To understand how this withdrawal, so big with results, was possible, and to do justice to Sir John French's command in regard to it, we must leave Lamaze and Vautier at grips with the two German corps on the Ourcq, and turn for a moment to the situation south of the Marne.

On September 3, the British Army lay just south of Meaux, from Lagny to Signy Signets, having destroyed the Marne bridges behind it at General Joffre's request. Kluck, as we have seen, was then approaching the river from the north-west, coming on at a great pace. Several of his staff officers, pelting eastward from Meaux in an armoured automobile at nightfall, did not see that the last arch of the Trilport bridge was broken, pitched over, and were drowned. A little study of the map will show that Kluck's rapid movement—his pontoon corps established bridges of boats across the Marne on the night of the 3rd, and the next day his patrols were beyond the Petit Morin and on the Grand Morin—required not simply a farther retreat, but a different direction of retreat, of the British force. To throw it up against the neighbouring French columns, those of the 5th Army (commanded by General Franchet d'Espérey since the evening of September 3) was exactly what Kluck was aiming at.

To avoid such a calamity, and perhaps to tempt the rash commander farther south, Joffre asked Sir John French to retire some 12 miles farther, drawing his right south-westward, pivoting on his left. This manoeuvre, which to the British commander could only seem the natural pursuance of the French Army Orders of September 2, by him received on the following day, was carried out on September 4. The Expeditionary Force, as it was called, had been on the Continent for hardly three weeks, had fought in that time two great battles and many smaller engagements, and had retreated 160 miles in twelve days, losing much material and nearly a fifth of its original strength, about 15,000 officers and men. Behind the Forest of Crecy, close to the rail-

The
OURCQ
Front.
Afternoon of
Sept. 6.

ϕϕ ϕ = GROUPS OF GERMAN ARTILLERY

(VouKLUCK)

IV. C.

CHÂTEAU THRY

III. C.

IV. R.C.

MARNE

To LAFERE

Villeneuveuil

St Fiacre

Trilport

Nanteuil Wood

Chargis

MEAUX

8D.

45D.

Penchard

MARNE

Claye

To PARIS

St Mesmes

Nantouillet

Iverny

Charny

Villeroy

Monthyon

Morbryor

Barcy

Gissy

Chambry

Trois Thieux

Juilly

To PARIS

Dammartin

Montge

St Soupplets

Ossery

Forfry

Thieux

Gesv Prezes

Lizine Luy

Acy

63 D.R.

79

Bouillancy Boi

61D.R.

Plessis Belleville

(MALNOURY) Prézy

Silly-le-Long

Le Haudouin

Nanteuil

1 Cav. C.

FOREST OF ERMEN ONVILLE

To SENLIS

FOREST OF VILLERS COTTERES

Betz

Villers-St Génc

Glubvelle

Nareuil-s-Ocq

Étavigny

IV Cav. D.

II C. (IV. D.)

To POLIVRES

ROSOY

GERGOGNE

May-en-Multien

Tuncye

Manociuvre

Plessis Placy

Pusieux

Etrepilly

Manociuvre

Douy

Izy

III. C.

MARNE

OURCQ

SOISSONS

way junctions south of Paris, it was able, on the night of September 4 and during the 5th, to pick up much-needed reinforcements, bringing its effective strength up to five divisions and five cavalry brigades, with guns and supplies.

At midday on September 5, when the battle of the Ourcq was beginning, the I German Army had reached the following positions:— Marwitz's IX Cavalry Division was north of Crécy, the II near Coulommiers. Richthofen's V Cavalry Division was at Choisy, south-west of La Ferté-Gaucher, the Guard Cavalry a little farther east, near Chartronges. The II Corps was extended from the Marne near Montceaux to the Grand Morin west of Coulommiers. The IV Corps was on the latter river about La Ferté-Gaucher. The III. Corps was on the great highroad about Sancy and Montceaux-les-Provins; and the IX north of Esternay. The general strategical significance of these dispositions will presently appear; for the moment, we are concerned with them specially in relation to Maunoury's and the British Armies.

Twelve hours later, Kluck's front was advanced a little farther, extending from near Crécy-en-Brie, along the Grand Morin, by Coulommiers and La Ferté-Gaucher, to Esternay, with the cavalry of Marwitz before the centre and left. The bulk of this force was aimed at the 5th French Army; but the II and part of the IV Active Corps faced the British. Such was the position at the moment when Kluck, informed of the danger to his rearguard, decided to send back to the Ourcq his II Corps, bringing the western wing of the invasion to a sudden and humiliating end.

Neither at French nor at British Headquarters were these dispositions exactly known; still less could the German commander's intentions be known. The last stage of the British retirement, asked for by General Joffre, had taken the body of Sir John French's troops out of direct contact with the enemy. They had to embody newly-arrived men and guns, and then to return over this ground Joffre's order of September 4 had named as the British line for the evening of the following day "the front Changis-Coulommiers, *facing east*, ready to attack in the general direction of Montmirail"—due east, that is to say, not north-east. It is evident, from this instruction, that the *generalissimo* (1) did not anticipate any serious resistance west or south of Coulommiers, for the British could not be fighting on their north flank while marching due east, and they could not start from Coulommiers when the enemy was 8 miles farther south; and (2) did not anticipate a sudden withdrawal of Kluck northward, which would require the British to turn thither in aid of Maunoury.

When Joffre and French met at Melun on September 5, the instruction was modified, but not radically; it was now, in Sir John's words, "to effect a change of front to my right -my left resting on the Marne, and my right on the 5th Army, to fill the gap between that army and the 6th." The right of the 5th Army, however, was not at Coulommiers—both Changis and Coulommiers were in the hands of the enemy—but Courtacon, 12 miles farther to the south-east; and to join the 6th and 5th Armies implied a north-easterly, not an easterly frontage. Joffre so far recognised the difficulty of filling this wide space with five divisions as to instruct Gallieni to send across the Marne the 8th Division of the French 4th Corps; and this came in, with prompt effect, between Meaux and Villiers-sur-Morin, 5 miles farther south, beside the British 3rd Corps, at 9 a.m. on September 6. There then still remained a space of over 20 miles between the 6th and 5th Armies, and it is, therefore, idle to suggest, as some zealous partisans of Gallieni have done, (see note at end of section), that the British commander was needlessly nervous as to the continuity of the line, when it became evident that considerable bodies of the enemy were spread across his path.

It was not till September 7 that any need appeared to help Maunoury. But, as we now know, Kluck ordered the withdrawal of his II Corps to the Ourcq at 3.30 a.m. on September 6—2½ hours before the beginning of the Allied offensive. The withdrawal was well covered, and was not observed for twenty-four hours. The change of direction of the British advance toward the north could not be effected with the instancy that paper strategists have imagined; and the necessity of keeping touch with d'Espérey continued. The question whether the British advance was timid and halting must be judged in the light of the facts not as we now know them, but as they revealed themselves from day to day; and in the light not of Gallieni's desires or needs only, but of the whole battle, and particularly of the instructions given to the British Army by General Joffre, who alone was responsible for the whole battle.

That Maunoury would be seriously engaged with Kluck's rearguard on the afternoon of the 5th was not anticipated by the French; it could not, then, be anticipated by the British. Since criticisms are raised as to one side of a converging movement, it must be pointed out that, if the French attack on the Ourcq had been delayed for twelve hours, and had not anticipated the general offensive, all would

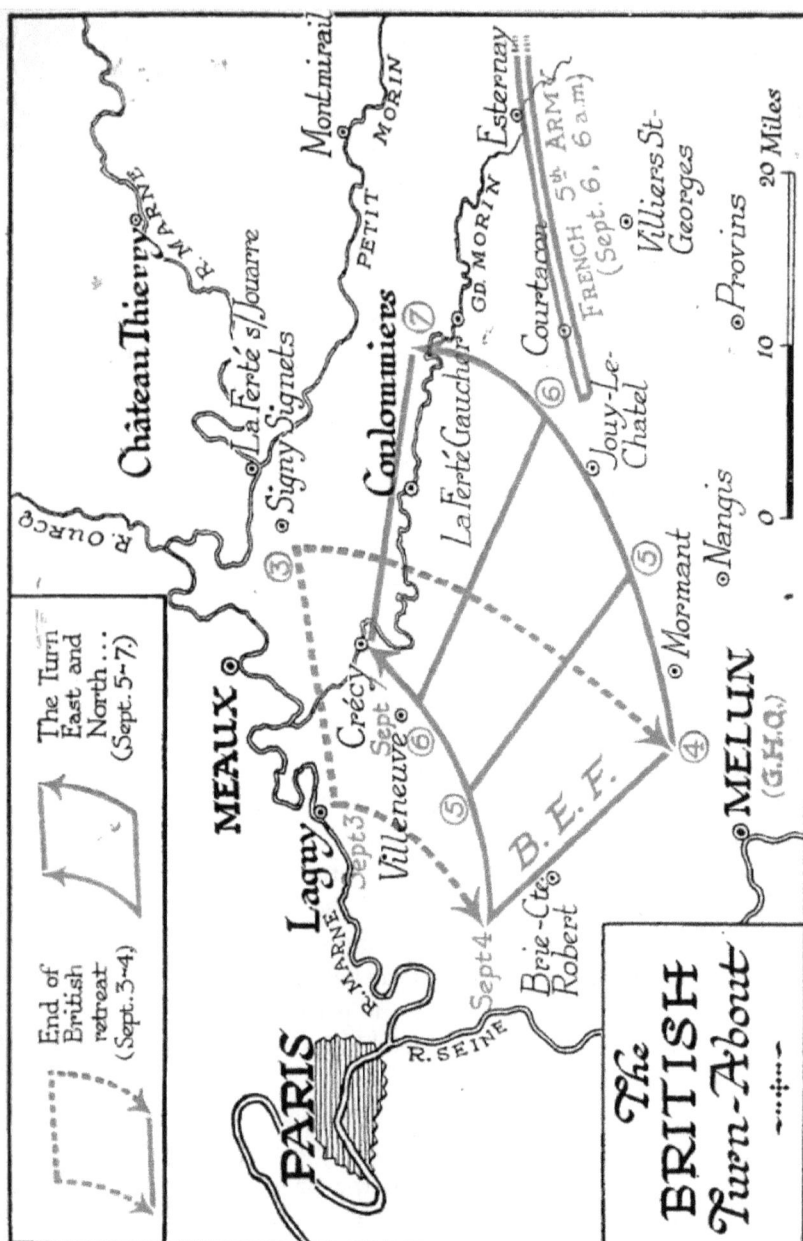

The
BRITISH
Turn-About

Legend:
End of British retreat (Sept. 3–4.)
The Turn East and North... (Sept. 5–7.)

PARIS

R. SEINE

R. MARNE

MEAUX

Lagny

Sept 3
Villeneuve
Sept 4

Crécy
Sept 3

Brie-Cte-Robert

MELUN
(G.H.Q.)

B.E.F.

⑤
⑥
④
⑤

R. OURCQ

Château Thierry

R. MARNE

La Ferté s/Jouarre

Signy Signets

③

La Ferté Gaucher

Coulommiers

⑦

PETIT MORIN

Montmirail

MORIN

GD. MORIN

Esternay

Courtaçon

FRENCH 5th ARMY
(Sept. 6, 6 a.m)

Villiers-St-Georges

Jouy-Le-Chatel

⑥

Mormant

Nangis

Provins

0   10   20 Miles

have been well. Kluck would have been unable to evade one assailant in order to throw all his force upon the other; and the tasks of Maunoury and the British would have been more advantageously divided. We are here, apparently, in face of one of those failures of information and agreement which are liable to occur, even under the best leadership, between armies of different nationality when plans are suddenly changed. It may now be recognised that the Battle of the Marne would have yielded a completer, cheaper, and speedier victory if the rectangular movement of the French 6th and British Armies had been more exactly designed and timed to a strict simultaneity. There was a lack of assimilation. Perhaps the British were slow in getting under weigh; it is much more certain that Gallieni was precipitate.

The front of the British 3rd (incomplete), 2nd, and 1st Corps at the opening of the offensive lay, then, from Villiers-sur-Morin, across the edge of the Forest of Crécy, by Mortcerf, Lumigny, Rozoy, and Gastins, to near the Forest of Jouy, where Conneau's Cavalry Corps connected with the infantry of the 5th Army. The battle here opened with an enemy attack. To mask its withdrawal to the Ourcq, a part of the German II Corps had delivered, early on the morning of September 6, a blow at the British right, and fighting was sharp till noon over the farmlands of the Brie plateau between Hautefeuille and Vaudoy—that is, 8 miles south-west of Coulommiers. Field-Marshal French says:—

> At this time I did not know that a retreat had really set in, or how the various German corps and divisions were placed.

Columns of the IV Active Corps were still farther south, to the east of Vaudoy, on the Provins road, with large forces of cavalry and the III Corps on their left. It was a delicate part of the front, the space between the British and 5th French Armies. During the afternoon, while the khaki line slowly progressed over the stubble fields and broken forest around the villages of Lumigny, Pezarches, and Touquin, unmistakable evidence began to come in that the German foreguard had become a rearguard, and that the body of the II Corps had been in retreat all day. The charred walls of the hamlets of Courchamps and Courtacon, destroyed with deliberate ferocity, marked the most southerly points of the invasion in the western field.[4] To the Allied soldiers

4. Four days later, in the village inn at Pezarches, *Madame*, an upstanding woman of about thirty, told me of the following incident: "On Sunday morning my mother had gone to church, and I remained at home with my father and my little boy. My father left us to get some tobacco. Going out for a moment with the child, I saw a group of horsemen in the street, and said to myself: 'We are saved. (Cont. next page).

who knew not Maunoury, it must have seemed that their offensive was commencing magically well. About 10 a.m., the British left and centre—the 4th Division and the 2nd Corps—had been surprised to find the pressure on their front suddenly relieved. On their right, the 1st Corps soon saw its way free, and strode northward. At 6.30 p.m., the IV Active Corps received orders to follow the II Corps back to the Ourcq. Thus, by evening on September 6, Sir John French was able to reach the Grand Morin, from Crécy-en-Brie eastward, with scouts beyond the stream at Maisoncelles. Coulommiers, where Kluck had had his headquarters, was occupied during the night.

The Allied plan was now fully revealed. Instead of presenting on the Grand Morin an ironclad face, safe in flank and rear, the I German Army had been suddenly thrown on to a rectangular defensive on a front of 50 miles between Betz and Courtacon, against attacks converging from the west, south-west, and south. That evening, at Joffre's request, the British line was directed more to the north, thus emphasising the effect of Maunoury's move. From this moment, the withdrawal of the whole of Kluck's forces over the Marne must have been envisaged. On the following day, September 7, in fact, the III and IX Corps (west of Montmirail), were preparing to follow the IV Active Corps across the Marne; but the Allies were then aware of what was happening.

Marwitz's Cavalry Corps covered the movement along the Grand Morin, with one division to the west, one to the east, and one 4 miles north of Coulommiers, while Richthofen's divisions operated farther east, all available artillery supporting them. The task was fulfilled with much resource and energy; but the position was not one that could be long maintained, for the British 3rd Corps was at Maisoncelles, 4 miles beyond the Grand Morin, and the French 8th Division threatened the

It is the Belgians!' When I returned, to my surprise, they were in the house, sitting in my room and in the *café*. An officer asked me to cook him a couple of eggs. I noticed that one of the men was wounded, and asked whether it was painful. He nodded, and I went to the kitchen. There I saw, on the windowsill, a spiked helmet. I nearly fainted! So they were Germans! I managed to take in the eggs. Then the officer asked mc, very politely, to show him my left hand, and, pointing to the wedding-ring, said: 'You are married?' 'Yes,' I replied, trembling. 'Your husband is a soldier?' 'Yes.' 'You have a child?' 'No, I have no children,' I said. 'But I saw him. You are hiding him because you have heard that the Germans cut off the hands of French children. That is false. We never hurt women or children. Bring your little boy.' But, as I persisted that it was not my child, he said no more. He and the others paid in German money for what they had, and left. A quarter of an hour later the firing began."

German flank at double this distance northward by occupying St. Fia-cre and Villemareuil. At noon, Marwitz gave way, falling back to the Petit Morin, from La Ferté-sous-Jouarre south-eastward. By evening, the British 3rd and 2nd Corps were beyond the Grand Morin at La Haute Maison and Aulnoy; the 1st was held back somewhat from Chailly to near La Ferté-Gaucher, in touch with the French 5th Army. General de Lisle's Cavalry Brigade, with the 9th Lancers and the 18th Hussars, showed especial vigour. The men were full of cheer, and ready for anything; but Sir John French was a careful commander. The meas-ure of the enemy's retreat could not be immediately taken through the curtain of cavalry and artillery—aviation was in its infancy in those days. All the strength available was in line; and it was so thin a line as to tempt surprise. The field-marshal considered the alternative of send-ing direct help round to Maunoury, but concluded that the best aid would be to drive rapidly to and across the Marne.[5]

★★★★★★

Note:—Several French volumes hint the first criticism, and it is expressed very definitely by General Bonnal in the article already re-ferred to on the battle of the Ourcq in La Renaissance of September 4, 1915. The substance of General Bonnal's charge is as follows:

> Unfortunately, the British Army, rather hesitant after its checks at Le Cateau, Landrecies, and Compiègne, lost time in displace-ments dictated by prudence, and did not give the 6th Army in time all the help desirable.

Maunoury had asked for it at noon on Sept. 4; and the *generalissi-mo's* directions of that night anticipated the British being at Coulom-miers and Changis on the evening of the 5th. But, on the afternoon of the 4th, the head of Sir John French's Staff had announced to Gallieni for that night:

> An order of movement the result of which was to distance the British Army at once from the 6th and the 5th Armies. (If this movement was not the further retirement asked for by Gen-eral Joffre, we do not know what is meant.) Marshal French occupied during the 5th positions north and south of Rozoy, facing east. But this disposition placed the British Army much to the rear, to the west, of the line first fixed, and permitted the German II Corps, reported in the morning at Coulommiers,

---

5. *1914*, ch. 4.

to repass the Marne and escape to the north-west. Fearing its appearance on the Ourcq, General Gallieni wrote on the 6th to Marshal French praying him at once to advance in accordance with the orders of General Joffre.

On his side, the latter telegraphed to General Maunoury, on the 6th, asking him constantly to support the British left. In consequence, the chief of the 6th Army sent to Meaux the same evening the 8th Division (4th Corps), which had just detrained at Paris. (This division actually came in on the morning of the 6th.) If the presence of the 8th Division on his left did not determine Marshal French immediately to take the offensive" (what this means we do not know, for the British offensive had commenced on the morning of the 6th), it was because at this moment he was much concerned as to the pretty considerable interval between his right and the left of the 5th Army. Yet this interval was watched by the Cavalry Corps of General Conneau.

On the evening of the 6th, the British Army reached the line of the Grand Morin, in contact on its right with the 5th Army. Unfortunately this contact was so close that the British Army thought it necessary to march level with and on the same lines as the 5th, which had great difficulty in assuring its route, having to drive before it four corps of Von Bülow's Army.

General Bonnal concludes his criticism with a not very amiable homily on the insufficient training of the old British Army, and the inadequacy of its Staff work. Generals not trained as in France and Germany had, he says, a tendency "to practise the linear order," to move their troops in deployed formation, supporting their flanks on neighbouring bodies, and taking a thousand precautions that lead to delay. That is why "the British Army, composed of officers and men full of strength, vigour, and energy, took more than two days to cover the 20 kilometres between the Grand Morin and the Marne, when, on the 6th, they ought to have marched on the nearest enemy."

For similar comments, see "*La Bataille de la Marne, Recit Succinct*," by General Canonge (*Le Correspondant*, September 25 and October 10, 1917), with details of the battle.

One sentence of M. Hanotaux is more to the point than all these criticisms and suppositions:

No doubt, if the encounter had not been produced, a little

prematurely perhaps, in the region of St. Soupplets-Penchard, at noon on the 5th, the whole army of Von Kluck would have been south of the Marne in the evening; while Maunoury would have taken it in reverse on the north bank. Kluck would then have been closed in. (*Histoire*, ch. 38).

An interesting attempt to justify Gallieni against Joffre, and to challenge the latter's strategy at this time, will be found in *La Genèse de la Bataille de la Marne*, by General H. Le Gros. He quotes Joffre as complaining to the government (on Sept. 4) that Gallieni was seeking to "push him into a premature offensive."

3. A RACE OF REINFORCEMENTS

On the Ourcq, each adversary was bringing up reserves, and was trying to turn the other by the north, with a slight advantage in time on the French, but a superiority of speed on the German, side. We left the centre of the 6th Army, on September 6, practically stationary about Marcilly and Barcy; while, moving from Brégy and Bouillancy, the 7th Corps gained Puisieux and Acy during the afternoon, and the 8th Division, thrown across the Marne, drove some enemy contingents into the woods of the river loop east of Meaux. Maunoury decided to attack frontally the three plateaux of Vareddes, Trocy-Vincy, and Etavigny, throwing picked columns into the valleys between, that of the Therouanne at Etrepilly and the Gergoyne ravine at Acy-en-Multien, in the hope of turning the hill positions. His field batteries were now in force at Bouillancy, Fosse-Martin, La Ramée, Marcilly, and Penchard; but he had no heavy artillery. Worse, from September 5, when his only aviator was brought down at Vareddes, to September 9, when Captain Pellegrin found a machine and discovered the nest of German mortars in the gullies by Trocy, he had no air scouts, so that, almost throughout the battle, the German gunners dominated the field.

On September 7, Schwerin's IV Reserve Corps, strengthened during the day by a part of the IV Active Corps, rallied against Lamaze's harassed men, who, still untutored to spade work, suffered heavily, but did not give way. Ditte's Moroccan Brigade commenced at dawn a new move toward Vareddes, was beaten off, spent the afternoon in a fearful hand to hand struggle on Hill 107, won it, but was finally driven back to Chambry. The Algerian troops of General Drude, the 45th Division, had come in on the right centre; and they were able, during the morning, to make a long stride forward east of Marcilly. Beyond

Barcy, however, they were immediately stopped; repeated charges were broken, many officers and men being left on the ground. During the night, under a brilliant moon, the north wing of the division cut its way into the village of Etrepilly, but could not carry the cemetery, 300 yards beyond, and had to fall back.

The 7th Corps was no more fortunate. After taking Etavigny and the hillsides above Acy with a rush, it was suddenly overwhelmed by a massive counter-attack of the newly arrived II Corps, and had to abandon both villages, re-forming before Bouillancy and Puisieux. Many units had lost nearly all their officers. A panic was threatened. At a moment when it seemed that the left of the army could not be saved, Colonel Nivelle, with five field batteries of the 5th Artillery regiment, gave a first exhibition of the qualities which, two years later, were to secure the defence of Verdun, and to bring him to the chief command. Carrying forward through the wavering ranks of the infantry a group of his field-guns, he set them firing at their utmost speed upon the close-packed columns of the enemy. The "75" is a murderous instrument in such circumstances; and those grey-coats who remained afoot broke in disorder.

It was an hour's relief; but manifestly this wild situation could not long continue. The enfeebled lines approached the extreme limit of endurance. And still the tide of slaughter swayed to and fro. Nogeon, Poligny, and Champfleury Farms—the first north, the others south, of Puisieux, large stone buildings topping the plateaux—were the scenes of most bloody and obstinate encounters. Nogeon, the largest of them, was stormed and lost three times at intervals during the day. Under sustained fire from Trocy, its massive walls were broken; the corn barns took fire and blazed across the expanse of the battlefield.

In the evening, Von Schwerin drew back his lines a little from the edge of the plateau, and the ruined farms and hamlets gave the French a precarious shelter. At the same time, a reciprocal attempt at envelopment by the north began to design itself. The 61st Reserve Division had just been brought up from Pointose; and Maunoury decided to throw it, with the 1st Cavalry Corps, out to his extreme left, the former at Villers St. Genest, the latter beyond Betz. Almost simultaneously, new German detachments reached the Ourcq, and were set to prolong to the north the front of the II and IV Corps, while a *Landwehr* Brigade acting as line of communication troops was summoned urgently from Senlis. There was now no question of the 6th Army fulfilling its original task; the utmost hope was that it might hold till the British came up, across the enemy's rear.

Maunoury had to cope with an equal mass in better positions—three strong corps, the IV, the II, and the IV Reserve, with the IV Cavalry Division—against Lamaze's two Reserve Divisions, Drude's Division, the 7th Corps, the 61st R.D., and the Cavalry Corps. Only the III and IX Corps and Marwitz's Cavalry remained beyond the Marne; and, though the British pressure was increasing, the enemy's withdrawal had not been seriously disturbed. Kluck's boldness, skill, and decision were undeniable. It was evident that he had recovered from the first shock, and meant, if possible, to overwhelm its authors. Exhausted, and tormented by thirst, it was with sinking hearts that the Army of Paris looked up to the smoking hills.

Viewed from French General Headquarters, however, the prospect was more favourable. The retreat of the I German Army was gravely compromising the position of its neighbour, the II; and its effects were beginning to show farther to the east. For three days, these two forces were moving in opposite directions—Kluck to the north-west, Bülow to the south-east. The task of exploiting the dislocation thus produced fell to the British and d'Espérey's Armies. The role of the 6th Army was thus radically changed by the development of events; but it remained as important as ever in the whole design. If Gallieni and Maunoury could have reviewed the field from the Ourcq to Verdun, they would have been well satisfied.

4. THE PARIS TAXI-CABS

I spent September 7 among the rear columns of the 6th Army. In the morning, the little town of Gagny, halfway between Paris and Claye (Maunoury's headquarters), and the last point one could reach by rail from the city, was full of men of the 103rd and 104th regiments, belonging to the 4th Corps (General Boëlle), just arrived from Sarrail's front. They sat in and before the *cafés*, lay on the grass of the villa gardens, lounged in the school playground, where their rifles were stacked and their knapsacks piled. Some had managed to get their wives and children to them, and were telling great tales of the first month of war. I went out into the deserted countryside toward the front, passing marching columns, motor-wagons, dispatch-riders, here a flock of sheep in charge of uniformed shepherds, there a woodland bivouac, and in the evening returned to Gagny.

More regiments had arrived; the town was boiling from end to end. In the main street, a battalion was already marching out to extend Vautier's left, a thin file of country folk watching them, waving handkerchiefs, the girls running beside the ranks to give some handsome lad a flower. Up the side roads, other columns waited their turn, standing at ease, or sitting on the edge of the pavement; a few men lay asleep, curled up against the houses. But the most curious thing was a long queue of Parisian taxi-cabs, a thousand or more of them, stretching through by-roads out of sight. The watchful and energetic Gallieni had discovered, at the cost of us *boulevardiers*, a new means of rushing reinforcements to the point where they were direly needed.

It was the idea of his chief of staff, General Clergerie. Joffre had at this moment only one remaining unit of the Regulars to give to Maunoury—a half of the 4th Corps, which had been brought round by rail from the Verdun front, and of which we have seen the 8th Division in action south of Meaux. The 7th Division had detrained in Paris during the afternoon of September 7. It was to be sent to Maunoury's extreme left, near Betz, 40 miles away. Everything might now depend upon speed. It was found that only about a half of the infantry could be carried quickly by train. Clergerie [6] thought the remaining 6000 men might be got out by means of taxi-cabs. The Military Government of Paris already had 100 of the "red boxes" at its disposal; 500 more were requisitioned within an hour, and at 6 p.m. they were lined up, to our astonishment, beside the Gagny railhead. Each cab was to carry five men, and to do the journey twice, by separate outward and return routes. Measures were taken in case of accident, but none occurred. This first considerable experiment in motor transport of men was a complete success; and at dawn the 7th Division was in its place on the battlefield.

On September 8, the British Expeditionary Force, steadily gathering momentum, reached, and in part crossed, the Petit Morin, taking their first considerable number of prisoners, to the general exhilaration. On the left, the 3rd Corps advanced rapidly to the junction of that river with the Marne; but the enemy had broken the bridges at La Ferté-sous-Jouarre, and held stubbornly to their barricades on the north bank through this night and the following day. Farther up the deep and thickly wooded valley, the 2nd Corps had some trouble between Jouarre and Orly; while, on the right, the 1st Corps, after routing the German rearguards at La Trétoire and Sablonnières, made the passage with the aid of a turning movement by some cavalry and two Guards battalions of the 1st Division.

---

6. *Le Petit Journal.* September 9, 1917.

The orders of this day for the 6th Army were to attack on the two wings—Drude's Algerian Division (relieving the exhausted 56th Reserve and the Moroccan Brigade), with the 55th Reserve, on the right, towards Etrepilly and Vareddes; the 61st Reserve Division, General Boëlle's 7th Division, and Sordêt's cavalry, on the left—while the 7th Corps stood firm at the centre, and, south of the Marne, the 8th Division pressed on from Villemareuil toward Trilport, in touch with the British. For neither side was the violence of the struggle rewarded with any decisive success. On the French right, the Germans had more seriously entrenched themselves, and had much strengthened their artillery. Lombard's Division of the 7th Corps was heavily engaged all day at Acy; at night the enemy still held the hamlet, while the *chasseurs* faced them in the small wood overlooking it.

On the left, the 7th Division of the 4th Corps had no sooner come into action than it had to meet a formidable assault by the IV Active Corps. This was repulsed; but the cavalry corps seems to have been unable to take an effective share in the battle. During the afternoon, German troops occupied Thury-en-Valois and Betz. Reinforcements were continually reaching them. At nightfall, although Boëlle's divisions were resisting heroically, and even progressing, the outlook on the French extreme left, bent back between Bouillancy and Nantheuil-le-Haudouin, had become alarming. Maunoury, however, obtained from General Gallieni the last substantial unit left in the entrenched camp of Paris, the 62nd Division of Reserve, and gave it instructions to organise, between Plessy-Belleville and Monthyon, a position to which the 6th Army could fall back in case of necessity. In course of the night, Gallieni sent out from Paris by motorcars a detachment of *Zouaves* to make a raid toward Creil and. Senlis.

It was a mere excursion; but the alarm caused is very comprehensible when the extreme attenuation of the supply lines of the German I Army is remembered. Marching 25 miles a day, and sometimes more, it had far overrun the normal methods of provisioning. During the advance, meat and wine had been found in plenty, vegetables and fruit to some extent, bread seldom; here, in the Valois, the army could not feed itself on the country, and convoys arrived slowly from the north. Artillery ammunition was rapidly running out. Hunger quickly deepens doubt to fear.

But Maunoury's men were at the end of their strength. On the morning of September 9, a determined attack by the IV Active Corps, supported by the right of the II, was delivered from Betz and Anthilly.

133

The 8th Division had been summoned back from the Marne, to be thrown to the French left. Apparently it could not be brought effectively into this action; and the 61st and 7th Divisions and the 7th Corps failing to stand, Nanteuil and Villers St. Genest were lost, the front being re-formed before Silly-le-Long. "A troop which can no longer advance must at any cost hold the ground won, and be slain rather than give way." Such a summons can only be repeated by a much-trusted chief. Maunoury repeated it in other words.

Thousands of men, grimy, ragged, with empty bellies and tongues parched by the torrid heat, had already gone down, willingly accepting the dire sentence. Few of them could hear or suppose that the enemy was in yet extremer plight. So it was. Early in the morning, Vareddes and Etrepilly had been found abandoned; greater news had been coming in for hours to Headquarters—some of it from the enemy himself by way of the Eiffel Tower in Paris, where the French "wireless" operators were picking up the conversations of the German commanders. Marwitz was particularly frank and insistent; his men were asleep in their saddles, his horses broken with overwork. He was apparently too much pressed to wait for his message to be properly coded. By such and other means, it was known that Kluck and Bülow were at loggerheads, that, even on the order of Berlin, the former would not submit himself to his colleague, and that, in consequence, Bülow in turn had begun to retreat before Franchet d'Espérey.

CHAPTER 7

The "Effect of Suction"

1. French and d'Espérey strike North

The unescapable dilemma of the Joffrean strategy had developed into a second and peremptory phase. In deciding to withdraw from the Brie plateau and the Marne, rather than risk his rear and communications for the chance of a victory on the Seine, Kluck, or his superiors, had, doubtless, chosen the lesser evil. The marching wing of the invasion was crippled before the offensive of the Allies had begun; but Gallieni's precipitancy had brought a premature arrest upon the 6th Army. Beside this double check, we have now to witness a race between two offensive movements—Bülow and Hansen pouring south with the impetuosity of desperation, while, along their right, the British Force and the French 5th Army struck north between the two western masses of the enemy with the fresh energy of an immense hope. Which will sooner effect a rupture?

Logically, there should be no doubt of the answer. Kluck was mainly occupied with Maunoury; Bülow, with Foch. Between them, there was no new army to engage the eight corps of Sir John French and Franchet d'Espérey. The cavalry and artillery force of Marwitz and Richthofen, strong as it was, could do no more than postpone the inevitable—always provided that Maunoury and Foch could hold out. Every day, the pull of Kluck to the north-west and of Bülow to the south-east must become more embarrassing. French writers have applied an expressive phrase to the influence of this pull—"*effet de ventouse*," effect of suction—though hardly appreciating its double direction. The maintenance of a continuous battle-line is axiomatic in modern military science. It follows from the size of the masses in action, the difficulty, even with steam and petrol transport, of moving them rapidly, and their dependence upon long lines of supply.

The soldier bred upon Napoleonic annals may long for the opportunity of free manoeuvre; all the evolution of warfare is against his dream. An army neither feeds nor directs itself; it is supplied and directed as part of a larger machine executing a predetermined plan. Superiority of force is increased by concentration, and achieves victory by envelopment of the enemy as a whole, or his disintegration by the piercing of gaps, a preliminary to retail envelopment or dispersal. A course which loses the initial superiority and requires a considerable change of plan is already a grave prejudice; when to this is added a necessary expedient leading to an extensive disturbance of the line, prudence dictates that the offensive should be suspended until the whole mass of attack has been reorganised in view of the new circumstances.

The German Command dare not risk such a pause. It persisted; and the penalty lengthened with every hour of its persistence. The more Kluck stretched his right in order to cover his communications by Compiègne and the Oise valley, the wider became the void between his left and the II Army, constantly moving in the opposite direction. When French and d'Espérey found this void, a like difficulty was presented to Bülow—to be enveloped on the right, or to close up thither, leaving a breach on his other flank, which the Saxon Army would be unable to fill. Thus, Maunoury's enterprise on the Ourcq, though falling short of full success, produced a series of voids, and, at length, a dislocation of the whole German line, which was only saved from utter disaster by a general retreat.

General Franchet d'Espérey, who had been brigadier in 1908, divisional commander in 1912, a gallant and energetic officer now fifty-eight years of age, successful with the 1st Corps at Dinant and St. Gerard in Belgium, and in the important battle of Guise, had, on September 3, succeeded Lanrezac at the head of the largest of the French armies, the 5th. Its task—in touch with Foch on the right, and with the British, through Conneau's cavalry corps, on the left—was to press north toward Montmirail, against Kluck's left (III and IX Corps, and Richthofen's cavalry divisions) and the right wing of Bülow (VII Corps and X Reserve Corps). In later stages of the war, the junction of two armies often showed itself to be a point of weakness to be aimed at.

With four active corps and three divisions of reserves in hand, d'Espérey had, even before the German withdrawal began, a consider-

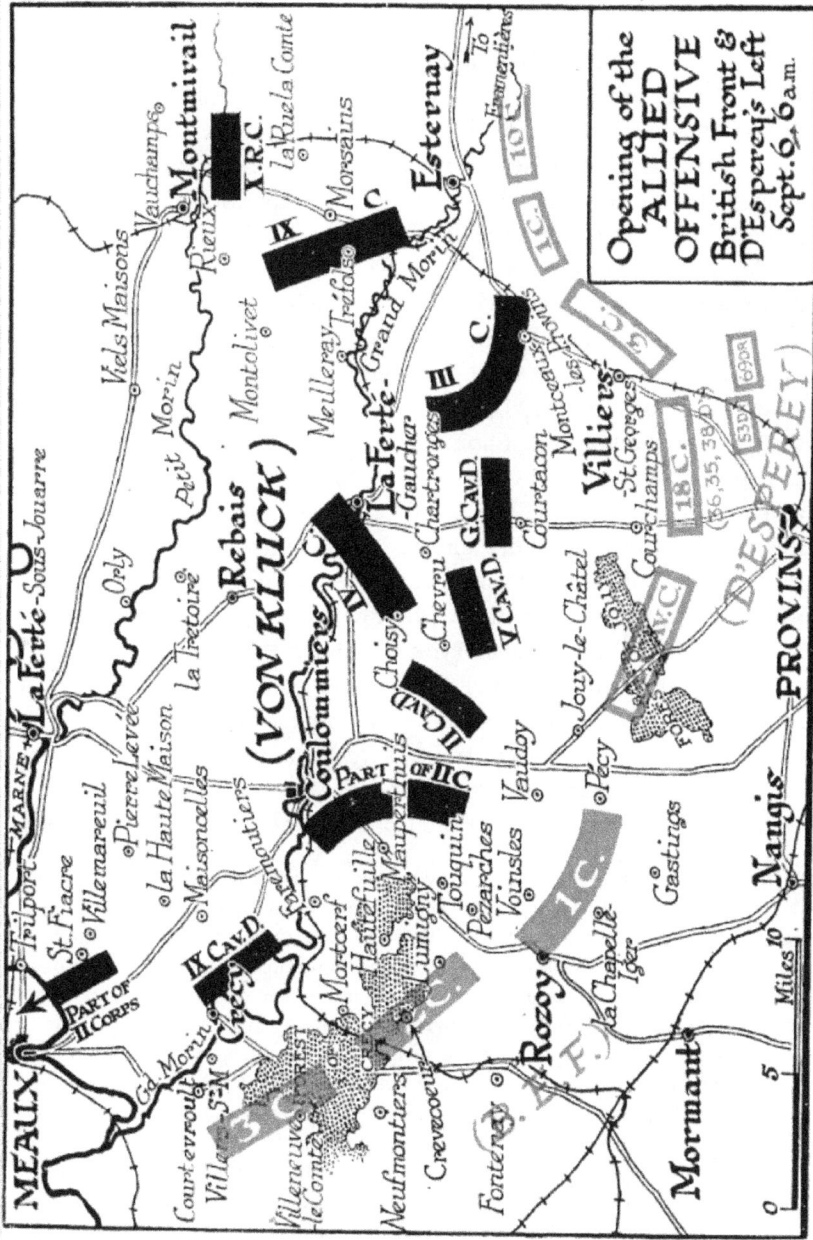

Opening of the
ALLIED
OFFENSIVE
British Front &
D'Esperey's Left
Sept. 6, 6 a.m.

MEAUX
St. Fiacre
Trilport
Villenareuil
Pierre-Levée
la Haute Maison
Maisoncelles
PART OF
II CORPS
Gd. Morin
Courtevroult
Villers S^te-M.
Crécy
IX Cav D.
Pecy
Mortcerf
Hautefeuille
Lumigny
Touquin
Pézarches
Vaudoy
Fontenay
La Chapelle-Iger
Rozoy
ROYAL
CRÉCY
Neufmontiers
Crèvecœur
Frémontiers
Maupertuis
(B.E.F.)
PROVINS
(D'ESPEREY)
Nangis
Mormant
0   5   10 Miles

MARNE
La Ferté-sous-Jouarre
Orly
la Trétoire
Petit Morin
Rebais
Montolivet
Viels Maisons
Vauchamps
Montmirail
Rieux
X.R.C.
IX
C.
la Recula Comte
Morsains
Trefols
Esternay
To Frognolivans
10 C.
5 C.
GQGR
53 D, 38 D)
(36, 35,
18 C.
St. Georges
Courchamps
Villiers
Montceaux-les-Provins
Courtacon
III
C.
la Ferté-Grand Morin
Meilleray
Chartronges
Chevru
G. Cav D.
V. Cav D.
Choisy
Jouy-le-Chatel
FOR.
W.C.
1 C.
Gastins
Pécy
Voinsles
Beautheil
(VON KLUCK)
Coulommiers
La Ferté-Gaucher
IV
II (Cav.)
PART OF III C.

able advantage—indicating Joffre's intention that it should be the second great arm of his offensive, that which should make the chief frontal attack. On the other hand, the enemy held strong positions along the Grand Morin, and, behind this, along the Vauchamps-Montmirail ridge of the Petit Morin. During their retreat the Allies had used the opportunity offered by the valleys of the Marne and its tributaries for delaying actions; these streams were now so many obstacles across their path. The first French movement, on September 6, was powerfully resisted. On the left, the cavalry occupied Courtacon.[1]

At the centre, the 18th and 3rd Corps co-operating (prophetic combination—Maud'huy, Mangin, and Petain!), the villages of Montceaux-les-Provins and Courgivaux, on the high road from Paris to Nancy, which was, as it were, the base of the whole battlefield, were taken by assault. On the right, the 1st Corps was stopped throughout the forenoon before Chatillon-sur-Morin by the X Reserve Corps. D'Espérey detached a division, with artillery, to make a wide detour and to fall, through the Wood of La Noue, upon the German defences east of Esternay. Thus threatened, the enemy gave way; and the market-town of Esternay was occupied early on the following morning. The 10th Corps continued the line toward the north-east, after suffering rather heavy losses beyond Sézanne.

On the morning of September 7, the air services of the 5th Army reported the commencement of Kluck's retreat; and soon afterwards a corresponding movement of Bülow's right was discovered to be going on behind a screen of cavalry and artillery, supported by some infantry elements. D'Espérey had no sooner ordered the piercing of this screen

---

1. In Courtacon, I found eighteen of the two dozen small brick houses completely destroyed by fire, after having been sacked. The pretext given was that villagers had betrayed the German troops—part of the Guard Cavalry Division—to the Allies. The single room of the village school presented an unforgettable exhibition of malice. Dirty straw, remnants of meals, torn books, and broken cartridge cases littered the floor. Piles of half-burnt straw showed that a hurried attempt had been made to destroy the building; there were two such piles under the bookcase and the tiny school museum, which consisted of a few bottles of metal and chemical specimens. Amid this filthy chaos, the low forms, the master's desk, and wall-charts inculcating "temperance, kindness, justice, and truth," stood as they had done on the day before the summer holidays. As I turned to leave, I saw, written across the blackboard in bold, fine writing, evidently as the lesson of that day, the words: "*À chaque jour suffit sa peine*"—"*Sufficient unto the day is the evil thereof*," as our English version has it. Under this motto, all unconscious of it, these brutes had slept and wakened to their incendiary work—men of a nation that boasted itself the pioneer in Europe of elementary schooling. Could any recording angel have conceived a more biting irony?

than news was brought in of the critical position of the neighbouring wing of Foch's Army, the 42nd Division and the 9th Corps, through which Bülow's X and Guard Corps were trying to break, from the St. Gond Marshes toward Sézanne. He at once diverted his 20th Division to threaten the western flank of this attack (which will be followed in the next section) about Villeneuve-lès-Charleville. Meanwhile, rapid progress was being made on the centre and left of the 5th Army. Between Esternay and Montmirail extend the close-set parklands called the Forest of Gault, with smaller woods outlying, a difficult country in which many groups of hungry German stragglers were picked up during the following days.

Through this district, the 1st Corps and the left of the 10th, with General Valabrègue's three divisions of reserves behind, beat their way; while, farther west, in the more open but broken fields between the Grand and the Petit Morin, the 18th and the 3rd Corps made six good miles, to the line Ferté-Gaucher-Trefols. More than a thousand prisoners were taken during the day, with a few machine-guns and some abandoned stores.

We have seen the British Expeditionary Force at the beginning of a like novel and exhilarating experience. Its five divisions, having seized Coulommiers on the night of September 6, had pressed on to the Petit Morin, and, from its junction with the Marne eastward to La Trétoire, where obstinate opposition was offered, had secured the crossings. D'Espérey's left wing thus found its task lightened; and the 18th and 3rd Corps were ordered to sweep aside the remaining German rearguards, and to strike across the Petit Morin on either side of Montmirail. September 8 was thus a day, rather of marching than fighting, except at Montmirail, on whose horse-shoe ridge the enemy held out for some hours.[2] In the evening, General Hache entered the picturesque town, and set up his quarters in the old *château* where Bülow's Staff had been housed on the previous day.

On the left, Maud'huy pushed the 18th Corps by Montolivet over the Petit Morin, and after a sharp action took the village of Marchais-en-Brie. On the right, the 1st Corps was checked at Courbetaux and Bergères, the German VII Corps having come into line; so that the 10th Corps, between Soigny and Corfelix, had to turn north-westward to its assistance. This was scarcely more than an eddy in the general stream of fortune. The moral effect of a happy manoeuvre

---

2. M. Madelin says that 7000 German corpses were found. The figure may be doubted.

goes for much in the result. The British and d'Espérey's men forgot all their sufferings and weariness in the spectacle of the enemy yielding. British aviators reported Kluck's columns as in general retreat, certain roads being much encumbered. Bülow had necessarily withdrawn his right to maintain contact; his centre and left must follow if the pressure were continued.

The hour of decision approached. During the morning of Wednesday, September 9, Sir John French's 2nd and 1st Corps crossed the Marne at Luzancy, Sââcy, Nanteuil, Charly, and Nogent-l'Artaud. This part of the valley was scarcely defended; and a brigade of the 3rd Division had progressed 4 miles beyond it by 9 a.m. Anxious news for the German Staff. Unfortunately, our right was arrested until afternoon by a threat of attack from Château-Thierry; and, lower down the river about La Ferté, the 3rd Corps, still represented only by the 4th Division and the 19th Brigade, was stopped until evening before the broken bridges and rifle-parapets on the northern bank. Some guns then carried over near Changis bombarded the German artillery positions beyond the Ourcq, a notice to quit that had prompt effect. Château-Thierry was left to the French 18th Corps, which occupied the town that night.

Meanwhile, Smith-Dorrien and Haig entered the hilly country about Bezu, Coupru, and Domptin, on the road from Château-Thierry to Lizy-sur-Ourcq. Marwitz vainly essayed to obstruct the northward movement. Beaten in an action near Montreuil-aux-Lions, he informed Kluck that he could do no more, and hurried back to the line of the little River Clignon, about Bussiares and Belleau, which were reached by 4 p.m. A little later, British aviators brought in word that the enemy had evacuated the whole angle between the east bank of the Ourcq and the Marne, and that, on the other hand, the withdrawal of the German I Army was creating a void beyond Château-Thierry: the cavalry of Richthofen, sent thither by Bülow, was in the same predicament as that of Marwitz farther west. At daybreak on September 10, Pulteney's Corps left the Marne behind. Meeting no serious resistance, the British crossed the Clignon valley, and by evening occupied La Ferté-Milon, Neuilly-St. Front, and Rocourt.

These were marching days for the 5th Army. Conneau's cavalry, reinforced by an infantry brigade and extra batteries, passed the Marne at Azy on the 9th, and, harrying Bülow's right flank, reached Oulchy-le-Château next day. The 18th Corps, with the reserve divisions in support, pushed on from Château-Thierry toward Fère-en-Tardenois;

and the 3rd Corps, which had occupied Montigny, halfway between Montmirail and the Marne, on the 9th, forced the passage, under heavy fire from the hills at Jaulgonne, on the 10th. The 1st Corps had a heavier task. Having progressed as far as the Vauchamps plateau, it was wheeled back to the south-east to help the 10th Corps, which d'Espérey had transferred to Foch's Army of the centre, now in the gravest peril.

2. Battle of the Marshes of St. Gond

While the 6th Army, within sight of the Ourcq, was suffering its great agony, while the "effect of suction" was showing itself in the Anglo-French pursuit of Kluck, very different were the first results at the centre of the long crescent of the Allied front. Kluck was saved by his quick resolution, together with Marwitz's able work in covering the rear. Bülow was in no such imminent danger. His communications with the north were at first perfectly safe. The situation of his right wing, which must either fall back or lose contact with the I Army, was awkward; but, doubtless, Kluck's success would soon re-establish it. The circumstances indicated for the remainder of the II Army and the neighbouring Saxon Corps an instant attempt to break through the French centre, or at least to cripple it, and, with it, all Joffre's offensive plan. The very strategic influence which helped the British and d'Espérey, therefore, at first threw a terrible burden upon Foch and the "detachment" which on September 5 was renamed the "9th Army"; yet it was by this same influence that, in the end, though by the narrowest of margins, he also won through.

The theatre of this struggle is the south-western corner of the flat, niggardly expanse of La Champagne Pouilleuse, lying between the depression called the Marshes of St. Gond and the Sézanne-Sommesous railway and highroad. It is very clearly bounded on the west by the sharp edge of the Brie plateau; on the east it is bordered by the Troyes-Châlons road and railway. Sézanne on the west, and Fère Champènoise at the centre, are considerable country towns; the right is marked by the permanent camp of Mailly. To the north of Sézanne, the hill of Mondemont, immediately overlooking the marshes and the plain, and the ravine of St. Prix, on the Epernay road, where the Petit Morin issues from the marshes and breaks into the plateau, are key positions. The Marshes of St. Gond (so called after a seventh-century priory, of which some ruins remain) witnessed several of the most poignant episodes of Napoleon's 1814 campaign "from the Rhine to

The MARNE RE-CROSSED.
Morning of Sept. 9.

(V. BÜLOW)

VII. C.

Condé-en-Brie

Montigny

1. C.

3. C.

18th C.

(D'ESPÉRÉ)

Dormans

R. Marne

Reuilly

Chartèves

Château Thierry

G. Cav. D.

IX. C.

Azy

Essomes

(VON KLUCK)

III. C.

Bezu-Ste Germain

Givry

Hautevesnes

Gandelu

Mézy-en-Multien

La Plessis Placy

IV. R. C.

Vendrest

Dhuisy

II Cav. D.

Bouresches

Do. V. Cav. D.

Montreuil-aux-Lions

Bezu-le-Gd

II Cav. D.

2nd C.

Charly

S. Marne

Mézy

Nogent-l'Artaud

Montmirail

Montvirot

Fromantières

Vauchamps

Marchais-en-Brie

Madaunay

Petit Morin

Sablonnières

Viels Maisons

Orly

Bussières

la Trétoire

COULOMMIERS

Rebais

Crécy

MÉAUX

Maisoncelles

la Haute Maison

Pierre-Levée

Villemareuil

Trilport

Signy-Signets

Changis

Varreddes

La Ferté s-Jouarre

3rd C.

1. C.

II Cav. D.

Liz ancy

Château

S. Mery

Etavigny

IV. R. C.

II. C.

Acy

Vincy

TO BETZ

(MAUNOURY)

l'Ourcq

Crouy-s-Ourcq

0   10   20   30 Miles

Fontainebleau."

They were then much more extensive. Between the villages of Fromentières and Champaubert, there survives the name, though little else, of the "*Bois du Desert*," where 3000 Russian grenadiers are said to have been slain or captured by Marmont's *cuirassiers*, while hundreds of others were drowned. A month later, Blücher was back from Laon attacking on the same ground; and Marmont and Mortier were in full retreat along the road to Fère Champènoise. Pachod's national guards, the "Marie Louises," turned north to the marches of St. Gond as to a refuge. The Russians and Prussians surrounded them; and only a few of the French lads escaped by the St. Prix road. Today the marshes are largely reclaimed and canalised; but this clay bed, extending a dozen miles east and west, and averaging more than a mile in breadth, fills easily under such a rainstorm as fell upon the region on the evening of September 9, 1914, and at all times it limits traffic to the three or four good roads crossing it. The chief of these, from Epernay to Sézanne and Fère Champènoise respectively, pass the ends of the marshes at St. Prix and Morains; the former is commanded by Mondemont, the latter by Mont Août, near Broussy.

Was this "last barrier providentially set across the route of the invasion"[3] forgotten? Joffre's earlier plan did, indeed, involve the abandonment of all the plain extending to the Aube; the decision to stand on the line of the marshes was a consequence of Gallieni's initiative. Foch's Army had been carried beyond them in its retreat, but, fortunately, not far beyond. On the morning of September 5, advance columns of Bülow's left had entered Baye; patrols had reached the Petit Morin bridge at St. Prix, and the north-centre of the marshes at Vert-la-Gravelle. A little more dash, and the Germans would have possessed themselves of all the commanding points. It was about 10 a.m. that Foch received the *generalissimo's* order closing the retreat:—

> The 9th Army will cover the right of the 5th Army, holding the southern passages of the Marshes of St. Gond, and placing a part of its forces on the plateau north of Sézanne.

Foch at once directed the appropriate movements; and, by the evening of September 5, the following positions were reached:

French Left.—Driven back from St. Prix by forces belonging to Bülow's X Active and Reserve Corps, the 42nd Division (General

---

3. Le Goffic, *Les Marais de St. Gond.*

Grossetti) held the neighbouring hills from Villeneuve-lès-Charleville and Soisy to Mondemont.

Centre.—During the afternoon, Dubois advanced the 9th Corps (Moroccan Division and 17th Division) from Fère Champènoise to Broussy and Bannes, and thence pushed two battalions over the marshes to Toulon-la-Montagne, Vert-la-Gravelle, and Aulnizeux in face of the Prussian Guard Corps, the main body of which was at Vertus. The Blondlat Brigade of the Moroccan Division attacked Congy, but failed, and fell back on Mondemont. The 52nd Reserve Division was in support about Connantre.

French Right.—The 11th Corps (General Eydoux) rested on the east end of the marshes at Morains-le-Petit, and from here stretched backward along the course of the Champagne Somme to Sommesous, with the 60th Reserve Division behind it. They had before them the Saxon XII Active Corps and one of its reserve divisions. At Sommesous, General de l'Espée's Cavalry Division covered a gap of about 12 miles between Foch's right and de Langle de Cary's left at Humbauville.

Thus, on the eve of the battle, the 9th Army, inferior to the enemy in strength, especially in artillery, presented to it an irregular convex front. Bülow was at Esternay on the west; Hausen was approaching the gap on its right flank; the centre was protruded uneasily to and beyond the St. Gond Marshes. The expectation of General Headquarters had, apparently, been that the German onset would fall principally on the right of the 5th Army. Foch was, therefore, instructed to give aid in that direction by pushing his left to the north-north-west, while the rest of his line stood firm until the pressure was relieved. In the event, these roles were reversed: it was d'Espérey who had to help Foch. The original dispositions, however, had a certain effect upon the course of the battle. They gave the 9th Army a pivot on the Sézanne plateau; and the obstinacy with which this advantage was retained seems to have diverted the German commanders, till it was too late, from concentrating their force on the other wing, the line of attack from which the French had most to fear.

Foch was the offensive incarnate; but, on the morning of September 6th, he could do no more than meet, and that with indifferent success, Bülow's attack upon his left-centre. He was weakest where the enemy was most strong: a large part of the French guns could not reach the field for the beginning of the combat; the 9th Corps, in particular, felt the lack of three groups of artillery it had left in Lorraine. Failing this support, the two battalions holding Toulon-la-Montagne were quickly shelled out of their positions. In vain Dubois, commanding the 9th Corps, ordered the Moroccan *tirailleurs* to march on Baye, and the 17th Division to retake the two lost points. A crack regiment, the 77th, crossed the marshes and entered Coizard village, Major de Beaufort, cane in hand, on a big bay horse, at its head, crying to his men, shaken by rifle fire from the houses: "Forward, boys! Courage! It is for France. Jeanne d'Arc is with us." The 2nd and 3rd battalions went on, and tried to climb Mount Toulon.

The fighting continued all day, ending in a painful retreat to Mont Août through two miles of swampy ground, in which the men plunged up to the waist rather than risk the shell-ploughed causeway. The Guard followed as far as Bannes, and the X Corps occupied Le Mesnil Broussy and Broussy-le-Petit, where the French batteries arrested them. Small French detachments clung to Morains and Aulnay through the day and night; otherwise, the north of the marshes was lost. Against the left, Bülow was less successful. The 42nd Division and the Moroccan Division withstood repeated assaults of the X Corps at Soisy-aux-Bois and on the edge of the St. Gond Wood. The struggle, however, was most severe: Villeneuve, occupied on the evening of September 5, was lost at 8 a.m. on the 6th, recaptured an hour later, lost again at noon, and recovered at night. On the right, the 11th Corps had to evacuate Ecury and Normée under heavy fire; Lenharrée and Sommesous were partially in flames, but still resisted.

Unawed, in his quarters at Pleurs, Foch wrote the following order for the morrow:—

> The General Commanding counts on all the troops of the 9th Army exerting the greatest activity and the utmost energy to extend and maintain beyond dispute the results obtained over a hard-pressed and venturesome enemy.

Many of the generals, lieutenants, and men may have thought these last words too highly coloured. Foch himself knew more of the real situation. He knew, as did Bülow, how gravely the latter was prejudiced by Kluck's predicament. Already, the prospect had arisen of the I German Army being gripped by the closing vice of Maunoury and the British. Already, d'Espérey's great force was moving north along Bülow's flank toward Montmirail. Joffre's masterstroke was revealed. Was the victory that Berlin and the armies counted as certain to slip

FOCH'S FRONT

– – – Sept. 6. morning
——— Sept. 7. night.

(Von Bülow)

X C. (Res.) Fromentieres Champaubert Bergères Epetus So To Châlons
Barnay. Congy Toulon-la-Mne. MME-SOULDE

X C. (Active) Pt. Morin. Bannay. Etoges GUARD CORPS Coizard. SOULDE

Charleville St. Prix Villevenard MARSHES Talus- St. Gond (Von HAUSEN)

Soizy. Oyes 42 D. St. Prix Coizard Reuves Bricot- IV C. Cav. SOMME XII C. (Res.)

10 C. of the (5th ARMY) Mondement Broyes Allemant Réas Linthes St. Loup Chapton Villeneuve Mt. Aout Puits XII C. (Act.) Normée Lenharrée Vésimont Haussimont

Sézanne Lintelles Coizard Chalmont Broussy-le-Gd Barres II C. Cav. Moreuis le-Pt. Aulnay Autruraux Vert-la-G. II C. Cav. Sommesous

To Anglure Pleurs Coniantre VAURE Fère Champenoise 18 D. Coniant.-les- II C. 60 D.R. Luxy 9 D. CAV.

MAURIENNE Gourgançon Ognes Corroy Faux Semoine Salon Mailly le Camp la folie

(FOCH) LA SUPERBE Villiers- Herbisse Herbisse Trouan-le-Pt. les Ferus

0   10   20   30 Miles

away at the eleventh hour? For the first time in a triumphant generation, a German Army was in danger of defeat; nay, all the armies were in danger. Astounding change of fortune! The grey-coat soldiery, dulling their weariness in the loot of cottages and farms, the subaltern officers, making free with the wine cellars of old manor houses, did not know it; but such was the fact. Their commanders were not the men easily to take alarm; yet, at this moment, alarm must have struck them.

3. Defence and Recapture of Mondemont

The grand manoeuvre of envelopment had failed. The alternative plan remained: to smash the French centre and roll up the lines on either side. On the morning of September 7, this effort began with a fierce onslaught across the ravine of the Petit Morin against the Sézanne plateau from Mondemont to Villeneuve.

On Foch's extreme left, nothing was gained. The 42nd Division was now receiving perceptible support from the 10th Corps of the 5th Army, which during the day, as we have seen, completed the clearance of the Forest of Gault, to the west of Villeneuve. Toward Mondemont, however, the X Active Corps made some progress, throwing the defenders back to the western borders of Soisy, again taking Villeneuve, and reaching through the St. Gond Wood nearly to the hamlet of Chapton. The bare crest called the Signal du Poirier gave the German gunners an excellent platform, with views over a large part of the French lines. One of their chief targets was the *château* of Mondemont, a two-storey mansion, dating from the sixteenth century, with pepper-pot corner towers, enclosing a large square courtyard. General Humbert had set up here his Staff quarters; but by noon the bombardment had become so severe that he had to leave it to advanced posts of the Moroccan Division, first, however, insisting on taking a proper lunch in the *salle-à-manger* with the trembling family. These were sent to the rear, and Humbert moved to the neighbouring *château* of Broyes.

In a later stage of the war, Humbert struck me rather as the thinker, a quiet, keen intelligence, and a fine gentleman. At this earlier time, one of the youngest generals in the French Army, he appears rather as the man of spirited action. Beaming with gay confidence, he abounded in the *gestes* that the French soldier so loves. Once several members of his escort were killed by a shell exploding in their midst; like Grossetti, afterwards to be known as "the Bull of the Yser," danger only stimulated him. "The Germans are bottled up," he said; "Mondemont is the

147

cork. It must be held at any price." At 5 p.m., a combined attack, by parts of the 42nd and Moroccan Divisions, with the 77th regiment of the 9th Corps, was made with the object of freeing the Mondemont position. Little ground was gained, and the losses were very heavy; it was a momentary relief, no more.

At length the German Command recognised that the French defence was weakest toward and beyond Fère Champènoise, and that a simultaneous attack by both their wings, with most strength on the east, might shatter it. First, however, the flank of the Guard Corps along the marshes must be cleared. This preliminary occupied the whole of September 7. On the west, Oyes was taken during the morning in the advance on Mondemont. On the east, the French companies outlying at Morains and Aulnay had to abandon these villages at 8 a.m., under threat of being taken in reverse along the railway. Morains is only four miles by highroad from Fère Champènoise; and here the picked infantry of the Guard were striking at the junction of the 9th and 11th Corps, with solid Saxon regiments closing in upon the latter to the south-east. Seeing their danger, Radiguet and Moussy concerted a movement by which, during the afternoon, Aulnizeux was taken and the German advance checked. In the evening, at the third attempt, the enemy recovered the village; and in the last hours of the night his general offensive along the Sézanne and Fère roads began. It will be convenient to follow first the western arm of the attack.

At 3 a.m. on September 8, after a sharp cannonade, the French machine-gunners on Mondemont Hill observed spectral forms approaching in open order—these were advanced parties belonging to the X Corps, with some elements of the Guard. They were easily repulsed; and, immediately afterwards, the much-thinned ranks of the 42nd and Moroccan Divisions, with the 77th regiment of the 9th Corps, were launched anew towards St. Prix. Although Bülow had received reinforcements, and had placed more batteries between Congy and Baye, the Moroccans occupied Oyes and its hill and the Signal du Poirier by 8 a.m., while the left of the 42nd carried Soisy at the point of the bayonet. Unfortunately, the debacle that was happening coincidently on Foch's right put any exploitation of this success out of the question. A fresh defensive front had to be created south of the marshes, facing east; the 77th regiment was recalled to St. Loup in the middle of the afternoon for this purpose. The 42nd Division seems to have been shaken by this removal of a sorely-needed support; and Bülow, promptly advised of it, ordered his columns forward once more.

On an islet in the west end of the marshes, between the villages of Villevenard and Oyes, stand a Rennaissance gateway and other remnants of the ancient Priory of St. Gond, and in their midst the humble dwelling of "the last hermit of St. Gond," as M. le Goffic calls him, the Abbé Millard, corresponding member of the French Antiquarian and Archaeological Societies. A victim of dropsy, the *abbé* was laid up when the approach of the Germans was announced. "So, then," he calmly remarked, "I shall renew my acquaintance with Attila." His housekeeper, a typically vigorous Frenchwoman, would have no such morbid curiosity. "You have no parishioners but the frogs. *Monsieur le Curé*; and they can take care of themselves against your Attila. Come along"—and, bundling some valuables into a wheelbarrow, and giving Father Millard a stick, she carried him off into safety. As they left, a body of Senegalese sharpshooters came up, and began to build across the highway an old-fashioned barricade of tree-trunks, carts, and blocks of stone. "Some barbed wire and a continuous trench, such as the Germans use, would have been better," remarks M. le Goffic; "but we remained faithful to our old errors, and, nearly everywhere, our men fought in the open or behind sheaves and tree trunks."

After hours of an ebb-and-flow of bayonet charges and hand to hand combats, the French lost in succession Broussy-le-Petit, Mesnil-Broussy, Reuves, and Oyes—all the morning's gain had vanished by nightfall. With the Germans entrenched a mile away, and only a single *Zouave* battalion in reserve, Humbert insisted that Mondemont must be held; and his corps commander, Dubois, desperately seeking to cover the void on his right with the 77th Regiment, told the officers that retreat was not to be thought of. Heavy rain fell during the evening, obstructing the movements of all the armies. On both sides, that night, the chiefs knew that the issue was a matter of hours, of very few hours.

We saw in the first section of this chapter that, on the evening of September 8, the left of the 5th French Army had passed, and its centre reached, the Petit Morin, while the 10th Corps immediately threatened Bülow's flank at Bannay, only 2 miles west of Baye. The "effect of suction" was working wonderfully. An order found during the day on a wounded officer, directing that the regimental trains should be drawn up facing north, showed the preoccupations of the German Staff. If the Guard and the Saxons could complete the rout of Foch's right-centre, they might yet win through; but there was no longer a moment to spare, for Bülow had no force capable of long withstanding d'Espérey's north-eastward thrust .

Against Foch's left, Bülow played his last stake at daybreak on September 9. A whole brigade, marching from Oyes under cover of mist, brushed aside the two battalions of sharpshooters, mounted Mondemont hill, and seized the *château* and village, which were rapidly provided with a garrison and machine-guns. The 42nd Division was in course of withdrawal at this time, its place being taken by the 51st Division of the neighbouring army. Humbert still would not take defeat: borrowing two battalions of *chasseurs* from Grossetti, he sent them to the assault of the promontory. They failed. At about 10.30 a.m., the 9th Corps lost Mont Août, the stronghold of Foch's centre, and fell back upon the lower hills between Allemant and Linthes. If the whole left and centre of the 9th Army were not to be swept, after its right, into the plain, the last footing on the Sézanne plateau must be held at any price

But how? Many companies of the Moroccan Division had lost all their officers and most of their men. The breakdown of his right had driven Foch to an extreme expedient which we will presently follow more closely—the transfer thither of the 42nd Division; all Grossetti could do for Humbert after his early morning failure, therefore, was to lend him his artillery for a couple of hours. From Dubois and his own corps, Humbert was able again to borrow the 77th Regiment. After a massed fire of preparation on the woods and slopes around the *château* of Mondemont by nine batteries, the hungry, haggard survivors of the 77th, divided into two bodies under Colonels Lestoquoi and Eon, approached the hill from the west and east, while four companies gathered to the south of the *château* as a storming force under Major de Beaufort,

We have already seen this only too chivalric officer defying the prime conditions of modern warfare in the capture of Coizard; here is a yet more pathetic exhibition of the ancient style of heroism. It was 2.30 of a bright afternoon, the air oppressive with heat, smoke, and dust. The *commandant* called a priest-soldier from the ranks, and asked him to give supreme absolution to the men who wished to receive it. They knelt, and rose. The major, putting on his white gloves, then gave the order to charge Bugles sounded; the men ran forward "in deep, close masses," shouting and singing. Many fell before reaching the garden of the *château*. De Beaufort, standing for a moment under a tree to consider the next step, was shot dead. A few men got through a breach in the garden wall, only to meet a rain of bullets from loop-holes in the house. A score of officers (including Captain de Secondat-Montesquieu, a descendant of the great French writer) were lost, with a third of the effectives. At 3.30, Colonel Eon withdrew the remainder of the storming party.

For a breathing space only. The *château* was, in fact, besieged. Three field-guns were brought within 400 yards of it; and at 6 p.m. three companies advanced upon the quadrangle of buildings, four others upon the village, at the foot of the hill. Forty minutes later. Colonel Lestoquoi led his last remaining company forward, crying: "Come on, boys; another tussle, and we are there." This time, *château*, park, farm, and churchyard, and finally the village, were carried. "I hold the village and the *château* of Mondemont," Lestoquoi reported to General Humbert; "I am installing myself for the night."

The Battle of Mondemont was over; one wild ebb-wave, and the peace of nature's fruitfulness fell for all our time upon the riven fields, the multitude of graves, the desolate marshes.

4. Foch's Centre broken

Far other and graver was the course of the eastern arm of the German attack, after the loss of the marsh villages by the French 9th Corps on September 7.

Dubois' shaky line, along the south of the marshes, was continued eastward by the 11th Corps (including, now, the 18th Division) from near Morains to Normée, and this by the 60th Reserve Division, thence to Sommesous, and the 9th Cavalry Division, reaching out to the left of de Langle's Army (the 17th Corps). These faced, respectively, the Prussian Guard Corps, the Saxon XII Active Corps, and part of its reserve. No great Inequality, so far; but Bülow and Hansen were bringing up reinforcements, and preparing a terrible surprise. Throughout September 7, the Saxons had been hammering at Eydoux' front along the Somme-Soude. Lenharrée, defended throughout the afternoon and evening by only two companies, became untenable during the night. All the officers had fallen, Captain Henri de Saint Bon last of them, crying to his Breton reservists of the 60th Division: "Keep off! Do not get killed to save me." On entering the village, and seeing what had happened, the Saxon commander ordered his men to march before the French wounded, saying: "Salute! They are brave fellows." So began the darkest episode, the nearest approach to a German victory, in the battle of the Marne.

An hour before—at 3 a.m. on September 8—their guns pushed forward under cover of darkness, the general assault by Bülow's and Hausen's armies had begun . It was well planned according to the information of those commanders, and, considering how serious an obstacle the marshes presented to their centre, remarkably conducted. On the west, the resolution of the defenders of Mondemont would have gone for nothing without the increasing support of d'Espérey's 10th Corps. At the left-centre, the marshes gave Dubois sufficient cover to enable him to wheel half his force eastward. Beyond that, the conditions favoured the enemy, for the only main roads converged upon Fère Champènoise; and, if the French were driven back, a dangerous block would inevitably be produced. Against the extreme right, the Saxons were not in great force; and, on that flank also, the neighbouring French Army gave vital aid.

So, in the misty dawn of September 8, the grey-coats, picked Prussians and burly Saxons, swarmed forward, seeming to renew themselves irresistibly. Foch, talking to his Staff overnight, had exclaimed that such desperation suggested the need of compensating for ill fortune elsewhere; and now he opened a black day with a characteristic phrase of stubborn cheer: "The situation is excellent; I order you again vigorously to take the offensive." The situation excellent! Foch would not use words of meaningless bravado; he may have been thinking of d'Espérey knocking at Bülow's side door.

At this hour (7 a.m.), he could not yet know that the loss of Lenharrée had been followed by the turning of two regiments of the 20th Division, and two others of the 60th Reserve Division, defending the passages of the Somme-Soude, and that the hues on either side were crumpling up. So it was. From a number of personal narratives, often contradictory and exaggerated, we can draw an outline of what occurred in the surprise of Fère Champènoise, without pretending to determine exactly where, or by what failing of exhausted men, the confusion originated.

Before Normée, outposts of the 11th Corps, scattered by the sudden fierceness of the onslaught, left uncovered the 35th Brigade (of the 18th Division), which lay bivouacked in the woods. One regiment, the 32nd, was surrounded, and only a half of its effectives, with a few junior officers, escaped. The 34th Brigade, behind it, had time to fall back without loss, through Connantre to Oeuvy, along with the survivors of the 35th. The remnants of the defenders of Lenharrée retreated toward Connantre, firing steadily. As far as Fère Champènoise,

FOCH'S FRONT
Sept. 8-9.

_ _ _ French line Sept. 8, noon.
——— Sept. 9, afternoon.
----→ Manœuvre of 42 D. (replaced by 51 D.R.) from left to centre.

XIX C.
To Vitry
Coole
9 D.CAV. Humbert C.
DE MAILLY
Trouan-le G⁰
M.MARAINS FARM

XII C.R.
Sompuis
MAILLY CAMP
Sommesous
Trouan-le D.
60 D.R.
Villers-Herbisse
Herbisse

SOUDE
To Châlons
Ecury
Normée
Lenharrée
Connantray
XII C. Corps
IV Cav Corps
Euvy
Gourgançon
Semoine
Salon
Broken Line of 21, 8, 22 D. (11 Corps)

Morains le P.
Fère Champenoise
Connantre
Corroy
Ognes
Courcelles
Fresnay
La Fanx
Fresnay
LA SUPERBE
Allibaudières
Plancy
Pouan
Arcis-S-Aube

MARSHES OF ST.GOND
GUARD Corps
MT.AOUT
Broussy-le-P.
Brussy-le-G.
Puits
S.Sophie
FERM
Connantre
Chalmont
Lintelles
Linthelles
Pleurs
Argiume
R. AUBE

Talus-S-Prix
A & R.C.
2 D.R.
la Villeneuve
Mondement C. (11 Corps)
Allemant (9 Corps)
Broyes
St.Loup
Baudement
Méry-sur-Seine

10 C.
X C.
5th Army
51 D.R.
Esternay
Sézanne
GD. MORIN
Chantemerle
Barbonne
R. SEINE
Romilly
S.Seine
R. SEINE

0   10   20 Miles

the chase ran fast along the four roads, from Bannes, Morains, Ecury, and Normée. In the little country town, crouched in a depression of the hills, and so indefensible, an army chaplain [4] was conducting service in the parish church, at 9 a.m., when bullets began to spatter on the walls, and the first cries of flying men were heard above the noise of breaking windows. At 10.30, the Prussian Guard entered the town, drums and fifes playing. Presently, with bodies of Saxons from Normée, they continued the pursuit, which proceeded more slowly toward Connantre and Oeuvy and the valley of the Maurienne. Here and there, small French groups turned at bay, because they could go no farther, or hoping to stem the retreat.

Thus, 200 men of the 66th and 32nd Regiments came to a stand in one of the dwarf-pine woods south of Fère. They had no officer among them; but a sergeant-major named Guerre took them in hand, and disposed them in four sections, "like the square at Waterloo," he said. One German attack was beaten off; but when a field-gun came up. Guerre decided that the only hope was to make a sortie. It cost the brave man his life. About 30 of his fellows got away, including two privates, Malveau and Bourgoin, who, after wandering in the German lines, and being directed by a dying German officer, brought the flag of the 32nd Regiment during the evening to the commander of the 35th Brigade.

Perhaps it was because of the convergence of roads upon Fère, noted above, that, whereas the original breakdown occurred on Foch's right, the pursuit became concentrated upon his centre. The most important consequence of this fact was that the German Command never discovered the weakest part of the French front, and the dislocated right was able to escape from restraint and to re-form. The greater part of the 60th Reserve Division, which had extended from Vassimont and Haussimont to Sommesous, where two regiments arrested the Saxon advance for two hours, rallied early in the afternoon between Semoine and Mailly. General de l'Espée's cavalry, with some infantry elements, held up a brigade of the Saxon XII Corps south of Sompuis; and the neighbouring army of de Langle effectively engaged the XIX Corps between Humbauville and Courdemange.

Westward of the main stream of pursuit, the position of Foch's left was more delicate and critical. At the extreme left, we have seen that, during the morning, the 42nd Division recaptured Villeneuve and

---

4. *Au Centre de la Bataille de la Marne*, by the Abbé Neret, Curé of Vertus, who gives the hours named.

Soisy, while the Moroccan Division reached St. Prix and the Signal du Poirier. The 42nd held its gains throughout the day; but the 9th Corps, shaken by frontal attack across the marshes, and left with its flank in the air by the breakdown of the 11th Corps, had no choice but to withdraw its right, and suffered heavily ere it could take up new positions. Coming on from Morains, the Prussian Guard took the homesteads called Grosse and Petit Fermes, on the way to Bannes, in reverse by the east. Three French regiments were here thrown into confusion, cavalry plunging into the batteries, and fugitives obstructing the roads. The panic, however, was soon over.

At 7.30 a.m., the retreat sounded; at 9 a.m., Moussy was reorganising the 17th Division on the line Mont Août-Puits, with the 52nd Reserve Division in support. Hither the faithful 77th Regiment was called from Mondemont during the morning to help form an angular front, across which the Germans passed south in pursuit of the scattered elements of the 11th Corps. The headquarters of the 9th Army were moved back from Pleurs to Plancy, on the Aube.

Thus, at noon on September 8, the shape of the vast battle was markedly changed. D'Espérey was on the Petit Morin near Montmirail, and his 10th Corps near Corfelix. From the latter point, Foch's left extended south-east to Connantre. His centre, broken in to a depth of ten miles, was floating indefinitely in the valley of the Maurienne. The right, supported by de Langle, giving no immediate anxiety, his first problem, therefore, was to save the centre without losing the solidity of the left. It is in such emergencies, when a few hours even of loose and unsuccessful resistance may turn the balance, that the virtues of a race and the value of traditions and training in an army reveal themselves.

The breakdown before Fère Champènoise did not degenerate into a rout. Eydoux pulled the fragments of the 11th Corps together on the line Corroy-Gourgancon-Semoine, and in the evening delivered a counter-attack which gave him momentary possession of the plateau of Oeuvy. Dubois aided this reaction by striking at the west flank of the German advance. Early in the afternoon, after a preparatory fire by 15 batteries near Linthes, the 52nd Reserve Division was thrown eastward toward Fère Champènoise. This effort failed, as did another in the evening; and Dubois had to withdraw slightly, first from Puits to Ste. Sophie Farm, then to Chalmont, while the Prussians held Connantre and Nozay Farm.

5. Fable and Fact of a bold Manoeuvre

That evening, Foch conceived a manoeuvre so characteristic of the man, so evidently after his own heart, that the facts of its execution have been hidden under a mass of sparkling fable. The master had said in one of his lectures:—

"If, by whatever mental vision we see a fissure in a dam of the defence, or a point of insufficient resistance, and if we are able to join to the regular and methodical action of the flood the effect of a blow with a ram capable of breaking the dam at a certain place, the equilibrium is destroyed, the mass hurls itself through the breach, and overwhelms all obstacles. Let us seek that place of weakness. That is the battle of manoeuvre. The defence, overthrown at one point, collapses everywhere. The barrier pierced, everything crumbles."

That it was Foch, not Bülow, who had been on the defensive makes no difference: Foch never thought of war in pure defensive terms. Now he saw his opportunity.

There was no subtlety in the object. A rush which fails to produce a complete breach opens a flank plainly inviting attack; and the Staff at Plancy had had its eyes fixed all day upon the new German flank, 6 miles long, from Mont Août to Corroy. Twice the 9th Corps had struck at it without success. The boldness of Foch's design lay, not in its objective, which was evident, but in the means proposed for its execution. The right of the 9th Corps could do no more; its left, the Moroccan Division, had lost the south bank of the marshes, and was hard put to it to hold the hills around Mondemont. Nothing remained but the 42nd Division, which, though greatly fatigued, was in somewhat better posture about Soisy. Two demands now competed in the mind of the French commander. He regarded Mondemont as a key-position to be defended at all costs; and the removal of Grossetti, without compensation, would gravely endanger it.

But more than in any position he believed in forcing a result by a well-directed blow when the enemy offered the chance. D'Espérey's 10th Corps, it is true, had before it the chance of breaking across Bülow's communications at St. Prix and Baye; it had otherwise no pressing call to make such a movement. Farther south, there were both need and opportunity—the need of relieving the 9th and 11th Corps, the opportunity of a decisive action. Grossetti, then, must come to Linthes, and d'Espérey's 51st Division, in reserve of the 10th Corps, must take his place west of Mondemont. D'Espérey's loyalty in agreeing to this arrangement cannot be too warmly praised. The comradeship of arms, so influential a factor in the victory of the Marne, was nowhere more admirably illustrated.

But dawn on September 9 broke upon a situation aggravated to the extreme, in which the projected manoeuvre might well seem a blunder of recklessness. Bülow and Hausen had summoned their exhausted men to undertake a last essay. On the French left, Mondemont fell at 3 a.m. Two hours later, the Guard and the two Saxon Corps burst upon the centre and right with all their remaining force. Neither the 9th nor the 11th Corps was in a condition to meet this trial; but, in general, they faced it bravely. At 9 a.m., the 21st Division (11th Corps) could resist no more, and fell back from Oeuvy to Hill 129, south of Corroy, whence its commander, Radiguet, wrote to Foch:—

My troops could not hold out any longer under a bombardment such as we have suffered for the last two hours. They are in retreat all along the line. It is the same with the 22nd Division. I am going to try, with my artillery and what I can gather of infantry, to rally on the plateau south of Corroy. My regiments have fought admirably, but they have an average of only four or five officers left.

Foch replied from Plancy. at 10.15:—

The 42nd Division will arrive on the front Linthes-Pleurs. Whatever be the position, more or less in retreat, of the 11th Corps, we count on resuming the offensive with the 42nd Division toward Connantre and Corroy, an offensive in which the 9th Corps will have to take part against the (German) right from Morains to Fère Champènoise. The 42nd Division has been on the way since 8.30, and will be ready to go into action about midday. The 10th Corps has liberated it. The 10th is at our disposition, and has orders to support the Moroccan Division to prevent the enemy penetrating to the west of the Marshes of St. Gond.

On receiving similar instructions, Dubois sent two squadrons of hussars to make a provisional link between the 9th and 11th Corps, and intimated to his divisional commanders not only that they must stand firm, but that, in the classic phrase of Joffre, "no failing will now be tolerated."

Blind words, only to be justified on the lines of Nogi's apophthegm:—

157

Victory is to him who can resist for another quarter of an hour.

They were hardly uttered when Mont Août, the north-eastern bastion of Dubois' line, stubbornly defended for five days, was lost. Much of the artillery of the Prussian Guard had been concentrated on this outlying watch-tower of the Sézanne hills; and, in those early days of the war, nerves were not so steeled that a position heavily bombarded and definitely turned could be long held. Of the two brigades of the 52nd Reserve Division, the 104th had been detached to Moussy's 17th Division; the 103rd remained under the command of General Battesti. Of the former, the 5th battalion, 320th Regiment, under Commandant Meau (known as an author under the pseudonym "Jean Saint-Yves") was posted on the north slopes of Mont Août; two companies of the 51st Chasseurs were on the east; and Lt.-Col. (afterwards General) Clandor, with the 6th battalion, was in the wood at the foot of the hill. Meau, with wounded head bound in bloody bandages, "like a Crimean veteran," as a combatant says, was keeping his men firm under a rain of light and heavy shells commencing at about 9.30 a.m., and Clandor was also determined to hold, when it suddenly became known that the 103rd Brigade, on their right, had received an order to retreat, apparently given by Battesi in alarm at the extent of the enemy's advance. [5]

First in twos and threes, then in masses, the reservists left the woods that cover the eastern slopes of the hill, and hurried westward, groups of horsemen galloping past them, and gun-teams plunging through the meadows. The whole line was thus shaken; and, shortly afterward, the two batteries which had hitherto sustained the men on the crest were silenced by German guns that had got round behind Ste. Sophie Farm. At 11.45 a.m., Moussy gave Mean and Clandor orders to fall back; but their obstinacy had its reward—Mont Août was never occupied by the enemy. The debris of Battesti's brigades were rallied

---

5. I rely upon the article by M. le Goffic, "*La Defense du Mont Août*," in *La Liberte*, September 7, 1918, embodying the narrative of an eye-witness, who mentions the following curious details: "A black cow, maddened by the bombardment, charged the trenches, leaped aside when a shell burst, sniffed the smoke, and stamped in the shell-holes. Slowly, a shepherd, a big, careless ruffian, climbed the slope with his five white sheep. For a moment he stopped level with us, 500 yards to the right. As though by accident, his five sheep were on his left, on our side; and immediately shells began to arrive in fours, the range lengthening each time by a hundred yards. But we were not in range." This perhaps rather imaginative correspondent thinks that the Germans mistook dead for living Frenchmen on the slopes of Mont Août, and that that is why they did not seek to occupy it.

during the early afternoon on the hills of Allemant and Chalmont. A part of Moussy's Division was driven south, and, after a gallant recoil at Ste. Sophie Farm, drew off to the west.

What had become of Grossetti and the 42nd, the last hope of the French centre? From Soisy to Linthes is a march of only 12 miles, and they were to have started at dawn—had started, Foch said, at 8.30 a.m. Exhaustion, hitches in the replacement by the 51st, and the needs of Mondemont may explain the harrowing delay. Messengers were sent out, without result. Foch, fuming at Plancy, issued note upon note to encourage his lieutenants. He wrote at noon:—

Information shows that the German Army, after having marched without rest since the beginning of the campaign, has reached the extreme limit of fatigue. Order no longer exists in their units; regiments are mixed together; the Command is confused. The vigorous offensive of our troops has thrown surprise into the ranks of the enemy, who thought we should not offer any further opposition. It is of the highest importance to profit by these circumstances. In the decisive hour when the honour and safety of the French Fatherland are at stake, officers and soldiers will draw from the energy of our race the strength to stand firm till the moment when the enemy will collapse, worn out. The disorder prevailing among the German troops is a sign of our coming victory; by continuing with all its force the effort begun, our army is certain to stop the march of the enemy and to drive him from our soil. But every one must share the conviction that success will fall to him who can endure longest.

There were, in fact, disorders in the invading host. All morning, Prussian and Saxon soldiery had been making public revel in Fère Champènoise, breaking open and pillaging houses and shops, drinking, dancing, and singing in the streets. Nevertheless, the fighting columns advanced steadily. At 1 p.m. the Guard reached Nozay and Ste. Sophie Farms and entered Connantre, and the Saxons Gourgancon. Radiguet's Division of the 11th Corps, after a brave stand at Oeuvy, drifted before them, first to Fresnay, then to Faux and Salon. Foch did not waver in his intentions. He wrote at 1 p.m:—

The 42nd Division is marching from Broyes to Pleurs. It should face east between Pleurs and Linthes, so as to attack afterward in the direction of the *trouée* between Oeuvy and Connantre. The attack will be supported on the right by the 11th Corps, on the left by all available elements of the 9th Corps, which will take for their objective the road between Fère Champènoise and Morains.

The meaning of the word *trouée* as here used must not be mistaken. It presumably meant the highroad to Fère Champènoise. There was no such "gap" between the Prussian and Saxon forces as some writers have imagined; and they were both, at the time of this note, three miles or more south of the line Oeuvy-Connantre.

Though the situation was not so simple as the idea of a "gap" would suggest, Foch had accurately gauged its character and the peculiar weakness of the German advance. It has been noted that this was at first inclined (partly by the lie of the roads) in a south-westerly direction. One result was to relieve the pressure on the French extreme right, where the 60th Reserve Division withdrew easily from Mailly to Villiers-Herbisse, while de l'Espée's cavalry received strong support from the neighbouring army. On their east flank, therefore, the Saxons had to move with care. On their right, the Prussian Guard had been attracted westward, and there checked, at 4 p.m. , by an attack of portions of the 9th Corps. The Saxons had progressed more easily, and had overrun the Prussians by several miles, thus prolonging the flank at which Foch intended to strike. There was no "fissure" at this time, but rather an overlapping; when, on the following day, a real gap opened between Bülow's and Hansen's Armies (on the Epernay and Châlons roads respectively), the retreat was too fast for the French to take advantage of it.

Foch's design was the classic combination of flank and frontal attack. Grossetti was to drive east-northeast from Linthes-Pleurs, beside the main road and railway, toward Fère Champènoise, while, on his left, Dubois gave what aid he could in the same direction, and Eydoux came up from the south. It was to be the same famous manoeuvre that Maunoury and the British had commenced three days before, without immediate success, but from which the whole "effect of suction," with its momentous consequences, had arisen. Thanks to those three days of heroic effort and sacrifice, Foch's success was instant and complete, though it was not such as the fables have it.[6] Indeed, the enemy did

6. General Canonge, in his historical sketch, confirms my own inquiries. The embryo of the myth is to be found in the "*Official Résumé*," published on June 8, 191 5, in the Bulletin des Armies, according to which, on the evening of September 9, Foch's Army, "moving from west to east toward Fère Champènoise, took in flank the Prussian Guard and the Saxon Corps which were attacking south-east of this locality. This audacious manoeuvre decided the success." This was presently elaborated, with various romantic decorations.

not wait for the assault. He bolted. A doubtful story goes that a German aviator observed the approach of Grossetti's columns, and gave Von Bülow's Staff timely warning. The truth appears to be that the German retreat had been ordered between 3 and 5 p.m. At 6, under a red sunset, the 42nd Division arrived, and, supported by three, later increased to five, groups of artillery, moved slowly forward from the line Linthes-Linthelles, to bivouac near Pleurs.[7]

The 9th Corps alone came into touch with the enemy; and a rearguard resistance was enough to impede its hastily re-formed ranks. At daybreak on the 10th, the 34th Brigade entered Fère Champènoise, which had been evacuated the previous evening, picking up 1500 stragglers; while the 42nd Division was occupying Connantre, where 500 men of the Grenadier Guards were made prisoner at the *château*. As Grossetti's columns crossed the hills in the dawn-light, the air was poisonous with rotting humanity, and spectral forms arose begging for a cup of water. They were men wounded in the surprise of the 8th who had lain in the open for nearly three days. The front of the 9th Army was restored; and, weary but exultant, it prepared to go forward to the general victory. Whether, in the end, the movement of the 42nd Division counted for anything in this result, we can know, if ever, only when the German archives are opened. The chief factor lay not in the form of any particular manoeuvre, but in the sheer persistence of the French centre. Foch and his men won by Nogi's "quarter of an hour."

---

7. Canonge, after two inquiries on the spot, and with written evidence in addition, says that the 42nd Division left Broyes between 2 and 3 p.m., reached Linthelles about 5 p.m., stopped there, and then bivouacked in the zone Linthes-Linthelles-Ognes Pleurs, passing the night there "in general reserve," and moving away only about 5 a.m. on September 10. Fère Champènoise, he adds, was evacuated by the Germans, after an orgy of 24 hours, at about 5.30 p.m. on the 9th, but was traversed during the greater part of the night by German troops coming from Connantre and Gourgancon. Connage thinks that, "on sight of the troops of the 42nd Division, those of General Dubois, certain now of support, advanced, and the division then stopped and turned back to night-quarters." Bülow, he believes, had ordered his retreat at 3.30 p.m. The first French detachment entered Fère Champènoise at 7 a.m. next day.

CHAPTER 8

From Vitry to Verdun

1. THE BATTLE OF VITRY-LE-FRANÇOIS

In the original design of the whole battle, the action of the right or eastern half of the Allied crescent was to be reciprocal to that of the left—while the centre held, Sarrail was to strike out from the region of Verdun westward against the flank of the Prince Imperial, as Maunoury struck out eastward from the region of Paris against that of Kluck. Something of this intention came into effect; but it was much modified by two circumstances. In the first place. General Joffre was driven both by major opportunity and by penury of means to make a choice. He decided that Verdun rather than Paris must run the greater risk, that Kluck's headlong advance made the west the chief theatre for his offensive; and, to make sure on the west, he further weakened the eastern armies. It was, then, on terms of something less than equality of numbers that Sarrail and de Langle had to meet the crown prince, the IV Army, and the Saxon left, with their greatly superior equipment. Secondly, the danger beyond the Meuse could not be ignored; and anxiety on this score necessarily handicapped Joffre's plan.

The German idea was to cut Verdun off on either side: no direct attack was made upon the fortress, the Crown Prince proceeding around the entrenched camp by the west, while the Lorraine armies approached on the east and the IV Army swept over the empty flats of Champagne. On September 5, the German V Army, coming down both sides of the Argonne, had reached the open country south of the forest of Belnoue, that is, from 20 to 30 miles south-west of Verdun, It was, doubtless, expected that the Meuse fortress would be abandoned, as, indeed, it must have been had the French retreat continued longer. Stopped as it was, the crown prince awoke from his dream of making a new and greater Sedan between Dijon and Nancy to find himself under the necessity of forming a double front, toward the east and the south, a very unfavourable position in which to continue an offensive, to say nothing of the possibility of defeat. So far, good; but the situation was anything but secure.

The French were perilously fixed on both sides of the Meuse in a long, sharp salient which had to be defended on three sides. Maunoury and the British, on the west, had escaped any danger of envelopment before the battle began. Without a battalion to spare, Sarrail and Langle stood throughout the struggle, the former with his back, the latter with his flank, to a wall that might give way at any moment. Even a small piercing of the French line between Verdun and Nancy would have involved the fall of the whole salient; while a still more disastrous realignment must have followed a failure of Castlenau and Dubail between Nancy and the Vosges. In these circumstances, Sarrail could not produce, Langle had not the benefit of, such an "effect of suction" as governed the issue farther west.

If the struggle could not be harder, it was more protracted. Partly because it became, when the French reinforcements arrived, a death-grapple of nearly equal masses—more or less than 400,000 men on either side—with little opportunity for manoeuvre, partly because it occurred over obscure countrysides, it has not been adequately appreciated. It is, however, no less important than the battles of the left and the centre; for, if there was involved in them the fate of the capital, here not only Verdun, but Nancy and Toul, with the armies of the eastern frontier, were in the scales. Langle and Sarrail share equally with Gallieni and Maunoury, French, d'Espérey, and Foch the honours of the total victory. The theatre of this part of the conflict forms a triangle, Vitry-Verdun-Bar-le-Duc, whose base is extended on the west to the Camp de Mailly, on the east to the hills on the farther bank of the Meuse.

It is naturally divided into two sectors of very different character: (1) the left, or western, stretching from Mailly to near Revigny, in which the French 4th Army had to meet on a level front the Saxon left and the IV Army of the Duke of Würtemberg; (2) the right, or eastern, including the southern Argonne, the salient of Verdun, and the Heights of the Meuse, held by Sarrail's 3rd Army against the V Army of the German Prince Imperial and a force from the Army of Metz. Both French groups had been greatly weakened to help other commands, Langle giving his 9th and 11th Corps to form Foch's army, while Sarrail surrendered the 42nd Division to Foch, and the 4th Corps to Maunoury.

These transfers, necessary to provision the *generalissimo's* offensive, were compensated just, and only just, in time; thanks to a better outlook on the eastern frontier, Langle de Cary received the 21st Corps from the Vosges on September 9, and on the 8th Sarrail received the 15th Corps from Lorraine, closing with it an alarming gap between the 3rd and 4th Armies. Sarrail then had about ten divisions to the crown prince's twelve; Langle's force was also slightly outnumbered.

On the evening of September 5, Langle's front stood thus: On his *left*, the 17th Corps faced the Saxon XIX Corps between the moorland camp of Mailly and the Sommesous-Vitry railway. At his *centre*, across what may be called the delta of Vitry-le-François, a wide alluvial plain where the merged waters of the Ornain and the Saulx join the Marne, some elements of the 12th Corps and the Colonial Corps stood against the VIII Corps, active and reserve, of the IV Army. Vitry, an important junction of railways, roads, and waterways, is completely dominated by the hills to the north of the delta; and the 12th Corps, to which its defence would have fallen, had been so punished during the retreat that the greater part of it had to be withdrawn to the Aube for reconstitution on the evening of September 5. The Germans, therefore, occupied the town without much difficulty, and rapidly gathered behind it a strong force of artillery.

While the French thus lost the cover of the Saulx and the Marne-Rhine Canal, they could still fall back upon the St. Dizier Canal and the Marne. The centre front, at the beginning of the battle, ran from the Mailly hills at Humbauville, through the villages of Huiron, Frignicourt, Vauclerc, and Favresse, to Blesmes railway junction. On Langle's right, the 2nd Corps had passed the Saulx and its tributary the Ornain, and the Marne-Rhine Canal, leaving only advanced posts on the north of the valley, toward Revigny. To it were opposed Duke Albrecht's VIII Reserve and XVIII Active Corps. The German programme was to break through by Vitry and Revigny into the upper valleys of the Seine, Aube, Marne, and Ornain. Langle's orders were to try to make headway northward, in co-ordination with Sarrail's attack toward the west. In fact, he was barely able to hold his ground until successes on either side relieved the pressure.

Happily, the German Command had not discovered the weakness of the junction between Foch's and Langle's forces; and the Saxons did not at first prove formidable. The 17th Corps was, therefore, able

FRONT of the FRENCH 4th ARMY, Evening Sept.7

C. = Corps
RC. = Reserve Corps
Cav.D.= Cavalry Division
Col.C.= Colonial Corps

Mairy-s-Marne

R.MARNE

Togny-aux-Bœufs

Possesse

To St.Menehould

Bettancourt

Villers-la-Sec Alliancelles

Heiltz-le-Maurupt

Sermaize

(WÜRTEMBERG)

XVIII C.

ORBAIN

Etrepy

D.

Bignicourt

Heiltz l'Eveque

R.SAULX

le Buisson

R.C.

Maurupt

MAURUPT WOOD

Blesmes

BLAISMES

Sorgy

Pringy

Soulanges

(P. of) Couvrot

Brussort

Marolles

Domprémy

VIII C.

Pargny

Ravesse

To St.Dizier

Perthes

Fontaine

Faux-sur-Coole

Maisons-en-Champagne

Vauclerc

Frignicourt

Etrennes

Matignicourt

Norrois

Blaise

Col.C.

VIII C.

Coole

To Paris

XII C. (V.HAUSEN) Vitry

Glannes

Huiron

Toudamp

17 C.

Chatel Raould

Humbauville

23D

13D

Sompuis

9 Cav.D.

(De LANGLE de CARY)

0   5   10   20 Miles

on September 6 to make a short advance west of Courdemanges, nearly to the railway. At the centre, the remaining battalions of the 12th Corps and Lefebvre's Colonials were attacked violently in the morning. Huiron and Courdemanges, at the foot of the hills, were lost, but retaken during the evening. The three delta hamlets of Frignicourt, Vauclerc, and Ecriennes were also lost, the last two to IV Army regulars who had crossed the St. Dizier road and canal.

On the right, the enemy forced the Marne-Rhine canal west of Le Buisson; and for a moment there was a danger of the Colonials being cut off from the 2nd Corps. To fill the breach. General Gerard transferred a brigade of the 4th Division from Pargny to near Favresse. Perhaps because of the consequent weakness of the right of the 2nd Corps, it could not hold the line of the canal from Le Buisson to Etrepy; and Von Tchenk's XVIII Corps entered Alliancelles, 5 miles west of Revigny, and crossed the Ornain, in the afternoon. Reinforced by his Reserve, Tchenk pushed his advance on the following day, September 7, seizing Etrepy village, where the Saulx and Ornain join across the Rhine canal, at dawn, and Sermaize a few hours later.

Langle was here faced with a grave danger. His centre was still holding pretty well: Huiron was again lost, but the Colonials had recovered Ecriennes. On his left, the 17th Corps slightly improved its position, albeit the hazardous thinness of this part of the French front could not be much longer concealed. It was for his wings, therefore, that he was most anxious; and thither the two promised corps of reinforcements, the 15th and 21st, were directed. The 15th reached the right, to prolong Sarrail's line, just in time. The enemy had, at a heavy cost, passed the Saulx-Ornain valley, with its many lesser water-courses, and had reached the edge of the wooded plateau of Trois-Fontaines, beyond which, ten miles south of Sermaize, lay the important town of St. Dizier. To break through thus far would be to cut off Sarrail at Bar-le-Duc from Langle at Vitry-le-François; it would be the doom of Verdun, and probably of the French centre. The greatness of the stake, the bitterness of the disappointment, afford the only explanation of the abnormal savagery shown by the Crown Prince's troops in this region.

On September 8, the fighting reached its fiercest intensity. Tchenk pressed furiously his attack against and around Pargny, which his men entered at 5 p.m., after suffering heavy losses. Maurupt was also taken, but Gerard quickly recaptured it. The crisis, though not the struggle, was over with the arrival of the 15th Corps between Couvonges and

Mognéville, threatening Tchenk's left flank if he should attempt any farther advance. At the centre, a reconstituted half of the 12th Corps and the Colonial Corps were engaged in desperate combats. Courdemanges, Ecriennes, and Mont Moret fell in the morning; but the hill was retaken at nightfall. Several times driven out of Favresse, a brigade of the 2nd Corps finally held the village, and arrested the progress of the VIII Reserve Corps towards Blesmes railway junction. With constant violence of give and take, these positions were little changed on the following day.

On the left, two regiments of the 17th Corps, pending the arrival of the other half of the 12th (23rd Division), bore throughout the 8th the onset of a fresh Saxon Division (xxiii of the XII Reserve Corps) to the west of Humbauville; while the remainder of the 17th Corps fell back a little before the XIX Corps, but advanced anew in the afternoon. In the evening, the balance was more than restored by the appearance of Baquet's Division of the 21st Corps at the extreme left of the army, which next day (September 9) drove the Saxon right back in disorder toward Sommesous, liberating Humbauville, and enabling the 17th Corps also to gain ground. The other Division of the 21st Corps (43rd) had now reached the scene; and, on the 10th, Langle was able to make a strong offensive on this side, in association with Foch's pursuit of the retreating Saxons.

2. Sarrail Holds the Meuse Salient

The French 3rd Army, when Sarrail took over its command from Ruffey on August 30, was a thing of shreds and patches. The 42nd Division of Sarrail's own 6th Corps was being sent to Foch, leaving behind two other divisions, and a brigade of a third which had been broken up. The 4th Corps was about to leave for Paris, to take part in the battle of the Ourcq. There remained the 5th and the diminished 6th Corps, General Paul Durand's Group of Divisions of Reserve (67, 75, and 65), formerly under Maunoury, the 72nd Reserve Division, forming part of the garrison of Verdun, and the 7th Cavalry Division. Verdun depending directly upon General Headquarters, Coutanceau and Heymann, the governor and the *divisionaire*, were not subject to Sarrail's orders; but they co-operated admirably. Yet another *southron*, Sarrail was fifty-eight years old, a tall, slight figure, with (at that time) short white beard and moustache, blue eyes, and a gentle manner bespeaking the scholar and thinker rather than the man of action he proved himself to be.

After service in Tunis and with the Foreign Legion, he had been advanced by Generals André and Picquart, and rose by steady stages from colonel in 1905 to corps commander. Across the mists of more painful days, I recall the strong impression he made upon me when I first met him at Verdun in December 1914.

From near the frontier, the 3rd Army had fallen back, at the end of August, westward to the Meuse between Stenay and Vilosnes, leaving the reserve group and garrison troops to make a thin line of defence on the east of the river, just beyond the radius of the entrenched camp and the edge of the Meuse Heights from Ornes to Vigneulles. "Entrenched camp" is the conventional name; but there were no serious entrenchments in those days, and scarcely any, as I can testify, three months later. The forts and thickly-wooded hills were sufficient, with the field army free, to determine the German Grand Staff to leave Verdun, as it was leaving Paris, aside. The French, however, could yet have no certainty on this score.

During the first days of September, the 5th and 6th Corps pivoted around the west of Verdun; and, when they had completed the semicircle, the problem had to be faced. The hazard of the old fortress was no mere matter of sentiment. Its fall would mean the loss of all it could contribute to the contemplated attack on the enemy's flank, and of a great strength of artillery and munitions that could not be removed, as well as of a formidable position. On the other hand, there lay Joffre's plan, and the reasoning that had saved the British Army from internment at Maubeuge. The *generalissimo's* orders were express: the 3rd Army must keep its liberty, and must, accordingly, retire to the north of Bar-le-Duc, and possibly as far as Joinville. It was not only Verdun, but his power of threatening the German flank, that Sarrail hoped to save. He resolved, therefore, to give ground as slowly as possible, keeping his right in touch with the fortress to the last moment, and to risk, up to a certain point, a breach of contact with de Langle de Cary. At daybreak on September 6, his forces were ranged over the broadly rolling fields and moorlands, facing westward, as follows:

Right.—Several regiments of the Verdun garrison were coming into line about Nixéville, and the three reserve divisions were spread thence along the Verdun-Bar highroad (afterwards famous as the "*Via Sacra*") and narrow-gauge railway as far as Issoncourt, having before them the German XVI Active Corps reinforced some hours later by the VI Reserve.

Centre.—The 6th Corps extended through Beauzée south-west-ward to near Vaubécourt, with d'Urbal's cavalry about Lisle-en-Barrois, facing the German XIII Corps.

Left.—The 5th Corps stood across the path of the German VI and part of the Duke of Würtemberg's XVIII Corps among the villages north of Revigny, from Villotte to Nettancourt.

Although the dispositions of the German V Army—one corps of which was detained 10 miles north, and another a like distance west, of Verdun—at this juncture do not suggest over-confidence, an order found on the field shows that the crown prince now believed himself sure of a dramatic victory. At 8 p.m. on Saturday the 5th, instructions had been issued for the XVI, XIII, and VI Corps (in this order from east to west), with the XVIII Reserve on their right, to drive resolutely south, and to seize Bar-le-Duc and the Marne crossings to and beyond Revigny, while the IV Cavalry Corps exploited the breach between Sarrail and Langle's forces, and hurried on "on the line Dijon-Besançon-Belfort." As a whole, this design at once failed. The German advance had hardly begun when Heymann's and Durand's reservists, on the north, threatened its line of supply by an attack toward Ville-sur-Cousance, St. André, and Ippecourt; while, at the centre, the 6th Corps pushed toward Pretz, Evres, and Sommaisne.

The small advantages gained were soon negatived, and at night the line was back at Rampont, Souhesmes, Souilly, Seraucourt, and Rembercourt; but a half of the crown prince's units were held, if not crippled. This must have been all the more irritating to him because of the rapid success of his VI Corps and the IV Army. During the morning, in fact, the French left was driven out of Laheycourt, Sommeilles, and Nettancourt, then from Brabant and Villers-aux-Vents, and before night from Laimont and the market-town of Revigny. The crown prince had reached the Marne just as Kluck was beginning to retire from it. General Micheler and the 5th Corps, mourning many of their men and a divisional chief. General Roques, but cheered to think that the first reinforcements from Lorraine would arrive on the morrow, drew together their ranks at Villotte, Louppy, and Vassincourt.

On September 7, the encounter became closer and more severe, without any marked change of position, the 67th and 75th Divisions, on the right, carrying Ippecourt by assault (to lose it next day), the 6th Corps resisting obstinately on either side of Rembercourt, and, on the left, the 5th Corps meeting furious attacks around Vassincourt.

In the evening, the 29th Division of Castelnau's 15th Corps passed the Marne to Combles and Fains, two battalions of *chasseurs* reaching Couvonges and the neighbouring woods. On the morning of the 8th, Sarrail's 5th Corps was supported and extended by the full strength of the 15th. One brigade of the latter was directed by Vassincourt toward Revigny, but could make no headway.

Other brigades came into action near Louppy and Mognéville; nevertheless, Villotte and Louppy-le-Chateau were lost. News arriving that de Langle's right had been driven back from Sermaize to Cheminon, and that Duke Albrecht's forces were at the foot of the Trois-Fontaines plateau, d'Urbal was ordered to take his cavalry corps round, and to harry the east flank of Tchenk's movement. No sooner had it reached the upper Saulx valley for this purpose than Sarrail hurried it back and away north-eastward to meet a yet extremer danger beyond the Meuse.

Below St. Mihiel, the river meanders beside a wall of steep hills, on the crests of which were situated a number of forts, dependencies of the Toul and Verdun systems, designed as observatories and points of arrest against an enemy march toward the principal crossings. The most important of these forts were Genicourt, Troyon, and the Roman Camp along the east, and Paroches on the west, banks. Troyon was an extensive square structure, sunk in a deep, wide moat, and garrisoned by about 450 men. Commanding the gap of Spada, it enjoyed, in its remote solitude, magnificent views over the plain of the Woevre as far as Metz, and the hills and valleys between St. Mihiel and Verdun. It has not been explained why the troops of Metz did not reach the Meuse earlier; probably their heavy artillery delayed them.

On the morning of September 7, there was no sign of trouble on the Heights, and the commander of Troyon, Captain Xavier Heym, went out partridge shooting. At noon, forces of infantry and cavalry, with thirty cannon, were reported on the roads from Hattonchatel and Heudicourt. The bombardment began at 2 p.m.; and before another day had passed, 400 heavy shells, some of them from 12-inch mortars, had been thrown upon the fort, putting seven guns out of action, and demolishing large parts of the casemates and galleries. This news was a crown to Sarrail's anxieties. He had no reserves left; the 3rd Army was wholly engaged. Its right might at any time be crushed, its left enveloped: now it was menaced in the rear. The dispatch thither of some tired cavalry was, of course, the merest bluff. Whatever might have been the fate of Verdun, the crossing of the Meuse at a higher

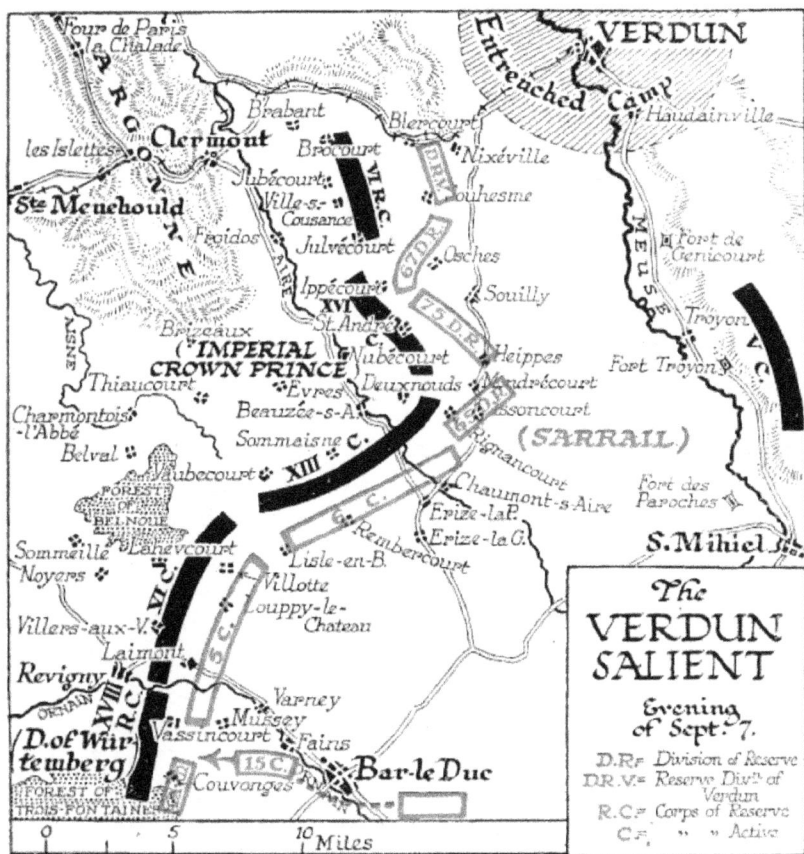

The VERDUN SALIENT

Evening of Sept. 7.

D.R^f = Division of Reserve
DR.V = Reserve Divⁿ of Verdun
R.C = Corps of Reserve
C = " " Active

VERDUN

Entrenched Camp

Four de Paris
la Chalade
les Islettes
Ste Menehould
Clermont
Brabant
Blercourt
Nixéville
Jouhesme
Haudainville
Brocourt
VI R.C.
Jubécourt
Ville-s-Cousance
Figidos
Julvécourt
Osches
Fort de Genicourt
Ippécourt
St. André
Brizeaux
IMPERIAL CROWN PRINCE
C.
Nubécourt
Souilly
Troyon
V.C.
Thiaucourt
Deuxnouds
Heippes
Mondrécourt
Fort Troyon
Charmontois-l'Abbé
Evres
Beauzée-s-A.
Issoncourt
(SARRAIL)
Belval
Sommaisne
C.
Vaubecourt
XIII
Pignancourt
Fort des Paroches
FOREST OF BEL-NOUE
Rembercourt
Chaumont-s-Aire
Erize-la P.
Erize-la G.
S. Mihiel
Sommeille
VI C.
Lisle-en-B.
Noyers
Lahéveourt
Villers-aux-V.
Villotte
Louppy-le-Chateau
Laimont
5 C.
Revigny
XVIII R.C.
ORNAIN
Varney
Mussey
D. of Würtemberg
Vassincourt
Fains
FOREST OF TROIS-FONTAINES
15 C.
Couvonges
Bar-le-Duc

0   5   10 Miles

point would have meant the withdrawal of Sarrail's right, and the opening for the crown prince of the shorter route for reinforcements and supplies which he so much needed.

On the evening of September 8, Joffre authorised the commander of the 3rd Army to draw back from Verdun along the west bank of the Meuse. Sarrail, who by this time knew of Kluck's retreat and the magnificent efforts of the French centre, was determined to hold on, at least till Troyon should fall; but the river bridges were cut and the forts left to their own resources. At 9 a.m. on the 9th, Verdun signalled that Fort Genicourt was being bombarded by heavy guns. At 11 o'clock, Troyon no longer had a piece in action. There were then in the neighbouring hills enemy columns amounting to the greater part of an army corps, with artillery, aviation parks, and convoys. Two infantry assaults were repelled by rifle and machine-gun fire. Meantime, General Durand's Reserve Divisions maintained their ground near Verdun, the 75th suffering severely in repeated attacks on the crown prince's fine of communications; and, on the left, part of the 15th Corps having pushed across the Saulx into the Trois-Fontaines Forest, and then struck north, Mognéville was captured by assault from two sides.

The turning-point of the battle had been reached. During the night of September 9, while his 6th Corps was repelling a furious attempt of the XIII and XVI Corps to break through, Sarrail learned that the British were well over the Marne, with d'Espérey nearly abreast of them, that Bülow had succumbed to Foch's will, and that the Saxons had begun to yield before Langle. Many an exhausted trooper, in lonely thickets, ditches, and broken farm buildings, only received the glad tidings two days later; yet the magic spark of a definite hope was lit. The 4th Army could now look after itself. The 3rd had failed to make good its first threat against the German flank. Even at this distance, however, the western "effect of suction" was at last faintly felt. The XVIII Reserve Corps was perceptibly weakening. During the 10th, the 15th Corps pushed through to the edge of the Trois-Fontaines Forest, approached Sermaize and Andernay, and sent some hundreds of prisoners to the rear.

If the right could only hold! In the afternoon the XIII and XVI were reinforced by the VI Reserve Corps (replaced by the V Reserve), Rembercourt, Courcelles, Seraucourt, and Souilly, were lost in succession. The struggle continued unrelaxed along a line but slightly withdrawn, from Condé-en-Barrois, through Erize-la-Petite and Neuville, to Rambluzin; and on the extreme right, about Vaudelaincourt, the

72nd Division performed prodigies. In the evening, the 67th and 75th Reserve Divisions were actually removed from the line, preparatory to an abandonment of Verdun. The enemy did not perceive the movement till too late.

And the gallant four hundred of Troyon continued to bar the way to the Meuse. Under cover of a flag, two German officers and a trumpeter rode up to the fort, and demanded its surrender. "Never!" replied Heym; "I shall blow it up sooner." And finally: "Get out, I've seen enough of you. *A bientôt, à Metz.*"[1] Who could imagine that "*bientôt*" was four years away?

---

1. Giraud (*Histoire*) gives a rather different report of this dialogue. I rely upon an article in *L'Illustration* of Jan. 9, 1915, containing a long passage from the diary of "an officer who was the soul of the defence"—doubtless. Captain Heym himself.

CHAPTER 9

Victory

It is now apparent that a record of the battle covering the whole front day by day would give no clear view of its development. The climax came not everywhere at the same hour, or even on the same day, but in a remarkable succession—beginning on the Ourcq about noon on September 9, and immediately afterward on Foch's front (the two areas most directly menaced by the advance of French and d'Espérey), reaching de Langle de Cary the next morning, and Sarrail only on the night of the 10th. It remains to trace the completion of the victory.

Maunoury had failed of his objective: after four days of grinding combat, he had advanced his centre some 10 miles eastward, but was, at noon on September 9, still an average of 6 miles short of the Ourcq, before Vareddes, Etrepilly, and Acy-en-Multien; while his left was painfully bent back from the last-named point westward to Silly-le-Long. Every effort to obtain an effective superiority of strength, and to break through or around the enemy's right, had been thwarted by Kluck's speed in supporting that flank. Looking at this part of the field only, it might be supposed that a substantial reinforcement of either side at this moment would have precipitated a disaster on the other. A wider view shows a very different balance.

If Maunoury could have found one or two fresh divisions, the German I Army might have been shattered; a further French withdrawal to and beyond the Marne would not have entailed any such grave consequences. In fact, both armies were exhausted; neither had any remaining reserve to call in. The decision came from the next sector of the front. Since Le Cateau, the little British Army had played only a secondary part; it was now to have the honour of saving the left wing of the Allies for the third time. From the moment it began to recross the Marne, solidly extended by d'Espérey, its intervention became a conclusive factor. It must have been during the morning of the 9th that the German Grand Staff reconciled itself to the necessity of a general retreat, at least from Senlis as far east as Fère Champènoise.

In after years, when the simple art of entrenchment had been elaborated and the men had become incredibly hardened to shell-fire, these same wooded hillsides would be contested foot by foot. At this time, freer and larger movements were required, especially when no considerable aid could be expected, when supplies were short, and the danger appeared on two sides. Kluck's very persistence, not having attained any positive result, told against him. His men might be persuaded that this was "not a retreat, but only a regrouping of forces for strategic reasons"[1]; all officers but the youngest knew that the "smashing blow "had been broken, the famous enveloping movement had failed, a new plan of campaign must be thought out. For that, rest must be found upon a naturally strong defensive position such as the line of the Aisne and the Laon mountains.

By noon on September 9—a gloomy, showery day—the call was urgent. The I Army could do no more. Its ammunition was nearly exhausted. Its best units were physically and morally broken. It had no longer the strength to bury its dead—they were unclothed and cast upon great pyres of straw and wood; and the odour of burning flesh added a new horror to the eastern part of the battlefield. Kluck's advance from Nanteuil and Betz, during the morning, was only a diversion, a last blow to secure liberty of movement. At 11 a.m., the French found Betz evacuated; Nanteuil and Etavigny were still held. Whipped on by headquarters, General Boëlle's two divisions of the 4th Corps crept forward again. During the afternoon, aviators observed long enemy convoys, followed by troop columns of all arms, crowding all the roads from the Ourcq to the Aisne. For several critical hours they were screened by a vigorous defence of the centre lines east of Etrepilly and Puisieux.

This and a slight reaction near Nanteuil were the final spasms of the battle of the Ourcq. We have seen that Marwitz, beaten by the 1st British Corps at Montreuil-aux-Lions, 13 miles due east of Etrepilly, in the early afternoon, had gone back to the Clignon, and that the whole angle of the Marne and Ourcq had been evacuated. Kluck could flatter himself to have held out to the last possible moment.

---

1. Colonel Feyler's *Avant-Propos Stratégiques* are particularly valuable for a pitiless analysis of the "moral manoeuvre" represented in early German accounts of the first part of the campaign.

Gradually the remainder of his artillery was removed from the Trocy plateau; and, under cover of night, all but rearguards made off to the north-east. The 6th Army seems to have been too weary to discover the flight of its redoubtable foe until daybreak on the following morning. The pursuit began at once, following both sides of the Ourcq. It was checked on the left by small detachments under cover of the Forest of Villers-Cotterets, an obstacle the importance of which was to be more fully proved in the last year of the war; while Kluck established new lines along the hills beyond the Aisne, from the Forest of Laigle to Soissons.

So the red tide of battle sank from the stubble-fields and coppices above Meaux; but burning farmsteads and hayricks, broken bridges, shattered churches and houses, many unburied dead, and piles of abandoned ammunition and stores spoke of the frightful frenzy that had passed over a scene marked a week before by quiet charm and happy labour. In the orchards and folds of the open land, the bodies of invader and defender lay over against each other, sometimes still grappling. Every here and there horses rotted on the roads and fields, presently to be burned on pyres of wood, for fear of pestilence arising. Most of the human victims had been buried where they fell; little wooden crosses sometimes marked their great common graves. On September 10, General Maunoury addressed to his troops the following message of congratulation and thanks:—

The 6th Army has supported for five full days, without interruption or slackening, the combat against a numerous enemy whose moral was heightened by previous success. The struggle has been hard; the losses under fire, from fatigue due to lack of sleep and sometimes of food, have surpassed what was to be anticipated. You have borne it all with a valour, firmness, and endurance that words are powerless to glorify as they deserve. Comrades I the Commander-in-Chief asked you in the name of the Fatherland to do more than your duty; you have responded to his appeal even beyond what seemed possible. Thanks to you, victory crowns our flags. Now that you know the glorious satisfaction of it, you will not let it slip away. As for me, if I have done some good, I have been repaid by the greatest honour that has been granted me in a long career, that of commanding such men as you.

Fifteen miles of high, open farmlands, cut by deep valleys, divide the Upper Ourcq from the Aisne. The British Army covered rather more than this distance on September 11 and 12, meeting serious opposition only at Braisne and on the high ground between the Vesle and the Aisne. The cavalry on the left, indeed, reached the latter river at Soissons on the evening of the 11th. Here the German retreat came to an abrupt end. Sir John French speaks loosely of the German losses as "enormous"; in fact, his 1st and 2nd Corps and cavalry took in one day 13 guns, 7 machine-guns, about 2000 prisoners, and many broken-down wagons. The spectacle of booty, always fallacious, was in this case peculiarly so. The main body of the enemy was defeated, but not routed; driven back, but not dispersed. From Courchamp to Soissons, the fullest measure of the retreat, is, by road, about 60 miles. Many stragglers gave themselves up along this route in a starving condition; many others hid for days in the woods of the Brie tableland and the Tardenois, where I witnessed several man-hunts conducted by French and British rearguards. In the final pursuit, Kluck may have lost 5000 or 6000 men—a small number compared with the costs to either side of the previous fighting.

The best of battle-plans is the most adaptable. Perhaps Joffre had not looked to the British Expeditionary Force for such a contribution to the general end. Maunoury, by his original orders, was to cross the Ourcq toward Chateau Thierry, driving Kluck up against Bülow; d'Espérey was to sweep up northward and meet him at right angles. The shifting of the greater part of the German I Army to the west of the Ourcq, and the consequent thinning of its connection with the II Army, displaced the action without changing its essential character. In the event, it was the British Army that led the northward movement [2]; d'Espérey, who, at the outset, had four active corps and three divisions of reserve for a front of only 25 miles (from Jouy-le-Chatel to Sézanne), while quickly compelling the withdrawal of Bülow's right, was able to give his neighbour, Foch, aid without which the whole victory would have been compromised.

On the evening of September 9, General Franchet d'Espérey is-

---

2. Major-General Maurice says: "I am convinced that history will decide that it was the crossing of the Marne in the early hours of the 9th by the British Army which turned the scale against Kluck and saved Maunoury at a time of crisis. . . . That an army which on August 21 had been all but surrounded by an enemy who outnumbered it by two to one should have fought its way out, retreated 170 miles, and then immediately turned about and taken a decisive part in the battle which changed the course of the campaign of 1914, is as wonderful an achievement as is to be found in the history of war" (Forty Days).

sued from his headquarters at Montmirail the following stirring message to his army:—

> Soldiers! On the memorable fields of Montmirail, Vauchamps, and Champaubert, which a century ago witnessed our ancestors' victories over the Prussians of Blücher, our vigorous offensive has triumphed over the German resistance. Held on his flanks, his centre broken, the enemy is now retreating toward the east and north by forced marches. The most redoubtable Corps of old Prussia, the Westphalian, Hanoverian, and Brandenburg contingents, are falling back hurriedly before you.
>
> This first success is only a prelude. The enemy is shaken, but not definitely beaten. You will still have to undergo severe hardships, to make long marches, to fight hard battles. May the image of your country soiled by barbarians be ever before your eyes! Never has a complete sacrifice for it been more necessary.
>
> While saluting the heroes who have fallen in the last few days, my thoughts turn toward you, the victors in the next battle.
>
> Forward, soldiers, for France!

At the time when the commander of the 5th Army penned these words, the situation was a singular one. The issue of the battle as a whole was, in fact, decided: the retreat of the three western, if not also of the next two, German armies had been ordered. Yet the only part of the Allied line that had been materially advanced was that before French and d'Espérey; and Foch, Langle, and Sarrail were still in a situation apparently desperate. Instead of being on the Marne between Epernay and Châlons, Foch's centre was lying in fragments 30 miles to the south, at Faux and Salon, after the debacle of Fère Champènoise. Why, then, did Bülow beat a hasty retreat at about 5 p.m. on that critical day? We have done justice to the manoeuvre of Grossetti's division; even if this had been executed six hours earlier, it could not have sufficed to produce a transformation so sudden and complete.

To understand the German collapse, a wider stretch of the front at the hour named must be scrutinised. Its chief feature will be found in the length of Bülow's right flank, extended no less than 40 miles from Chateau Thierry to Corroy. Over against this flank were gathered three corps of the 5th and five divisions of the 9th Armies; while the German thrust was being made by only four Prussian corps with a few Saxon detachments. The disparity was greater in quality than in numbers. D'Espérey's Corps were relatively fresh, and in high spirits;

Bülow's were fagged and to some extent disorganised. In these circumstances, the detachment of the 10th Corps to Foch, and the attack of the 1st Corps at Corfelix and Le Thoult, would probably have an effect upon the German Command which the transfer of the 42nd Division to Linthes would emphasise. Grossetti's movement might be risked; the possibility of a larger blow from the west against a flank of 40 miles could not be faced. On a smaller scale, the Saxons were in like danger from the east, where the 21st Corps, just detrained from the Vosges, had made a disturbing appearance during the day. The German centre had had too much and too little success—too little to give an immediate decision, too much, and at too heavy a price, for the security of its own formation.

That evening it blew a half-gale, and poured cats-and-dogs, along the Marne valley and the Sézanne hills. The clay pocket of St. Gond became a quagmire; the few roads crossing the west part of the marshes were covered by the French "75's," and the slaughter they wrought gave rise to legends recalling what happened a century before. The 10th Corps, extended by the 51st Reserve Division, struck out eastward during the night from Champaubert, Baye, and Soizy, and on September 10 cleared the plain between the marshes and the Châlons highroad. At 5 a.m. on the 10th, the Moroccan Division and the 9th Corps reached the east end of the marshes, but were stopped before Pierre-Morains and Ecury, where a sharp engagement took place. The 42nd Division was also checked on the Somme before Normée and Lenharrée, as was the 11th Corps, which had come up on its right, before Vassimont and Haussimont.

On Friday, September 11, the French entered Epernay, the champagne capital; and on the following day the enemy evacuated the city of Rheims, continuing to hold the neighbouring hill forts. Thousands of men and large quantities of ammunition and material were abandoned; but it soon became evident that the retreat was not an aimless flight. On September 11, 12, and 13, the German gunners on Mt. Berru and Nogent l'Abbesse bombarded the ancient and beautiful city. The *façade* of the cathedral, with its precious sculptures and windows, received irreparable damage; the choir-stalls and other fine woodwork within were destroyed, the Archiepiscopal Palace, the City Hall, and neighbouring buildings burned down. The establishment of a solid German rampart extending from the Oise across the Laon hills, dipping to the outlying forts of the old Rheims defences, and then reaching across Champagne, through the Argonne, and around

Verdun, to Metz, was to prove one of the great achievements of the war, a defiance through nearly four years of sacrifice.

For a moment, at the end of the Battle of the Marne, it seemed that such a possibility might be averted. Conneau's 2nd Cavalry Corps, the 18th Corps, and the 53rd and 69th Reserve Divisions had all passed the Aisne, between Bourg and Berry -au-Bac, on September 14. Conneau now found himself supporting a frontal attack of d'Espérey's 18th Corps and reserves upon the abrupt cliffs by which the Aisne hills fall to the flats of Champagne, the Craonne plateau. A force from Lorraine under General von Heeringen was to be brought into this vital sector, between Kluck and Bülow; meanwhile, the connection was uncertain. While, a little farther west, Sir Douglas Haig was boldly reaching up to the Chemin des Dames, d'Espérey sent Conneau north-eastward as far as Sissonne; and thence one of his divisions was ordered to take in reverse the German troops posted above Craonne. Success seemed assured, when the 18th Corps and the reserve divisions were beaten back; and Conneau, fearing to be isolated on the north of the river, recrossed it. All the energy of General Maud'huy was needed to preserve a foothold on the right bank. Within a fortnight, the long deadlock of trench warfare had begun, and a new phase of the war had opened in the north-west.

At 7 a.m. on September 12, a patrol of chasseurs of the 9th Army entered Châlons, the Saxons hurrying off before them to the Suippes Valley; a few hours later, General Foch established his headquarters in the old garrison town. The Saxon Army was now in a condition worse than that of the British after Le Cateau; and it disappeared as an independent command with the fixing of the lines in Champagne, Foch's rapid march to the north-east made the German positions south of the Argonne impossible. From September 11, Langle was able to devote himself wholly to the IV Army, By noon that day, they had evacuated their defences in and around Vitry-le-François; and in the evening, the left of the 4th Army (21st, 17th, and 12th Corps) reached the Marne between Sogny and Couvrot, while the Colonial Corps passed the Saulx near Heiltz-l'Evêque, and the 2nd held the Ornain from Etrepy to Sermaize, in touch with the 15th Corps of Sarrail's Army, which was approaching Revigny.

When, on September 12, General Espinasse's troops entered that town, it had been systematically destroyed. The central streets presented an extraordinary scene of devastation. Nothing remained except parts of the lower walls and, within, masses of stone, brick, and mortar broken small, with scraps of iron and charred wood. The town hall, a graceful building in French classic style, had about a half of its outer fabric standing. The church, which was of historic interest, was roofless and much damaged within. Houses and shops had been first pillaged, and then fired. Most of the neighbouring villages had been similarly treated. One scene stands out in my memory. Sermaize-les-Bains was a pleasant town of 4000 inhabitants, on the Saulx, with a mineral spring, a large sugar refinery, and a handsome old church. It had been demolished from end to end by skilled incendiarism.

Of 500 houses, only half a dozen remained standing. Except a few chimneys and pieces of wall, the rest was a rubbish heap, recalling Pompeii before the antiquaries cleared it up. There had been an ironmonger's shop—you could trace it by the masses of molten iron and clotted nails. There had been a glass and china shop—you could trace it by the lumps of milky coagulate that stuck out among the litter of brick. When I arrived, a few of the inhabitants were returning, women, children, and old men, carrying with them large, rough loaves of bread, or wheeling barrows of firewood. The church was roofless and gutted, the nave piled with fragments of stone. The curb's house was also burned out. In the middle of a grass-plot behind it stood a white statue of the Virgin, turning clasped hands toward the ruins.

How much these and other indulgences impeded the military effort of the crown prince's men, how much they strengthened the spirit of the French soldiers, may be supposed, but not measured. They mark with an odious emphasis for history the hour not only of a signal defeat, but of a profound disillusionment, which was to deepen slowly to the utter discredit of a system and an idea hitherto not seriously challenged. The game was played; with rage, the Prince Imperial submitted. Having held his left impassive for a day, while the right pivoted slowly backward toward the Argonne, on the night of September 12 the order was given for a general and rapid withdrawal; and on the following days, the French 4th and 3rd Armies found themselves in face of new enemy lines drawn from the Moronvilliers hills near Rheims, by Souain, Ville-sur-Tourbe, and Varennes, to the Meuse at Forges, 8 miles north of Verdun. The Châlons-Verdun road and railway were disengaged, a result of great importance, and the old fortress, with its outposts on the Meuse Heights, was definitively relieved. The Crown Prince pitched his tent on the feudal eyrie of Montfaucon. General Sarrail picked up his direct communications with Paris, faced round to Metz and the north, and prepared for the future.

And the master of the victorious host? On September 11, he had issued the following "*Ordre general* No. 15":

The battle that has been proceeding for five days is ending in incontestable victory. The retreat of the German I, II, and III Armies is accentuated before our left and our centre. In its turn, the IV enemy Army has begun to fall hack to the north of Vitry-le-François and Sermaize. Everywhere the enemy is leaving on the ground many wounded and quantities of munitions. Everywhere prisoners are being taken. While they advance our troops note the marks of the intensity of the struggle, and the importance of the means employed by the Germans to resist our onset. The vigorous renewal of the offensive determined our success. Officers and soldiers, you have all answered my appeal. You have deserved well of the Fatherland.

In a telegram to the Minister of War, he added:—

The Government of the Republic may be proud of the armies it has organised.

Neither then nor later did any phrase more worthy of the occasion than these fall from the pen or the lips of the *generalissimo*. In success as in failure, he was the same silent, weighty, cheerful figure—Joffre the Taciturn, to the end.

CHAPTER 10

The Defence of the East

General Joffre's Instruction of September 1 had prescribed that the whole offensive should pivot upon the right. The defence of the eastern front, as a wall protecting the western and central armies, and the pivot of their recoil—essential condition of the general success—was assigned to Generals de Castelnau and Dubail. The 2nd and 1st Armies had been severely punished at the outset of the campaign; and, evidently, a heavy task now lay before them.

The second of the German princes, Ruprecht of Bavaria, with the last corps of the Bavarian Army, could not be given other than a principal role; and Heeringen, chief of the 7th Army, Prussian War Minister during a critical part of the period of preparation, was also a veteran of the Grand Staff, with which he had worked for more than thirty years.

On September 6, the Grand Quartier General specified that Castlenau and Dubail should remain on their positions defensively till the end of the battle of the Marne.

We have seen that, after the failure of the offensives of Morhange-Sarrebourg and Mulhouse, the two armies retreated rapidly, but in such a way that, taking up an angular formation from the Grand Couronné of Nancy southward to the Gap of Charmes, and thence eastward to the Donon, they were able, on August 25, to fall upon the two flanks of the advancing enemy with instant effect. There was then a pause, due in part to heavy fogs, for several days, in which either side prepared for a new encounter.

The circumstances differed considerably from those in the west. For their abortive offensives, the two armies had been given a distinct superiority of force on the eastern frontier; but, after the successful defence of the Gap of Charmes, this superiority had been drawn upon repeatedly by the *generalissimo* to feed his main design. Thus, Castlenau had sent from the 2nd Army: on August 15, the 18th Corps, to Lanrezac, for the advance to the Sambre; on August 18 and September 4, the 9th Corps, to the 4th Army, from which it was detached to Foch's Army of the centre; on September 3, the 15th Corps, to Sarrail; and on September 1, the greater part of the 2nd Cavalry Corps, to the space between the British and French 5th Armies.

At the same time, Dubail, while absorbing gradually the body of Pau's "Army of Alsace," sent the 21st Corps, on September 4, to Langle's left, and the 13th Corps, on September 9, to the region of Compiègne for the battle of the Aisne; after which, in the middle of September, when the great victory had been won, the 1st Army took over the whole of the Nancy front from the 2nd Army. These deplacements were necessary, and remarkably timed and executed; but they represent a not inconsiderable diminution of effective strength at a grave juncture. To compensate for their losses, the High Command could only send to the Lorraine Armies divisions of reserves. Their performance surpassed all French, and rather justified German, anticipations. It is, however, to be remarked that the opposed forces of the Bavarian Crown Prince and Heeringen underwent a similar transformation.

In addition to their reserve divisions, they received between them, at the end of August and the beginning of September, something like 100,000 men of the *Ersatz* and *Landwehr*. An *Ersatz* division of the Guard was engaged near Lunéville, and Bavarian and Saxon *Ersatz* divisions appeared on the Upper Meurthe.

A large part of the Bavarian and Rhenish *Landwehr* was also used in Lorraine. Heeringen's army, itself constituted in Alsace, moved northward after Dubail, and, when arrested on the Upper Mortagne and the Northern Vosges, detached two of its corps to the Bavarian Army for the crucial attack on the Grand Couronné. Metz, Strasbourg, and the garrison towns of Alsace were used as reservoirs on the German side, just as were Toul, Epinal, and Belfort on the French, until both antagonists had drawn their last possible reinforcement, and the invasion failed by exhaustion.

For the actions now to be followed, the opposed forces, from north to south, were as follows:—

2nd ARMY (General de CASTEL-NAU).

73rd Division Reserve (General Chatelain).
From Toul. In the Moselle valley, south of Pont-à-Mousson.

2nd Group of Divisions of Reserve (General Leon Durand).
59th, 68th (General Aubignose), 70th (General Fayolle). From Ste. Geneviève to near Réméréville, the centre of the Nancy front.

64th Division Reserve (General Compagnon). Supporting the 70th before Nancy.

20th Corps (General Balfourier, succeeding General Foch).
39th and 11th Divisions, with a Colonial brigade attached. Across the Sanon, from Haraucourt to near Vitrimont.

74th Division Reserve (General Bigot).
Astride the Mortagne, from Mont to Xermamenil.

16th Corps (General Taverna).
32nd and 31st Divisions. On the Mortagne, between Einvaux and Gerbéviller.

1st ARMY (General DUBAIL).

8th Corps (General de Castelli), with 8 groups of Alpinist reserves added. From Gerbéviller southward.

6th Cavalry Division.
Till September 8.

13th Corps (General Alix).
At the centre, till September 10.

58th Division Reserve.

57th Division Reserve (General Bernard).

71st Division Reserve.
In support, south of Bruyères.

14th Corps.
West of the St. Dié valley.

44th Division (General Soyer).
From the Army of Alsace.

41st Division.
South of St. Dié and east of the Meurthe.

VI ARMY (CROWN PRINCE OF BAVARIA).

33rd Division Reserve.
From Metz, for the movement in the Woevre. South of Pont-à-Mousson.

2 or 3 Landwehr Divisions, south of Nomeny.

II Bavarian Corps (General von Martini).
Between the Sanon and the Vezouse.

Guard Ersatz Division.

III Bavarian Corps (General von Gebsattel).
Between the Seille and the Sanon.

XXI Corps.
Between the Meurthe and the Mortagne.

I Bavarian Corps (General von Xylander).

I Bavarian Corps Reserve (General von Fasbender).

VII ARMY (General von HEERINGEN, till the night of September 6).

XIV Corps (General von Hoeningen).
West of Baccarat.

XIV Corps Reserve.
Both the above were transferred to the VI Army on September 6.

XV Corps (General von Deimling).
Detached, September 7, with Heeringen, to the Aisne.

XV Corps Reserve.
At first only the 30th Division Reserve; later the 39th Division Reserve arrived. In the St. Dié valley.

Ersatz and Landwehr Brigades.

Uncertainty as to some German units, and the continual transfer on both sides, make an accurate comparison of strength impossible. M. Hanotaux [1] estimates the French forces at their maximum at 532,000, and the German at 530,000 men. This was during the battle of the Gap of Charmes, and at the end of August.

On September 4, Castlenau had lost 70,000 men or more, and the 1st Army was similarly reduced in the following days. On the other hand, Heeringen took the 15th Corps with him to the Aisne on September 7. It is probable that, during the crucial struggle before the Grand Couronné, Castlenau was considerably outnumbered; and the French were markedly inferior in artillery, even when the heavy fortress guns had been brought into the field.

So long as they stood on the defensive, however, the French had the great advantage of a range of positions naturally formidable, and improved by some passable field-works. General de Curières de Castlenau, a particular star of the old aristocratic-military school, was unorthodox in one vital matter. In a study written in the spring of 1914,[2] he had concluded that the French concentration would be completed as soon as, or a little sooner than, the German. Nevertheless, he had declared for the strategical defensive; and, foreseeing a decisive battle on the Grand Couronné, the heights bordering the Gap of Charmes, and the west bank of the Mortagne, he had planned, for when the German attack should be worn down, the reaction north and south of the Forest of Vitremont which he was actually to conduct some months later. In this, Castlenau was one of the far-sighted few. The defensive idea favoured in the period when the military inferiority of France was most acutely felt had sunk into disrepute. "M. Hanotaux says:—

The system of offensive strategy, of 'striking out,' gained adepts, especially among the young officers. Certainly the system of awaiting strategy had not lost all its partisans: General de Castlenau represented a strong and reasoned doctrine when he advocated, for the east in particular, the offensive-defensive, and the preparation of a stand on the Meurthe at the outset, then on the Mortagne.

He was overborne in favour of the daring and gifted lieutenant and teacher who, in 1900, had insisted that "movement is the law of strat-

---

1. Hanotaux, *Histoire Illustrée*, vol. vii.
2. *Idem.*

egy," that the shock must be sought, not waited for, and that, "in a war with Germany, we must go to Berlin by way of Mayence."[3] Instead of leading to Mayence and Berlin, the French march upon Morhange and Sarrebourg had led back to the Gap of Charmes and the Grand Couronné. Tragically justified, Castlenau now had his chance. For the first time, the invaders found themselves faced by entrenchments, wire-fields, gun-pits, and observatories prepared as well as the time available had allowed.

Such a line, extending 60 miles from near Pont-à-Mousson to the north-western spurs of the Vosges, might well have followed straightly the high western banks of the Moselle, Meurthe, and Mortagne, having the fortresses of Toul and Epinal close behind. The abandonment of the beautiful city of Nancy—a garrison town, but in no sense a fortress—had usually been contemplated in the event of war: that is, perhaps, why the *Kaiser* so ostentatiously prepared for his ceremonial entry. Castelnau was resolved against this sacrifice. No positions, he thought, could be better defended than the crescent of hills called the Grand Couronné, of which the two horns point north-east from Nancy and the Meurthe, as though in anticipation, the northern horn ending in the twin mounts of Amance (410 and 370 metres), and the southern in a ridge extending from the Rambétant (330 m.) to the Bois de Crevic (251 m.); while the space between the tips is covered by the forest-plateau of Champenoux.

On the north, the Nancy crescent is supported by the Moselle Heights, from La Rochette (406 m.), above Bouxières, to Sainte Geneviève (382 m.); and the river is closed in by sharp and thickly-wooded slopes on both banks. On the south, beyond the River Sanon, the crescent is extended by the hills of Flainval and Anthelupt, and, within a wide loop of the Meurthe, by the great bulk of Vitrimont Forest, reaching near to the large town of Lunéville. Farther south, Dubail's divisions stretched along the high western bank of the Mortagne, and then, at an obtuse angle from Rambervillers, into the passes of the Vosges giving upon Raon-l'Etape and St, Dié.

We will follow the attack as it came up from this southern region, beginning with what must be regarded as a heavy demonstration preparatory and secondary to the chief affair, that of the Grand Couronné. After the failure to penetrate the Gap of Charmes, Heeringen had been charged to break through, or to make a feint of breaking through, the French 1st Army toward Epinal. Reinforced by the 41st

3. Foch, *Des Principes de la Guerre.*

187

and 44th Divisions and four divisions of reserves, Dubail was well resisting this pressure when, on September 4, he was required to give up his 21st Corps. At the same time, Heeringen's XIV Corps and other troops, from the valley of the Upper Meurthe, made a desperate effort to force the two mountain ways by which alone large bodies of men could reach the Moselle valley from the northern Vosges, namely, the road from Raon-l'Etape across the Col de la Chipote to Rambervillers, and thence to Charmes or Epinal by easy routes; and the road from St. Dié, through the mountain Forest of the Mortagne, to Bruyères, and thence to Epinal. Sharp fighting, in which the French lost heavily, especially in officers, took place on September 4 and 5 at the Chipote—a bare red hump barring the pass, surrounded by fir-clad cliffs—on the twin hills by Nompatelize, and on the lesser passes south of St. Dié. The real intention of the German Command was probably no more than to pin down Dubail's forces; it could hardly hope to pierce such a depth of mountain fastnesses in time to affect the general issue.

On the left of the 1st Army, on September 5, the German XXI Corps drove Castelnau's 16th and Dubail's 8th Corps out of Gerbéviller and Moyen, and passed on to the west bank of the Mortagne; but the French recovered most of this ground the same evening. On the right, the 14th Corps had to abandon the Passé du Renard and several neighbouring hills south of Nompatelize; and the 41st Division was driven up the St. Dié valley to the crest above Mandray, and beyond. On the following day, these positions also were won back in a reaction that began to threaten the German line of communications in the St. Dié valley. From this moment, the combats of the Upper Meurthe slackened and gradually expired.

The battle had been definitely deplaced to the north. Heeringen, with one of his active corps, was ordered to the Chemin des Dames, where he was to stop the threatening progress of the British Army—a most significant move; two remaining corps were about to be transferred to the Bavarian Command for the struggle before Nancy, the last and greatest effort on the east. On the night of September 7, the 8th Corps repassed the poisoned waters of the Mortagne at Magnières and St. Pierremont; and everything pointed to a sweeping advance, when Dubail was summoned by the General Staff to surrender another of his best units, the 13th Corps, to re-form his whole line, and to stand still with what remained. The danger-point now lay elsewhere.

Castelnau had hardly filled the spaces left by the removal of his

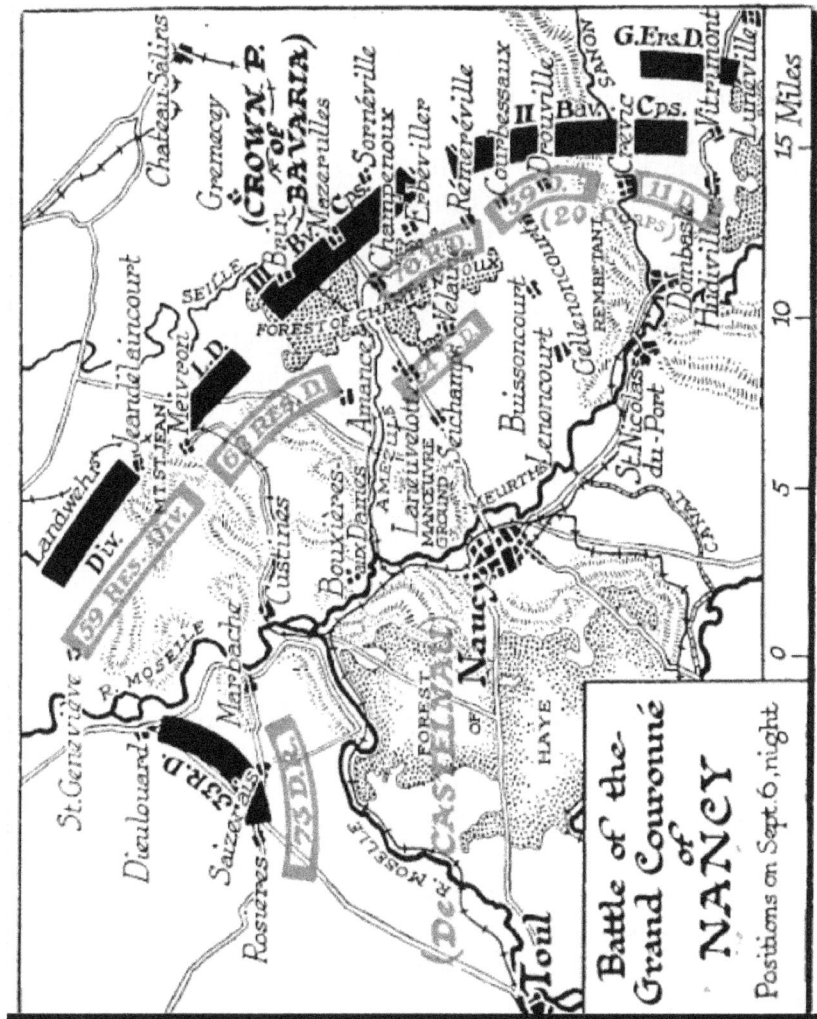

Battle of the
Grand Couronné
of
NANCY

Positions on Sept. 6, night

St.Geneviève
Dieulouard
Saizerais
Rosières
Marbache
R. MOSELLE
33R.D.
73 D.E.
(De CASTELNAU)
FOREST of HAYE
Toul
R. MOSELLE

Landwehr
Jeandélaincourt
Chateau Salins
Gremecey
Div.
St.Jean
Melveort
59 RES. DIV.
Custines
Bouxières-aux-Dames
Amance
Ameuf
Lanéuveloitz
MANŒUVRE GROUND
Seichamp
Velau
JOLIX
SEILLE
FOREST OF
Mazarulles
Sornéville
Réméréville
Champenoux
E.Bheviller
Buissoncourt
Lenoncourt
Cerceuil
Callencourt
REMEREANT
I.D.
GT. RES. D.
FORT.
59 D.
(20 CAPS.)
II D. CORPS
St.Nicolas du-Port
CANAL
Du Dombas
Hautville
(CROWN P.
of BAVARIA)
III Bav.
C ps.
II Bav.
Courbessaux
Drouville
Crevic
SANON
G.Ers.D.
C ps.
Vitrimont
Lunéville

NEURTHE

Nancy

0   5   10   15 Miles

15th and 9th Corps when, in the early afternoon of September 4, a cannonade of a violence hitherto unknown broke over the positions of the 2nd Army before Mont Amance, across the eastern side of Champenoux Forest, by Réméréville, Courbessaux, Drouville, and Maixe, to the east edge of the Forest of Vitrimont. The first attack came upon the right of this front, waves of Bavarian infantry flooding upon the barricaded farms and hamlets and the trenched hillsides. Behind Serres and in advance of Maixe, the 39th Division was pressed back; but, as a whole, the front of the 20th Corps was little changed; and, on its right, the 16th Corps was not yet disturbed. While this hell-fire was being lit, Kluck was racing southward across the Marne and a regiment of Cuirassiers, in full array, was marching through the streets of Metz, under the eyes of the Emperor, who, after visiting the Verdun front, was waiting for the hour of his triumphal entry into Nancy.

At nightfall the conflict waxed more furious. The German plan, as it was presently revealed, was to burst through the opening of the Grand Couronné, and, while maintaining a strong pressure upon the southern horn of the crescent, to envelop the northern horn by a rapid push from Pont-à-Mousson up the Moselle valley, this move by fresh troops from Metz furnishing the precious element of surprise.[4]

Throughout the night of the 4th, the storm raged about the rampart of Nancy. Doubtless the German Command had chosen the way between the Champenoux Forest and the Rambétant as the least difficult for the first phase of its last effort; and, although night attacks are manifestly dangerous, the calculation in this case that the defenders would suffer most from confusion appears to have been justified. Boldly adventuring by dark forest paths and misty vales, the Bavarian Corps of Martini ejected the fore-posts of the 20th Corps from the hills near Lunéville, from Einville Wood, and the ridges between Serres and Drouville. Maixe and Réméréville were lost, retaken, and lost again. Erbéviller, Courbessaux, lesser hamlets, and farmsteads flamed across the countryside, a fantastic spectacle that deepened the terror of the remaining inhabitants, who had taken refuge in their cellars or the fields. General Fayolle's reservists of the 70th Division stood bravely

---

4. M. Hanotaux regards this last part of the plan as "pure folly," as "a few thousand resolute men holding the defiles, crests, and cliffs would break whole armies before Nancy was attained." This appears to be an exaggeration; but it is highly probable that before Nancy, as before Mons and on other occasions at the beginning of the war, the German Armies lost, through the traditional belief in envelopment, what they might have gained by concentration on the central attack.

on the east edge of Saint Paul Forest and at Courbessaux.

On their left the 68th lost Champenoux village at dawn, but re-captured it a few hours later; while, behind it, the 64th busied itself in completing another line of resistance from the important point of the Amezule gorge (on the highroad from Nancy to Château-Salins, midway between Laneuvelotte and Champenoux), by Velaine and Cerceuil, to the Rambétant.

At midnight on the 4th, Prince Ruprecht endeavoured to broaden his attack southward by striking from Lunéville across the loop of the Meurthe. Here, the 74th Reserve Division was prepared, having dug three successive lines of trenches between Blainville and Mont. At Rehainviller and Xermamenil, the right bank of the Mortagne be-came untenable by reason of enfilade fire. The 16th Corps, therefore, withdrew to the west bank. Just before dawn on September 5, the XXI Corps succeeded in getting a small body of men across the river below Gerbéviller. During the afternoon, these were thrown back by a combined push of the 16th Corps from the north and the Dubail's 8th Corps from the south. This success was confirmed and extend-ed on September 6, when the 16th Corps passed the Mortagne, and drove the enemy out of Gerbéviller, and through the woods above the ruined town. Thus the line of the Mortagne, so essential to the French defence, was restored, and in such solid fashion that it might become the base of a thrust against the German flank about Lunéville.

None so happy was the outlook at Castelnau's centre. During the morning of September 5, the Bavarians worked round the north end of Champenoux Forest as far as the foot of Mount Amance, where, after making five desperate assaults, they were stopped. In the evening, the 20th Corps was driven back to the line Vitrimont-Flainval-Crev-ic-Haraucourt-Buissoncourt: that is to say, half of the south horn of the crescent was overrun. The morrow witnessed a rally, the 70th Re-serve Division touching Réméréville, the 39th Active carrying the village of Crevic and progressing toward Drouville, and the 11th re-occupying Vitrimont Forest. But the grey tide still beat upon the foot of Amance.

At this juncture, when it seemed that the plateau of Champe-noux must be turned on both sides, and Castelnau's centre pierced, a no less alarming threat appeared in the attempt to turn the whole Nancy system by the north. Two French reserve divisions had been set facing Metz on either side of the Moselle—the 73rd on the west, between Pont-à-Mousson and Dieulouard, the 59th before the Seille, from Loisy, by the sharp rise of Ste. Geneviève, to Meivrons, where it joined the 68th. A single battalion (of the 314th Regiment, 59 D.R.), and a single battery (of the 33rd, 9th Corps) were posted on the extremity, at Loisy and Ste. Genevieve, of this outer buttress of the Grand Couronné, when, at noon on September 5, amid a thunder of guns, columns of the German XXXIII Reserve Division were observed traversing Pont-a-Mousson, and marching south. The cannonade and the deployment occupied the rest of the day; and next morning the invasion seemed to have passed westward. In fact, it had made rapid way, although at material cost, on the left bank of the Moselle, passing Dieulouard and reaching Marbache, which is only 6 miles north of Nancy, and Saizerais, 8 miles from Toul.

Few as they numbered, the guns and well-entrenched riflemen on the Ste. Genevieve spur, now an acute salient, were a thorn in the side of this success—a very troublesome thorn. At 7 p.m. a German force of about seven battalions debouched from the wooded lowland and began to mount the hillside. Hundreds of them had been mown down ere Captain Langlade and his eight remaining gunners would shift their hot pieces to a safer place behind. Commandant de Montlebert's battalion conducted throughout the night a more than Spartan defence. Time after time, urged on by fife and drum, the grey ranks rose, only to break like spume in the moonlight before the trenches could be reached. It was one of the occasions when the deadly power of the "75's" was shown to the full. At one o'clock in the morning the combat ceased: the assailants had withdrawn in a state of panic. They are said to have left 1200 dead behind them. The French battalion had lost 80 men.

A rare episode this: in general, the battle becomes more confused as the culmination is reached. Indeed, it is difficult to find an exact time or place of the climax. Each side saw its own trouble, but could hardly guess at the condition of the other. The last reserves of the 2nd Army were in play. Castelnau had warned the G.Q.G. that he might have to abandon Nancy, in order to cover Toul. The reply was an injunction to keep touch with Sarrail's right in the direction of St, Mihiel, whither—failing Epinal, failing Charmes, failing Nancy—the enemy now seemed to be turning. On September 7, the German host gathered itself together for its last and greatest effort. The Emperor, escorted by his guard of Cuirassiers, left Metz by the Nancy highroad, crossed the frontier, and took his stand on a sunny hill near Moncel (probably by St. Jean Farm, at the corner of Morel Wood), to watch the bombardment of Mount Amance, which was to prepare the way for the breach of the French centre by way of the Amezule defile.[5]

The gap was duly rushed at the first attempt, made by about ten battalions of infantry, in the morning. The left of the 68th Division fell back to the foot of Mount Amance, the right to Velaine, and the 70th Division to Cerceuil, The 20th Corps, ordered to move north and menace the German flank, was pushed aside; and by noon, the Bavarians had full possession of Champenoux Forest. This bulwark gone, everything depended upon Amance. Most of the artillery on the Grand Couronné (which included twenty 5-inch cannon, and eight 6-inch mortars) flashed upon its approaches; and here the momentary triumph expired. The authority of the crown prince, the presence of the emperor, could effect no more. Old Castelnau began to hope; hearing that the Metz troops had further advanced toward Toul as far as Rozières, he unhesitatingly took the 2nd Cavalry Division out of the line, and sent it off to the neighbourhood of St. Mihiel, whither it was to be followed next day by the 73rd Reserve Division.

The struggle dragged on with an increasing appearance of exhaustion and deadlock. On September 8, the Bavarians tried twice to break through the front of the 20th Corps, without success. Again they bent to the slopes of Mount Amance; the *poilus* let them approach, then staggered out of their holes, and, in a spasm of battle-madness, swept them back. La Bouzule Farm, dominating the narrowest part of the Amezule defile, and other strong points, changed hands repeatedly. On the right, in face of Lunéville, the 74th Reserve Division carried Rehainviller by assault, and the 32nd and 31st Divisions pressed from Gerbéviller nearly to the Meurthe—a severe pin-prick in the German left flank. On September 9 there were obscure fragmentary combats in the glades of Champenoux and St. Paul which we cannot attempt to follow. It will be safe to suppose that the German Command was now governed by the news from the west. Whether the Nancy front could have held without that aid, it is impossible to say. Though Castelnau ordered a counter-offensive all along the line, his men could

---

5. "*Choses Vues a Metz,*" *Revue Hebdomadaire*, December 18, 1915. Colonel Feyler quotes from the *Lokal Anzeiger* of Berlin the following commentary on one of the *Kaiser's* earlier appearances at the Front: "The presence of the emperor demonstrates clearly what a development events have taken. . . . The emperor would never have gone into France if those responsible had envisaged the possibility of the German Army being thrown back beyond the frontier. His presence among his troops in enemy country will not fail to produce a deep impression in Germany as well as abroad.

respond only feebly.

In the evening an armistice of four hours was arranged for the collection of wounded and the burial of dead. The French claimed to have found 40,000 German dead on the ground; the total losses will probably never be known. The *Kaiser* had left his observatory; the rebel heart of Metz leaped to see his disillusioned return. The defenders of Nancy could not know this; but there was a visible sign of failure, now easy to interpret: at midnight on September 8, amid a heavy thunderstorm, a German battery, told off for the purpose, threw eighty shells into Nancy—67 explosive shells and 14 shrapnel, to be precise, according to the diary of the officer responsible [6]—a silly outrage like the first bombardments of Rheims.

The "smashing blow" was failing at the same moment on the Ourcq, on the Marne, at Fère Champènoise, and here before the hill-bastion of the eastern marches. News ran slowly through the armies in those days; but some invigorating breeze of victory must soon have reached the trenches in Lorraine. For Prince Ruprecht it remained only to guard his main lines of retreat, in particular the roads from Nancy, Dombasle, and Lunéville to the frontier; and, as his troops had dug themselves well in, this was not difficult. Three French columns of assault, composed of relatively fresh troops, and supported by the 64th and 68th Reserve Divisions, after a powerful artillery preparation, advanced on the morning of September 10 against the Amezule and neighbouring positions; but they could not make much headway.

On the morrow the order was repeated, to better effect, especially on the wings. That night the German retreat in Lorraine began. Castelnau's men gazed incredulous into spaces suddenly calm and empty. One of them says:—

> Our soldiers, hungry, harassed, haggard, could hardly stand upright. They marched like spectres. Visibly, we were at our last breath. We could hold out only a few hours more. And then, O prodigy, calm fell, on the 12th, upon the whole of the stricken field. The enemy gave up, retreated for good, abandoned everything, Champenoux, so frantically contested, and the entire front he had occupied. He fell back in dense columns, without even a pretence of further resistance.

The grand adventure was finished,

Pont-à-Mousson, Nomeny, Réméréville, Lunéville, Baccarat,

---

6. Quoted in *Un Village Lorrain en Août-Septembre 1914. Réméréville*, by C. Berlet.

Raon-l'Etape, and St. Dié were evacuated in rapid succession. Before the war fell into the entrenched lines which were to hold with little change for four years, most of Lorraine up to the old frontier and a long slice of Alsace had been recovered. But with what wounds may be read, for instance, in the report of the French Commission of Inquiry into the devastation wrought by the enemy in the department of Meurthe and Moselle. As though the destruction of farmsteads and villages in course of the fighting were not sufficient, the Bavarian infantry had been guilty at many places of almost incredible acts of ferocity. At Nomeny, the 2nd and 3rd Bavarian regiments, after sacking the village, set it on fire, and then, as the villagers fled from their cellars, shot them down—old men, women, and children—50 being killed and many more wounded.

At Lunéville, during the three weeks' occupation, the Hotel de Ville, the Synagogue, and about seventy houses were burned down with torches, petrol, and other incendiary apparatus; and 17 men and women were shot in cold blood in the streets. Under dire threats, signed shamelessly by General Von Fosbender, a "contribution" of 650,000 *francs* was paid by the inhabitants. On August 24, practically the whole of the small town of Gerbéviller was destroyed by fire (more than 400 houses), and at least 36 civilians, men and women, were slaughtered. At Baccarat, 112 houses were burned down, after the whole place had been pillaged under the supervision of General Fabricius, commanding the artillery of the XIV Baden Corps, and other officers. This feature of the campaign cannot be ignored in our chronicle. Good men had supposed war itself to be the uttermost barbarism; it was left to the disciplined armies of the Hohenzollern Empire to prove that educated hands may lower it to depths of wickedness.

On September 18, General Curières de Castlenau was made Grand Officer of the Legion of Honour on the ground that:—

> "Since the beginning of the war, his army has fought without cessation, and he has obtained from his troops sustained efforts and important results. General Castlenau has had, since the beginning of the campaign, two sons killed and a third wounded; nevertheless, he continued to exercise his command with energy."

CHAPTER 11

Summing-Up

The Battle of the Marne closed a definite phase of the Great War, and perhaps—in so far as it was marked by open and rapid movement, and as it finally exposed certain gross military errors—a phase of warfare in general. A fresh examination of the plans of the preceding years and the events of the preceding month immensely enhances the interest of the whole development; for it shows the real "miracle of the Marne" to have been an uprush of intelligence and patriotic will in which grave faults of strategy and tactics were corrected, and the victory to be the logical reward of a true conception, executed with unfailing skill through a new instrument created while the conditions of the struggle were being equalised. In whatever sense we may speak of a "greatest" battle of history, this was assuredly, of all clashes of force, that in which reason was most conspicuously vindicated. Insanely presumptuous as was her ambition of reducing France, Russia, and Britain, Germany had at the outset some remarkable advantages. Chief among these must be counted the power of surprise, due to her long secret preparation, and a complete unity of command in face of dispersed Allies,

The German forces concentrated on the west were not numerically superior to those of France, Britain, and Belgium; their effective superiority was considerable. Half of the active corps, which alone the French expected as troops of shock, were doubled with thoroughly trained reserve formations, giving a mass of attack of 34 corps, instead of 22, a difference larger than the two armies of the enveloping movement. Their strength was also increased by a clear superiority in several branches of armament and field service (the French field-gun and the use by the Allies of the French railways being notable exceptions), and in some particulars of tactical practice, especially the prudent use of field defences. The basic idea being to strike France down before Russia and Britain could effectually interfere, speed was a principal condition of success; and the plan of the Western campaign was probably the only one on which it could be realised. One-third of the whole force was to hold the old Franco-German frontier in a provisional defence, while one-third attacked through Luxembourg and the Belgian Ardennes, and the remainder was thrown across the Meuse and the open plain of Flanders, toward the French capital.

This unprecedented enlargement of the offensive front, the outstanding feature of the plan, secured the most rapid deployment of the maximum forces; it alone could yield the great element of surprise; it alone provided the opportunity of envelopment dear to the German military mind. Its boldness, aided by terrorism in the invaded regions, astounded the world, and so seemed to favour the scheme of conquest. It might ultimately provoke a full development of British power; even in case of failure, it would cripple France and Belgium for many years. Its immediate weakness arose from the wide extension of forces not larger, except at certain points, allowing no general reserve and no large reinforcement, and from the necessity of great speed. The plan ignored many possibilities, from the Alps to Lille; once in motion, however, it could not be considerably or rapidly changed. Berlin, confident in the superiority of the war-machine to which it had devoted its best resources and thought, believed there would be no delay and no need of change.

France had been inevitably handicapped by the need of renouncing any initiative that could throw doubt upon her moral position, by the independence of her British and Belgian Allies, and by uncertainty as to Italy. This last doubt was, however, quickly removed; the Belgian Army delayed the invasion by a full week; and our "Old Contemptibles" gave most precious aid. A united Command at that time might have done little more than strengthen the instrument and confirm the doctrine whose imperfections we have traced. The instrument was inferior not only in effective strength, not only in some vital elements of arms and organisation, but in the system and spirit of its direction. The doctrine of the offensive, general, continuous, and unrestrained, had become an established orthodoxy during the previous decade, when the Russian alliance and the British Entente were fixed, when service was extended to three years, the 75 mm. gun was perfected, and a new method of railway mobilisation promised that the armies would be brought into action at least as rapidly as those of the enemy.

Before a shot was fired, it had prejudiced the military information services—whence the scepticism of the Staff as to a large German movement west of the Meuse, and as to the German use of army corps of reserve in the first line; whence the ignorance of the German use of aeroplanes and wired entrenchment.

No answer was prepared to the German heavy artillery. While unable to create the means to a successful general offensive, the French Command had discounted, if not positively discredited, modern methods of defence and delaying manoeuvre, methods peculiarly indicated in this case, since France had the same reasons for postponing a decision as Germany had for hastening it. The only hope of the Allies at the outset lay in a combination of defence and manoeuvre: there was no adequate defence, and no considerable manoeuvre, but only a general headlong attack on a continuous line. Of the consequences of this lamentable beginning, an accomplished and sober French officer says:

It is just to speak of the Battle of the Frontiers as calamitous, for this battle not only doomed to total or partial ruin nine of our richest departments: insufficiently repaired by the fine recovery on the Marne, it weighed heavily upon the whole course of the war. It paralysed our strategy. From September 1914, our High Command was necessarily absorbed in the task, first, of limiting, then of reducing, the enormous pocket cut in our territory. Ever obsessed by the fear of abandoning to devastation a new band of country, we were condemned for nearly four years to a hideous trench warfare for which we were infinitely less prepared and less apt than the invader, and that we were able to sustain only by force of heroism.[1]

Any one of the errors that have been indicated would have been grave; in combination, they are accountable for the heavy losses of the three abortive inroads into Alsace, Lorraine, and the Ardennes, and for the dispositions which necessitated the long retreat from the north. That the German armies suffered in these operations is, of course, to be remembered; but for France it was more urgent to economise her strength. In strategy infatuated, in tactics reckless, in preparation unequal to the accomplishment of its own designs, the then French Command must be held responsible in large measure for the collapse of the national forces in the first actions of the campaign.

---

1. Lt.-Col. Thomasson, *Le Revers*, introduction.

Joffre, who had been named *generalissimo* designate three years before, almost by accident, who was an organiser rather than a strategist, had inherited, with the imperfect instrument, the imprudent doctrine and plan. There was not the time, and he was hardly the man, to attempt radically to change them; nor has he yet recognised in words that there was any large strategical error to correct. But the facts speak clearly enough: from the evening of August 23, when the general retreat from the north was ordered, we enter upon a profoundly changed situation, in which the native shrewdness and solid character of the French commander-in-chief are the dominant factor.

The defence that should have been prepared could not be extemporised. The armies must be disengaged and re-formed. A large sacrifice of territory was therefore unavoidable. To delay the critical encounter till the balance of forces should be rectified was the first requirement. On August 24, Headquarters issued a series of tactical admonitions, prelude to a clean sweep of no less than thirty-three generals and many subordinate officers. Next day followed the "General Instruction" in which will be found the germ of the ultimate victory. The rule of blind, universal, unceasing offensive disappeared, without honour or ceremony; arose that of manoeuvre, informed, elastic, resourceful, prudent but energetic.

At once there was precipitated a conception which governed not only the battle of the Marne, but the whole after-development of the war. There must be no more rash adventures on the east; from Belfort to Verdun, the front would be held defensively, with a minimum of strength, to fulfil the purpose for which its fortifications were built, and to protect the main forces, which would operate henceforth in the centre and west. The importance of the north-west coast, and the fact that Kluck was not approaching it, plainly suggested the creation of a new mass of manoeuvre on this side to menace the German flank: this new body was Maunoury's 6th Army. These two features of the Allied riposte—defence on the east, offence from the west—were to be permanent. The French centre must be strengthened to bear the impact of Bülow, the Saxons, and the Duke of Würtemberg. Foch's Army, created to this end, to come in between those of d'Espérey (Lanrezac's successor) and de Langle, had the further effect of preserving the full offensive strength of the 5th Army.

For these purposes, large numbers of men had to be transferred from the east to the west and centre. Joffre at first hoped to stand on the Somme, and then on the Oise. But the new forces were not ready;

the defence of the east was not secured; the British Army was momentarily out of action; Kluck threatened the Allied communications; the line was a hazardous zigzag. The *generalissimo* would not again err on the side of premature attack.

The pursuit was not an unbroken course of victory for the invaders. Before the Gap of Charmes, on August 24-26, Castlenau and Dubail administered the first great German set-back of the war. At the same time, the Prince Imperial received a severe check at Etain; and, although Smith-Dorrien's stand at Le Cateau on August 26 disabled the British Force for some days, it did much to save the Allied left wing. On August 28, the German IV Army was sharply arrested at Novion Porcien; and next day took place the combats of Proyart and Dun-sur-Meuse, and the Battle of Guise. In these and many lesser actions, the spirit of the armies was prepared for the hour when the issue should be fairly joined.

The Fabian strategy was soon and progressively justified. Weaknesses inherent in the German plan began to appear. Every day of their unsuccessful chase aggravated the problem of supplying the armies, removed them from their heavy artillery, stretched and thinned their infantry lines, weakened their liaison, bred weariness and doubt (which were too often drowned in drink), while the French, on the contrary, were shortening their communications, and generally pulling themselves together. "It is the old phenomenon of the wearing down of forces in case of an offensive which we here encounter anew," says Freytag-Loringhoven. Two or three corps had to be left behind to mask Antwerp and to besiege Maubeuge; the Grand Staff could not altogether resist the Russian scare. There was increasing dislocation: in particular, Kluck had got dangerously out of touch with Bülow. And there was something worse than "wearing down" and dislocation.

The historian Meinecke imagines[2]:—

Perhaps our programme would not have collapsed if we had carried through our original strategical idea with perfect strictness, keeping our main forces firmly together, and, for the time, abandoning East Prussia.

This cannot be admitted. So far from being pursued more strictly, the original German idea soon could not be pursued at all. Its boldest feature had become inapplicable to circumstances more and more

---

2. Professor Friedrich Meinecke, of Freiburg University, in the *Frankfürter Zeitung*, December 31, 1916.

subject to another will. On September 1, when the Somme had been passed, and while Joffre was ordering the extension of the retreat to the Seine and the Aube, Moltke was engaged in changing radically the direction of the marching wing of the invasion, Kluck's I Army. Failing successively on the Sambre, the Somme, the Oise, and finally stultified by the superior courage that staked the capital itself upon the chance of a victorious recoil farther south, the greatest of all essays in envelopment ended in a recognised fiasco.

With the appearance on the southern horizon of the fortress of Verdun and the city of Paris, and the entry of the Allied armies between them as into a corridor, the whole problem, in fact, was transformed. The German Command suddenly found itself in face of a fatal dilemma. As Paris obstructed the way of Kluck, so Verdun challenged the Prussian Crown Prince. To enter the corridor without first reducing these two unknown quantities would be to risk serious trouble on both flanks; to stay to reduce them would involve delay, or dispersal of force, either of which would be disastrous. The course of argument by which the Grand Staff decided this deadly question has not been revealed They chose the first alternative.

Kluck was ordered to pass south-eastward of the one "entrenched camp," the Imperial Crown Prince south-westward of the other, both, and the three armies between them, to overtake the Allies and force them to a frontal encounter, while a fresh effort was made to break through the eastern defences. A heavy price must be paid for such large re-establishments and changes of plan in face of an alert enemy. Kluck has been too much blamed for what followed. He may have been guilty of recklessness, over-reaching ambition, and specific disobedience. But here, as in the Battle of the Frontiers, it is the authors, not the executants, of the offensive operation who must be held chiefly responsible for consequences that are in the logic of the case.

Joffre's hour had come. He had laboured to win three elements of an equal struggle lacking in the north: (a) a more favourable balance of numbers and armament—this was gained by the "wearing down" of the enemy, and the reinforcement of the Allied line, in course of the retreat, so that the Battle of the Marne commenced with something more than an equality, and ended with a distinct Allied superiority in the area of decision; (b) a favourable terrain—this was reached on the classic ground between the capital and the middle Meuse, under cover of the eastern armies, and subject to the dilemma of Paris-Verdun; (c) a sound strategic initiative. For this, the 6th Army had been prepared, and the 5th kept at full strength.

The failure of the enveloping movement and the change of the German plan provided the opportunity. To reduce the distended front of the invasion, at one time no less than 140 miles (Amiens to Dun-sur-Meuse) , to one of 100 miles (Crécy-en-Brie to Revigny), Kluck had boldly crossed the face of the 6th Army, and on the evening of September 5 presented a moving flank of more than 40 miles long to Maunoury, French, and d'Espérey's left. Joffre seems to have hesitated for a moment as to whether it were best to continue the retreat, as arranged, to the Seine, and then to have given way to Gallieni's importunity. "We cannot count on better conditions for our offensive," he told the government.

The order of battle was issued on the evening of September 4. "Advantage must be taken of the adventurous situation of the I German Army (right wing)." it started: this was to be the factor of surprise. Positions would be taken on the 5th in order that the general movement might begin at dawn on the following day. The 6th Army and the British were to strike east on either side of the Marne, toward Château-Thierry and Montmirail respectively, while the 5th Army attacked due northward: thus, it was hoped, Kluck would be taken in flank and front, and crushed by superior force. The central armies (9th and 4th) would move north against Bülow, the Saxons, and the Duke of Würtemberg; and Sarrail would break westward from Verdun against the exposed flank of the Crown Prince. The function of Foch's, the smallest of the French armies concerned, and of de Langle's, the next smallest, must be regarded as primarily defensive, the chief offensive role being entrusted to d'Espérey's, by far the strongest, and Maunoury's, with the small British force linking them. Sarrail had not the means to exploit his advantage of position. The essence of the plan lay in the rectangular attack of the left.

The design was perfect: Kluck's columns, stretched out from the Ourcq to near Esternay, should have been smashed in, the western part of the German communications overwhelmed, the other armies put to flight. These results were not obtained; the whole battle was, indeed, compromised, before it was well begun, by the unreadiness of the Allied left and the precipitancy of General Gallieni. When Lamaze's reservists stumbled upon Schwerin's outposts north of Meaux, at midday on September 5—eighteen hours before the offensive was timed to open—Maunoury had only three divisions in line, and on the following day he had only two more. Kluck had instantly taken alarm;

his II Corps was actually on its way back to the Ourcq while the main body of the Allied armies was commencing their grand operation. The benefit of surprise was thus sacrificed; and Kluck was able to move one after another of his corps to meet Maunoury's reinforcements as they arrived upon the field. Certain French partisans of the then Governor of Paris have attempted to shift the responsibility for this miscarriage to the shoulders of the British commander-in-chief.

The Expeditionary Force deserves more scrupulous justice. It had retired and was re-forming behind the Forest of Crécy, at the request of General Joffre, when the order of September 4 arrived. The positions therein named to be reached on the following day (Changis-Coulommiers) were unattainable, being too far away, and solidly held by the enemy. The instructions for Marshal French were to attack eastward toward Montmirail on the 6th; neither to him nor to the French Staff was it known till the afternoon of that day that Kluck was withdrawing across the Marne. No need appeared of helping Maunoury until September 7. By that time the field-marshal had again changed his direction at Joffre's request, facing north beside d'Espérey, instead of east beside Maunoury; and, from the moment when Kluck's withdrawal was discovered, rapid progress was made.

The German Staff now seems to have completely lost control of its two chief Commanders. The fatal fault is plainly exhibited in Bülow's *"Bericht zur Marneschlacht"*—significantly, withheld from publication for five years. Though weakened by a premature start, unreadiness, and imperfect coordination, the French attack on the Ourcq necessarily produced not merely a local shock, but a disturbance reverberating eastward by what has been called its "effect of suction." To double this with the strain of Bülow's continued offensive—disastrously successful in the surprise of Fère Champènoise—was the most reckless gambling. With the I Army pulling north-west, the II Army pulling south-east, and 60 miles between the points where they were seeking a decision, how could anything more than a pretence of liaison be kept up? But it was precisely before this interval that Joffre had aligned a full third of the strength of the French crescent—the 20 divisions of the French 5th and British armies. In the separation of the two masses of the German right, and the entry between them of this powerful body, lies the governing cause of the victory.

All the rest is a prodigy of endurance. The Battle of the Ourcq was no sooner joined than it resolved itself into a race of reinforcements, and a stubborn, swaying combat over a few miles of open farmland,

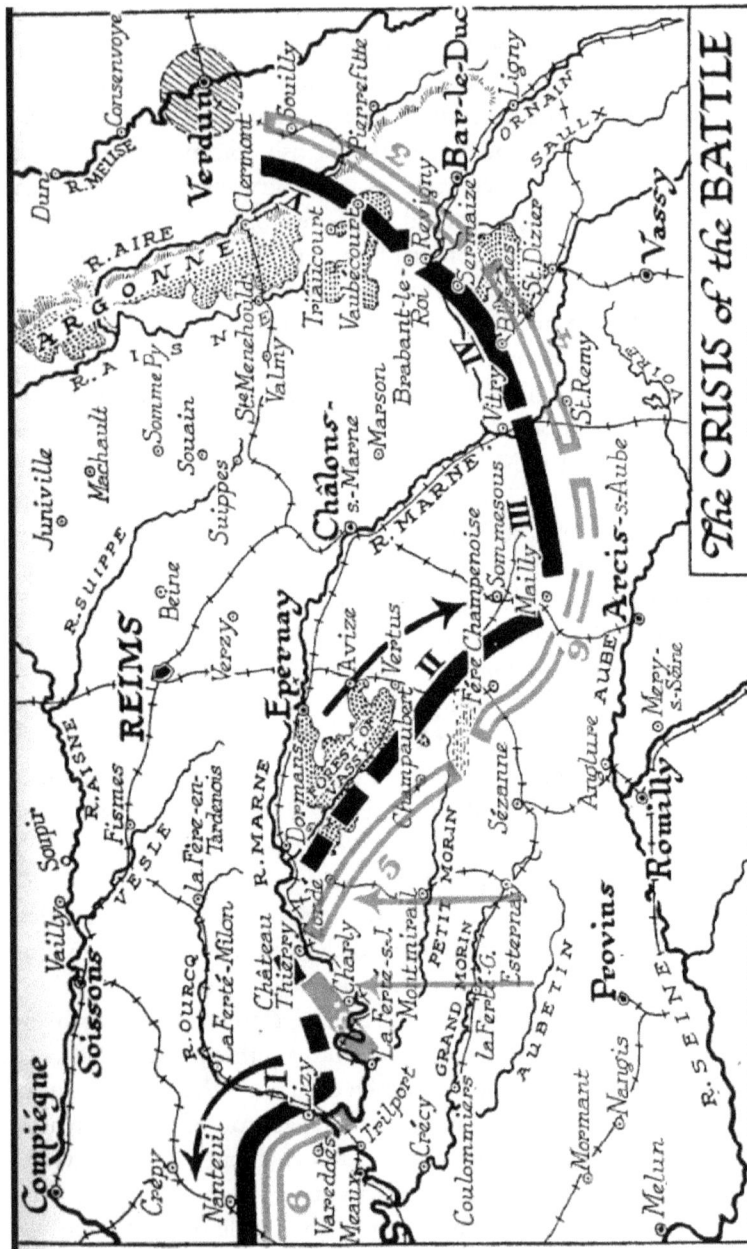

The CRISIS of the BATTLE
Mid-day, Sept. 9.

Compiègne
Soissons
Vailly
Soupir
R.AISNE
Fismes
VESLE
la Fère-en-Tardenois
R.OURCQ
LaFerté-Milon
Crépy
Nanteuil
II
Varreddes
Lizy
Meaux
Trilport
6
Crécy
Coulommiers
la Ferté-G.
Château Thierry
R.MARNE
Charly
La Ferté-s.-J.
Montmirail
PETIT MORIN
GRAND MORIN
AUBETIN
Estaprès
Mormant
Nangis
Provins
R.SEINE
Melun
Romilly
R.SEINE
Mégny-s.-Seine
Anglure
AUBE
Arcis-s-Aube
Sézanne
Fère Champenoise
Sommesous
Mailly
III
5
9
Champaubert
Vertus
II
Avize
VASSY
Dormans
Epernay
R.MARNE
Châlons-s.-Marne
Marson
Vertus
Brabant-le-Roi
Vitry
Vaubecourt
Triaucourt
Revigny
IV
St.Remy
Sermaize
St.Dizier
ORNAIN
Ligny
Bar-le-Duc
SAULX
Vassy
Valmy
Ste.Menehould
N
Somme P.y
Souain
Machault
Juniville
R.SUIPPE
Béine
Verzy
REIMS
Suippes
R.AISNE
ARGONNE
R.AIRE
R.AIRE
R.MEUSE
Dun
Verdun
Souilly
Clermont
Pierrefitte
Consenvoye

REIMS

Miles
0   10   20   30   60

with little of manoeuvre, save reciprocal attempts at envelopment by the north. The story of the battle of the Marshes of St. Gond is the epic of Foch's obstinacy, of Humbert's defence of the pivot on the Sézanne plateau, the loss of the swampy barrier and Mont Aout, the agonising breakdown about Fere Champenoise on September 8, and the devices of the following day to close the breach. Between these points of strangulation, the real offensive arm of the Allies progressed with comparative ease. On the night of September 8, when d'Espérey's 3rd Corps entered Montmirail, it was exactly midway between them. On the morning of the 9th, when the British 1st and 2nd Corps passed the Marne, Kluck and Bülow were more definitely divided.

At noon, Smith-Dorrien and Haig were on the Lizy-Château-Thierry road; and in the evening d'Espérey's 18th Corps held Château-Thierry, No last moment success of the enemy on the Ourcq or in Champagne could have greatly affected the course of this development. The necessity of a retreat of the three Western armies was probably accepted by the German Grand Staff in the morning of September 9; but it may be that a considerable success by either or both of the crown princes on that day would have modified the decision as regards the rest of the front. At 11 a.m. Betz was evacuated; and during the afternoon great convoys were seen hurrying from the Ourcq to the Aisne. Bülow's orders, inspired by fear of flank attack by d'Espérey's 10th and 1st Corps, rather than by the 42nd Division, seem to have been given about 3 p.m. Fère Champènoise was abandoned in the evening, and Foch's anxiously prepared manoeuvre could not be carried out. The 6th and 9th Armies were too much exhausted to attempt a serious pursuit till next morning; and the German right reached the Aisne without inordinate losses.

Every part of the French line had contributed to this result, for every other army had been cut or kept down to serve the major opportunity. And, if it stood relatively immobile, no less heroism and resource were shown on the eastern than on the western wing of the Allied crescent. Sarrail and de Langle were able to keep a rectangular disposition like that of Maunoury and the B.E.F., forcing the crown prince to fight on a double front; but they had not even a numerical equality of force with which to exploit it. The 4th Army, in holding foot by foot the Ornain-Saulx valley from Vitry to Sermaize, and the 3rd in its defence of the long salient of the Meuse, were also weighed upon by this peculiar anxiety: a comparatively small force might pierce their frail river guard, or the wall of the Lorraine armies might collapse beside them.

They were helped to success by three errors of omission on the part of the German armies concerned: (1) Verdun was not directly attacked, the crown prince being confident that it would fall automatically while his cavalry were reaching Dijon; (2) the attempt to force the Meuse at Troyon was feeble and tardy; (3) the thinly-covered gap on Langle's left was not discovered until the 21st Corps had been brought up. All along the line, the fighting was of a sustained violence. The 15th Corps arrived from Lorraine on September 8 just in time to save the junction of the 3rd and 4th Armies. It was, however, not till noon on the 11th that the Duke of Würtemberg abandoned Vitry; and only on the night of the 12th did the Prince Imperial order a retreat which definitely relieved Verdun, and reopened the Châlons road and railway.

In resting his plan upon a defence of the eastern pivot of the retreat and the recoil, Joffre was accepting an accomplished fact. The great attack upon the Couronné of Nancy began on the evening of September 4, thirty-six hours before the Allied offensive. It may be supposed, therefore, that the German Staff had decided to get the Bavarian Army into a position in which it could co-operate effectively with the Imperial Crown Prince when he came up level on the west. Heeringen's push from the St. Dié region toward Epinal, and the attack on the Mortagne, were probably intended to hide this design, and to pin down Dubail's forces. The promptitude with which Heeringen was sent off to the Aisne, on the night of September 6, that is, as soon as the danger of Kluck's position was realised, is significant. In itself, the presence of the *Kaiser* during the Bavarian attack on the Grand Couronné proves nothing. His ceremonial entry into Nancy would have grievously hurt French pride; but the sacrifice of the city had always been contemplated, Toul being the real redoubt of the Moselle defences.

The prize was to be larger; the prestige of three royal personages was to be satisfied. The Crown Princes of Prussia and Bavaria, ingeniously linked, had been so directed that in the crisis they had the whole Verdun-Toul system between them, and apparently at their mercy. The assault of the Amezule defile and Mount Amance was reciprocal to the adventure which Sarrail arrested 50 miles farther west. For five days and nights the battle raged about the entrenched crescent of the Nancy hills, with fiery wings outspread to Gerbéviller on the south-east, and Rozières on the north-west . No more dreadful struggle can be recorded. The German effort ceased on the night of September 9; and on the 11th the general withdrawal to the old frontier began. Like Foch, Langle, and Sarrail, Castlenau had won through by the narrowest of margins; but his, pre-eminently, was a victory of foresight and preparation. With all their power of heavy artillery (and here the resources of Metz and Strasbourg were at hand), it is remarkable that the German Staff never attempted to repeat in Lorraine the *coup* of Liège. As the French respected Metz, they respected Verdun; and the manoeuvre of the double approach to Toul, from east and west, proves their fears. These were, as we now know, well justified. Freytag-Loringhoven says:—

> It is certain that the old-fashioned fortresses are worthless, and, moreover, that the earlier notion, handed down from the Middle Ages, that positions have to be secured by means of fortresses, must be discarded. . . . But it will not be possible to dispense with certain previously prepared fortified points at places where only defensive tactics can be employed. The fortifications of the French eastern frontier, above all Verdun and the Moselle defences, have demonstrated how valuable these may be. . . . It is a question of constructing not a continuous system of fortifications, but a succession of central points of defence, and this not in the shape of fortified towns, but of entrenchment of important areas.

> The intention was to effect an envelopment from two sides. The envelopment by the left wing was, however, brought to a standstill before the fortifications of the French eastern frontier, which, in view of the prompt successes in Belgium, it had been hoped to overcome. . . . The defensive tactics of the chiefs of the French Army were rendered very much easier by the support these fortifications gave to their wing, as well as by the possibility of effecting rapid transfers of troops afforded by a very convenient network of railways, and a very large number of motor-wagons upon good roads. . . . . The war has proved that the assertion often made in time of peace, that the spade digs the grave of the offensive, is not correct.

One day, toward the end of the battle, I came upon a ring of peasants digging a pit for the carcasses of two horses that lay near by. They had already buried fourteen others, but seemed happy at their gruesome task—just such sententious fellows as the master took for his models in a famous scene. One of them guided me uphill to a small chalk-pit, at the bottom of which a mound of fresh earth, surmounted by a couple of sticks tied crosswise with string, marked the grave of two English lads unnamed. A thicket shaded the hollow; but all around the sunshine played over rolling stubble-fields. Ere the grave-diggers had finished, a threshing-machine was working at the farm across the highway. Some men were ploughing the upper ridge of the battlefield; and, as I left, a procession of high-prowed carts, full of women and children sitting atop their household goods, brought back home a first party of refugees. The harvest of death seemed already to give way to the harvest of life.

First of many still-born hopes. The Christmas that was to be the festival of peace passed, and another, and another. Interminably, the war prolonged itself through new scenes, more ingenious forms of slaughter, new abysms of pain, till the armies had fallen into a temper of iron endurance. But, even in such extremities, the heart will seek its food. Month after month, by day and night, coming from beleaguered Verdun or the gateways of Alsace to reach the Oise and Flanders, I passed down the long sparkling valleys of the Marne; every turn grew familiar, and their green folds whispered of the gain in loss and the quiet within the storm.

Like all religion, patriotism, for the many, speaks in symbols; what symbol more eloquent than the strong stream, endlessly renewed to cleanse, to nourish, and to heal? Through those stony years, most of the convoys crossed the Marne at some point—lumbering carts, succeeded by wagons white with a slime of dust and petrol; fussy Staff cars and hurried ambulances; gun-trains, their helmeted riders swaying spectrally in the misty air of dawn; columns of heavy-packed infantry, dreaming of their loves left in trembling cities far behind. In turn, all the armies of France, and some of those of Britain, America, and Italy, came this way; and into their minds, unconsciously, must have fallen something of the spirit of the Marne, and of those frightened apprentices of the war who first saved France, and dammed an infamous aggression.

So much the *poilus* knew; that comfort supported them. Most of the high company of Joffre's captains were still with them, winning fresh laurels—Foch, Petain, and Haig, Castlenau, Humbert, Langle, Sarrail, Franchet d'Espérey, Mangin, Guillaumat, Pulteney, Nivelle, Maud'huy, Micheler, and many another. Soon the world at large understood that this strange overturn of fortune was the base of all subsequent victories in the same good cause. More than this—that a man had conceived, designed, organised, and controlled it, and so earned enduring fame—might be vaguely felt, but could not be certainly known until the passage of time allowed it to be said that, as surely as there were warts on Cromwell's nose, there were shadows to the lights of the record of victory. At length, a true picture is possible; and instead of a play of blind forces, or a senseless "miracle," we see a supremely dramatic revolt of outraged reason, nobly led, and justly triumphing.

The German conspiracy failed on the Marne not by any partial fault or executive error, but by the logic of its most essential characteristics. It was a masterpiece of diabolical preparation: it failed, when the quickly-awakened French mind grappled with it, from dependence upon a rigid mechanism, and the inability of its authors to adjust it to unexpected circumstances. It was a wager on speed—for the enveloping movement bore in it the germs of the ultimate disturbance; that is to say, it presumed the stupidity or pusillanimity of the Republican Command, and this presumption proved fatal.

These faults were aggravated by disunion among the army leaders and disillusion among the men, while the Allies were inspired to an almost perfect cooperation. Already delayed and weakened in Belgium, the invading armies saw their surplus strength evaporating in the long pursuit, their dislocated line caught in a sudden recoil, and to be saved from being rent asunder only by closing the adventure. In the disastrous moment when Kluck and Bülow turned in opposite directions, the proudest war school in the world was beaten, and humiliated, by a stout *burgess* of Rivesaltes. Long before the war itself became hateful, this thought worked bitterly. Criminals do not make the best soldiers. Moltke was cashiered, with him Kluck and Hansen, and we know not how many more. It was the twilight of the heathen gods.

In the long run, mankind cherishes the reasonable, in faith or action; and, of the barbarous trial of war, this is all that remains in the memory of future ages. The Marne was a signal triumph for Right, won, not by weight of force or by accident, but by superior intelligence and will. That is its essential title to our attention, and its most pregnant meaning for posterity. So immense a trial was it, and a triumph so vitally necessary to civilisation, that all the heroic episodes of our Western history pale before it, to serve henceforth for little, faint, but comprehensible analogies; in the French mind even the *epopée* of the great Emperor is at last eclipsed. The combatants themselves could not see it thus. Afterwards, the war and those doomed to continue it became sophisticated—governments and the press told them what to expect, and followed them with praise and some care.

In this first phase, there is a strange *naïveté*; it is nearly all headlong extemporisation; masses of men constantly plunged from one into another term of the unknown. The "front" was never fixed; there were few of the features of combat later most characteristic—no trenches or dugouts, no bombs or helmets, no poison-gas, no mines, no Stokes guns, no swarm of buzzing 'planes across the sky, no field railways, few hot meals, and fewer ambulance cars. The armies did not come up to their tasks through zones devastated by the enemy, and then reorganised by engineers into so many monstrous war-factories. The forests they crossed were undisturbed, the orchards blossoming, the towns intact. They knew nothing of "camouflage": on the contrary, they saw and sought the individual foe, and by him were seen individually. Very often, and quickly, they came to bodily grips; commonly, the conflict ceased, or slackened, at sunset. What would afterward have seemed a moderate bombardment terrorised them, for it was worse than anything they had heard of.

In sum, with less of horror and less of protection, they felt as much as, and more freshly than, those who followed. War had not yet become habitual—there was neither the half-sceptical stoicism nor the profound comradeship of later days. Only a month had passed since this first million lads had left home. Every hour had brought some new shock. Resentment was fresh and fierce in them. No romantic illusion fed it; but deep offence called to the depths of dignity of an aged nation for answer, and the answer came. There stood the Boche, arrogant and formidable, polluting the soil of Brie and Champagne, the heart of France—what argument could there be? They did not think of one spot as more sacred than another, as, afterwards, thousands fell to hold Ypres and Arras, Soissons, Rheims, and Verdun. Like the process, the inspiration was simpler. The fields of the Marne were France, the land that had nurtured them, its freedom and grace of life and thought, the long Latin heritage, the virtues that a new Barbarism had dared to dispute and outrage. For this great all, they gave straightway their little all.

Rivers of blood, the old, rich Gallic blood that mingled Roman experience and Mediterranean fire with the peasant vigour of the North, tempered through centuries of labour and exaltation. The best must needs suffer most; and France, historic guardian of ancient treasuries, standard-bearer of European civilisation, must suffer in chief for the weaknesses of the Western world. To those who knew her, there was ever something of worship in their love, as in our regard for the fullest type of womanhood. The earth thrilled with anger to see her so foully stricken, and breathed freely only when her sons had shown the pure nobility of their response. No frenzies of meliorism, no Carmagnoles of murderous ambition, no Danton or Robespierre, no La Vendée and no Buonaparte have marred the story of the defence of the Third Republic. Democracy, Reason, slow-growing Law, are justified of their children.

Men raised by such achievement into an immortality of human gratitude, the young limbs and hearts so swiftly girded up, so soon loosed upon eternity, should evoke no common mourning.

> *Knows he who tills this lonely field,*
> *To reap its scanty corn,*
> *What mystic fruit his acres yield?*

Not their own soil only, they enriched with their blood, but the universal mind. In saving the best in dream and reality that France means to the world, they saved the whole future, as short reflection upon the alternative will show. The victory of the Marne sealed the brotherhood of France and England, and did much toward bringing America and the Dominions into the comity of nations. It was the basis of the completer victory to follow, and of the only possibilities of future peace and liberal progress. For ever, this example will call to youth everywhere—"*that from these honoured dead we take increased devotion, that we here highly resolve that these dead shall not have lived in vain.*" May there not again be need to pass through such a Gehenna; but it is surer that the world will only be made "safe for democracy," or even for elementary order, by the vigilance and chivalry of each oncoming generation. For these, for ever, ghostly bugles will blow through the woods and hamlets of the Marne.

> *Ames des chevaliers, revenes-vous encor?*
> *Est-ce vous qui parlez avec la voix du cor?*
> *Roncevaux! Roncevaux! dans ta sombre vallée*
> *L'ombre du grand Roland, n'est-elle pas console?*

LEONAUR

ALSO FROM LEONAUR
AVAILABLE IN SOFTCOVER OR HARDCOVER WITH DUST JACKET

THE FALL OF THE MOGHUL EMPIRE OF HINDUSTAN *by H. G. Keene*—By the beginning of the nineteenth century, as British and Indian armies under Lake and Wellesley dominated the scene, a little over half a century of conflict brought the Moghul Empire to its knees.

LADY SALE'S AFGHANISTAN *by Florentia Sale*—An Indomitable Victorian Lady's Account of the Retreat from Kabul During the First Afghan War.

THE CAMPAIGN OF MAGENTA AND SOLFERINO 1859 *by Harold Carmichael Wylly*—The Decisive Conflict for the Unification of Italy.

FRENCH'S CAVALRY CAMPAIGN *by J. G. Maydon*—A Special Correspondent's View of British Army Mounted Troops During the Boer War.

CAVALRY AT WATERLOO *by Sir Evelyn Wood*—British Mounted Troops During the Campaign of 1815.

THE SUBALTERN *by George Robert Gleig*—The Experiences of an Officer of the 85th Light Infantry During the Peninsular War.

NAPOLEON AT BAY, 1814 *by F. Loraine Petre*—The Campaigns to the Fall of the First Empire.

NAPOLEON AND THE CAMPAIGN OF 1806 *by Colonel Vachée*—The Napoleonic Method of Organisation and Command to the Battles of Jena & Auerstädt.

THE COMPLETE ADVENTURES IN THE CONNAUGHT RANGERS *by William Grattan*—The 88th Regiment during the Napoleonic Wars by a Serving Officer.

BUGLER AND OFFICER OF THE RIFLES *by William Green & Harry Smith*—With the 95th (Rifles) during the Peninsular & Waterloo Campaigns of the Napoleonic Wars.

NAPOLEONIC WAR STORIES *by Sir Arthur Quiller-Couch*—Tales of soldiers, spies, battles & sieges from the Peninsular & Waterloo campaingns.

CAPTAIN OF THE 95TH (RIFLES) *by Jonathan Leach*—An officer of Wellington's sharpshooters during the Peninsular, South of France and Waterloo campaigns of the Napoleonic wars.

RIFLEMAN COSTELLO *by Edward Costello*—The adventures of a soldier of the 95th (Rifles) in the Peninsular & Waterloo Campaigns of the Napoleonic wars.

www.ingramcontent.com/pod-product-compliance
Lightning Source LLC
Chambersburg PA
CBHW032055080426
42733CB00006B/281